TOO SIMPLE TO FAIL

A Case for Educational Change

R. BARKER BAUSELL, PH.D.

OXFORD
UNIVERSITY PRESS

2011

OXFORD
UNIVERSITY PRESS

Oxford University Press, Inc., publishes works that further
Oxford University's objective of excellence
in research, scholarship, and education.

Oxford   New York
Auckland   Cape Town   Dar es Salaam   Hong Kong   Karachi
Kuala Lumpur   Madrid   Melbourne   Mexico City   Nairobi
New Delhi   Shanghai   Taipei   Toronto

With offices in
Argentina   Austria   Brazil   Chile   Czech Republic   France   Greece
Guatemala   Hungary   Italy   Japan   Poland   Portugal   Singapore
South Korea   Switzerland   Thailand   Turkey   Ukraine   Vietnam

Published by Oxford University Press, Inc.
198 Madison Avenue, New York, New York 10016

www.oup.com

Oxford is a registered trademark of Oxford University Press

Library of Congress Cataloging-in-Publication Data
Bausell, R. Barker, 1942-
Too simple to fail : a case for educational change / R. Barker Bausell.
p. cm.
Includes bibliographical references.
ISBN 978-0-19-974432-9
1. Effective teaching.   2. Motivation in education.
3. Teachers–Conduct of life.   I. Title.
LB1025.3.B3894 2010
371.2'07–dc22
2010014549

1 3 5 7 9 8 6 4 2

Printed in the United States of America
on acid-free paper

Dedicated to

Nellie B. Bausell
Rufus B. Bausell
Devoted Parents and
Great Elementary School Teachers

CONTENTS

ACKNOWLEDGEMENTS

I would like to thank my graduate advisor and collaborator, William B. Moody, for giving me the opportunity to conduct much of the research that, decades later, largely informed the theory of school learning introduced here. Appreciation is also extended to Jodi Narde (Assistant Editor at Oxford) and Jais Alphonse (Project Manager) for their competence and conscientiousness in smoothly guiding the production process to fruition. The book was greatly improved by Marion Osmun's sage advice in helping me to shape its direction (and for reviewing multiple versions) before encouraging me to submit it to Oxford University Press. And finally a special acknowledgment to my editor, Abby Gross, for her unwavering support, enthusiasm, and belief in the importance of the project.

Thirty-five students sit facing a single teacher. The teacher has just provided a brief but coherent introduction to a new topic, but one portion of
her class couldn't follow what she was saying because they have had too
little previous instruction on the subject at hand. Another portion of the
class is terminally bored because they had previously learned 90% of everything the teacher said (or will say during the upcoming school year).
A third contingent is distracted by two misbehaving boys seated at the
rear of the room.

Recognizing these problems, and hoping to reinforce the main points
of her lecture, she reseats the two boys on opposite sides of the room and
has all the students open their textbooks to read the same page.
Unfortunately, the same part of her class who couldn't follow her lecture,
along with a significant portion of the students who were distracted, also
has trouble reading the textbook. And of course the students who already
knew what she was talking about already know everything contained on
that particular page in their textbook.

Sensing that something is amiss, the teacher decides to vary her routine
a bit and have everyone come to the front of the room and sit on the floor
surrounding the chalkboard. Following a few minutes of jostling and con-
fusion, the class then watches a student attempt to solve a math problem
based upon what has just been taught and read about (by some). This particular student fails miserably and can't follow the teacher's attempts to
help him "discover" his error. The remainder of the class isn't at all interested in this process since some of them would have never made such an

egregious mistake, some of them can't follow the teacher's explanation, and some simply aren't paying attention.

Later, with the students back at their desks, the teacher poses a question to the class on the topic. Some students raise their hand whether they know the answer or not; some wave their arms frantically because they are sure they have the correct answer (or simply want the attention); and everyone else waits for either the correct or the incorrect answer, or pays more attention to the myriad other competing activities that are constantly going on in the classroom, somewhat analogous to a cocktail party in which we stand in a crowded room with sounds and conversations going on all around us and must decide to what we will direct out attention and to what we will only pretend to do so.[1]

What these and most other classroom instructional activities have in common is their mind-boggling inefficiency, the amount of time they consume, and the fact that at any given point in time only a portion of the students involved will be actually attending to them—either because the instruction isn't keyed to their particular needs or they are free to attend to competing activities that they find more interesting. And as if all of this were not enough, the teacher herself is most likely ill trained for her job. She probably graduated from a university-based school of education, which may have been staffed by faculty who knew very little about how to maintain order in a public school classroom, make instruction relevant for as large a percentage of such a classroom as possible, foster learning under typical classroom conditions, or even how to teach the types of content she is now charged with covering. And if teaching children to read is part of our teacher's duties, she may have never even been given a cursory lesson on basic phonics instruction. In fact, it is possible that this teacher may never have enrolled in a single course that actually prepared her to teach children to read, to write, or to understand mathematics—perhaps because *her* faculty were never taught that themselves. An accident of history, perhaps, due to the discipline's early thinkers (such as Herbert Spencer, John Dewey) who were less concerned about increasing the amount students *learned* than they were about the philosophical and social implications of schooling.[2] Or, of later popular theorists such as Jean Piaget, whose work would ultimately wind up having no recognizable application to classroom instruction.

But returning to the 35-student classroom, our intrepid teacher realizes that she can't spend any more time on this particular lesson and must move on whether everyone is ready or not. She therefore announces a quiz on the topic for the next day and hands out a worksheet that she painstaking constructed herself and assigns it as homework in preparation for the impending quiz. Naturally, by now, she knows that some of her students will complete the worksheet conscientiously and some won't because (a) they don't have the requisite skills; (b) their parents don't have them either, so they can't help their children with the assignment; or (c) there is no one in the children's home who has accepted the role of delivering supplementary instruction or monitoring homework completion, believing instead that these tasks are the school's job.

But the teacher doesn't feel too badly about the job she's doing. One portion of her class is doing quite well, primarily those who listen in class, complete their homework, and whose parents are themselves adequately educated (and consequently recognize the necessity of being involved in their children's education). What our teacher probably doesn't realize is that if an age-appropriate aptitude or cognitive test of any sort had been administered to her students when they were three years old, the resulting scores would have very nicely predicted the identity of the children who do and do not complete their homework assignments—and probably even who will and will not graduate from college.

For, in truth, classroom instruction adds surprisingly little value to the preparation that parents provide their children in the home. True, new topics are introduced and old ones embellished during the 12,000-plus hours that children spend in school, but years before school begins some parents also contribute thousands of instructional hours to their children's education by exposing them to a challenging vocabulary, talking to them about the world, reading to them, instilling in them the importance of learning, limiting their television viewing to educational programming, and teaching them the alphabet, their numbers, word recognition, and often even how to read fluently. After school begins, these same parents also monitor what is going on in the classroom and, if the schools are not meeting their expectation, do not hesitate to intervene by requesting a new teacher, providing supplementary instruction (either themselves or by engaging tutors), ensuring that homework assignments are completed, or sending their children to private schools if necessary. And, not surprisingly, it is the children from these homes who do the best in school and who so please our hypothetical teacher by their performance in her classroom.

It is also the children from these homes who help disguise just how abysmally obsolete the classroom model has become over the years. For it is the presence of such children (and the schools they attend) that allows educators to remain entrenched in their practices and to support business as usual, pointing to the performance of these children and their schools as proof that classroom instruction does indeed work well under the right conditions. Of course, these conditions always involve the presence of students who come from learning-enriched home environments and can read as many words on their first day of school as their counterparts from economically deprived environments (who not coincidentally also happen to be assigned to attend "poorly performing schools") will be able to read by the end of their first *year*. And so what if these poor-performing elementary schools feed even worse performing middle schools and high schools until another generation of adolescents graduates without being able to read a newspaper or write a coherent sentence? At least, our current schools work well for *some* children.

But do they? What if no children arrived on the first day of school with any previous academic instruction? Would this permit the same degree of complacency? Could we afford to tolerate the resulting performance from our obsolete instructional system?

The sad truth is that no one knows just how *little* value classroom instruction adds to children's education, but it is the performances of our inner city schools serving children from home environments providing little or no supplementary instruction that probably give us the best indication. For here, at least, we can see the pathetic results of 12,000 hours of *classroom* instruction delivered to children who do *not* receive thousands of hours of extra-school parental *tutoring*.

But while everyone who knows anything about education knows how important these early home-learning factors are, absolutely *none of us* knows how much sheer human potential is squandered by our continued reliance upon classroom instruction delivered in the form of a poorly equipped, poorly trained teacher standing technologically naked in front of 35 diverse students. No highly educated parent bothers to look at the results of a typical inner city school district and say, "there but by the grace of God goes *my* child." On the other side of the coin, however, few people look at the graduates of one of our well-regarded suburban (or private) high schools and ask, "how much more potential would these educationally fortunate young people possess if they hadn't been taught in such an obsolete manner?"

We certainly can't rely upon our current testing system to give us any hint about any of this, for our tests are as obsolete as our classrooms. Indeed, our "achievement" tests aren't even designed to assess what is learned in school. Instead, they were developed via an obsolete century-old intelligence testing model designed primarily to rank order students based upon the types of home environments they came from.

One wonders how even the most demented committee conceivable could have designed a more *inefficient* mode of instruction or a more disingenuous method of disguising that inefficiency. Yet, educators seem completely committed to this woefully obsolete model, in part through simple inertia and a desire to avoid the effort that change always entails, in part because we are all so wedded to the concept of one teacher standing in front of a group of students that we are blind to the obvious option staring us in the face. But as recent history has shown, sometimes change is inevitable when it is technologically driven and obviously superior to business as usual.

What I propose to do in this book, therefore, is to explain what science tells us about the direction in which this inevitable change must move. In so doing, I will present the simplest conceivable theory of school learning and the equally simple (but not necessarily obvious) instructional principles that flow from it—all of which has one purpose: to show how our current obsolete mode of classrooms can be transformed into a learning environment capable of dramatically improving the education of *all* society's children. And, while I have chosen to concentrate on elementary school *instruction* because of the crucial importance of mastering the basic academic skills taught there, the principles I will present here are equally applicable to middle and secondary schools as well.

From a personal perspective, this book represents the culmination of an interrupted intellectual journey that began many years ago. It presents the synthesis of the entire field of school-based learning that has simmered uncompleted, like a low-grade irritant in the back of my mind for three decades. A synthesis that ultimately reduces to the preeminent importance of increasing both the *amount* and the *relevance* of the instructional time we provide our children.

My particular journey actually began in 1968, with my enrollment in a doctoral program in the University of Delaware's College of Education and with the subsequently unparalleled, exhilarating opportunity this provided me to conduct research into the factors influencing classroom learning. From that research, and the work of other researchers who came before and after, I came to realize that something was very wrong with how we herded our children into boxes in order to teach them. I also came to realize that something was very wrong with how we explained—both to ourselves as educators and to the world at large—why some children appeared to learn with such greater ease than others. But, for some reason, it took me a long time to realize that the solution to increasing school learning (as well as to explaining why some children perform so much better on standardized tests than others) boils down to the one simple factor: *relevant instructional time.*

Why it took me so long to fit the pieces together of this exceedingly simple puzzle, I do not know. Perhaps it was due to the happenstance that forced me into a field of research outside of education, thereby distracting me from addressing the puzzle's solution. Or, perhaps it was simply difficult for me to accept the fact that the entire discipline in which I had been trained boiled down to a single elemental concept—*time*—and that everything else proposed to explain school learning was nothing more than a chimera, a proxy for this single variable.

But, for whatever the reasons, hopefully the journey ends here with a completed theory of classroom learning and the crucial (and unavoidable) implications it provides for guiding us to exponentially increase school learning. For, after all of these years, I would not bother with the effort if I did not believe that we *now* have the technological capability for not only improving school learning, but also for eliminating the educational disparities that our obsolete classroom methods accentuate. Nicholas Lemann perhaps best articulates the problem when he says that this country has "channeled opportunity through the educational system and then . . . failed to create schools . . . that would work for *everybody*, because that was very expensive and voters didn't want to pay for it."[3] To which I would add: "nor did educators have any idea *how* to create such schools."

As will become clear in the chapters that follow, however, education is an exceedingly simple discipline—far more so than anyone realizes—thus, it follows that any theory emanating from it capable of solving our schools' inadequacies must be simple as well. Educational research is equally straightforward, so while I will briefly discuss a few of my own experiments (as well as some truly seminal work conducted by others) to illustrate the scientific basis for the direction we must take, this book isn't really about research, science, *or* theory. It is about how we can solve one of the most bedeviling problems facing us as a society: how to make the schooling process more productive for *all* of our children.

Of course, anyone who follows educational issues over the years knows that there has been no lack of opinions regarding how we should reform our schools. I will even touch on some of the more promising of these, although most have no scientific basis and stop short of informing us about anything that will actually impact *learning*.

Fortunately, however, both the theories and the research that informed them, share one characteristic: Unlike the more sophisticated sciences that must employ complicated mathematical formulations or complex neurobiological processes to explain their principles, everything associated with education and school learning is exceedingly *simple*. As an author, this provides me with a huge advantage, for not only do I have uncomplicated subject matter to discuss, my audience is exceedingly knowledgeable and experienced, having spent a significant portion of their lives receiving classroom instruction.

But, just because something is simple does not mean that it is either self-evident or unimportant. The success or failure of our schools has far-reaching implications, not only for the children who attend them but for everyone with an interest in the well-being and future of our society. Parents, because they entrust their children to the schools to prepare them for a future increasingly dependent upon knowledge and the ability to apply it; society because, at this very moment, we may well have a potential Newton, Darwin, Gandhi, Shakespeare, Mozart, or Einstein spending her childhood moving from one obsolete classroom to another in an inner-city school. And no one anywhere can believe that such a child could realize even a fraction of her enormous potential in such a place.

So, my sole intent in this book is to enumerate principles and strategies to increase school-based *learning*. I recognize the importance of philosophical, social, and political issues involved in the educational process, and I realize that the schools exist for purposes in addition to the production of learning.[4] I will, however, leave these larger societal issues to those wiser than I, and deal with my limited area of expertise: learning. I wouldn't even hazard a guess as to how we can produce future scientific, artistic, or social leaders, such as the luminaries just mentioned. What this book deals with is making sure that *all* of our children have the opportunity to learn to (a) read fluently, (b) write coherently, and (c) apply mathematical concepts in their lives. It is also very much about providing *all* of our children with the opportunity to realize their ultimate potential for contributing to our society and maximizing their chances for attaining a high quality of life therein.

CHAPTER 1

The Science of Learning

To improve learning, we must first understand what it is. Although scientists are beginning to make exciting inroads into identifying the chemical and biological changes that occur in the brain during the learning process, we are light years away from being able to apply any of their findings to classroom instruction. But fortunately, from a behavioral (as opposed to a biological) perspective, learning has been the subject of serious study for the past century, and although some of this research occurred in one of the most artificial learning settings imaginable—laboratories employing both animals and undergraduate psychology students—even this work has generated principles that have direct applicability to optimizing classroom learning.[1]

CLASSIC LEARNING RESEARCH

Ultimately, learning entails a neurobiological response to a stimulus of some sort. This unobserved neurological response is translated to an observable behavioral response, which can encompass anything from avoiding the stimulus in the future to correctly answering a test item. Classic learning research (as well as educational research in general) primarily concerns itself with changes in such behavioral responses (*learning*) following the presentation of visual or oral stimuli (*instruction*). Thus, if students are able to correctly answer test questions following instruction that they couldn't answer correctly beforehand, then we *infer* that learning has occurred.

Just as all learning basically involves some type of observable/measurable behavioral response, instruction also always boils down to a stimulus that is capable of eliciting such a response. From this perspective, then, instruction can take the form of (but is not limited to) such diverse stimuli as:

- Being lectured to in a classroom setting
- Completing computerized/online instructional modules
- Being presented a word, phrase, or nonsense syllable and told to memorize it
- Completing homework
- Engaging in self-study
- Reading
- Being read to
- Watching television
- Surfing the internet
- Listening to others (whether in class or at the dinner table)
- Being the beneficiaries of direct parental teaching
- Being corrected by parents
- Observing and subsequently modeling parental or peer group behaviors
- Observing the environment
- Visiting institutions with instructional agendas such as a churches, museums, and science centers

To control as many factors as possible in their research and to avoid teaching something that their subjects had already learned, classic learning studies often employed the visual presentation of nonsense syllables via a technique called *paired-associate learning trials*. Experimental subjects (typically, college undergraduates) were taught, via repeated presentations—often involving a slide projector or its equivalent—to "pair" these syllables (or sometimes conceptually unrelated words) until this arbitrary association was successfully "learned." To avoid as much error as possible in inferring that learning had occurred (and to measure it as precisely as humanly possible), testing involved exactly the same processes that were used in instruction (i.e., the syllables, words, or whatever, presented via the same medium in which they were learned).

As obsolete as current classroom instruction is, present-day teaching isn't quite this rote. Still, unlike classroom research, these experiments employed a form of instruction and a method of measuring learning that could be controlled and repeated quite consistently. This meant that scientists could have a great deal of confidence in any learning principles they unearthed. Whether these principles would apply to all types of learning, no one knew for sure, but the best guess was (and is) that the same neurobiological processes are associated with all types of learning resulting from all types of instruction, rote or creative, interesting or dull.

So, at the risk of oversimplification, three facets of learning were inferred by these studies, based on how many trials (or how quickly) students mastered the paired-associate tasks for which they received "instruction." These learning facets or parameters were:

- *Original learning,* which is identical to what we mean when we refer to school learning;
- *Retention,* which refers to how long what was learned is remembered—or to the circumstances under which forgetting occurs; and
- *Transfer of learning,* which in classic learning theory refers to the fact that previous learning can sometimes facilitate (and sometimes even impede) subsequent learning.

And, if you think about it, these three behaviors pretty much reflect what we expect students to take from the schooling process: learning what is taught (otherwise attending school is a total waste of time), remembering what is taught (because if we don't remember what we've learned, we might as well have not learned it in the first place), and being able to apply what is learned to new situations (because supplying correct responses to test items would be worthless if we can't assume that this will ultimately be related to other types of innovative, creative, or compliant behaviors of societal importance).

In a nutshell, then, the principles emanating from this type of research that were most relevant to classroom instruction and student learning were:

1. The more times the paired-associate tasks were repeated (that is, the more *instructional time* supplied), the more learning occurred. This was the strongest and most consistent relationship that this line of investigation ever uncovered: more relevant time on task (or more presentations of the stimuli) results in more learning. It was so pervasive, in fact, that some researchers embraced a "total-time

hypothesis," which basically postulated that, within reasonable limits, the same amount will be learned in a given amount of time regardless of the number of trials presented within that time period.[2]

2. Some forgetting almost always occurs, but the more time on task (or the more presentations of the stimuli), the longer the association (or learning) was retained (remembered). Retention can also be improved by (a) increasing the meaningfulness (or relevance) of the content and/or (b) continuing to present the stimuli even after they are learned (which was called *over-learning*). Of course, this still reduces to time on task (or increased instructional time) since the presentation of a stimulus is a form of instruction.

3. Transfer of learning (one form of which was called "learning to learn") proved to be a more tenuous affair, but it does occur as a function of instruction under certain conditions. For example, transfer was facilitated by over-learning, and it occurred most reliably when the training conditions were most similar to the ultimate testing conditions (which in schooling terms is reflected by practices such as teaching to the test or teaching test-taking skills) and when the original learning task possessed certain components in common with the transfer task (such as teaching a child the sound representing a certain vowel to facilitate the learning of a word containing that vowel). However, we still haven't learned enough about this concept to stretch it to what we mean by such attributes as creativity (or innovativeness), and this remains a major gap in our understanding of the instructional–learning process. Suffice it to say that the occurrence of learning is a prerequisite for both retention (and transferring that learned knowledge to novel applications), but learning is no guarantor of either.[3]

Now, admittedly, this brief overview does not do justice to classic learning research. Other variables were involved[4] but, generally speaking, most of the work in classical learning research, as in educational research in general, never transcended what educational researchers in my day called the "grandmother principle," which can be summed up in the following succinct generalization:

You never discover anything in educational research that your grand-mother didn't already know.

Still, our grandmothers weren't always right about everything, so it doesn't hurt to subject some of their opinions to scientific tests. Thus, in summary, far and away the most important finding emanating from this classic research (as well as from learning research that involved rats navigating mazes) was that the strongest determinant of laboratory learning is the *amount* of instruction delivered. More instruction, more learning; more time spent studying, more learning; more time on task, more learning; the more time an author spends repeating something, the more likely the reader is to learn it—to remember it—and to apply it.

CLASSIC SCHOOLING RESEARCH

Understandably, researchers interested in studying classroom instruction couldn't help questioning the broader relevance of the classic laboratory investigations of undergraduates paid to memorize nonsense syllables. They felt a need to study children actually being taught in a classroom setting. Thus, they tended to do their research based upon what real teachers did with real students within real classrooms.

In so doing, these researchers both gained and lost something. What they gained was the ability to observe learning in the real-life school settings in which they were primarily interested and to which they aspired to generalize their research. What they lost was any real degree of control over the research setting, in the sense that they had to deal with (a) much more diverse students who, unlike the undergraduates participating in paired-associate experiments, could not always read or understand directions; (b) teachers who potentially could vary in their instructional ability and conscientiousness; and (c) tests that weren't designed to match what students were taught (i.e., standardized achievement measures).

Still, some of this research, much of it conducted before the field's steroidal boosts in the mid to late 1970s—which I attribute to (a) Gene Glass' popularization of meta-analysis[5] (that, among other things, definitively demonstrated the positive learning effects of small class size[6]) and (b) Benjamin Bloom's emergence as the preeminent learning theorists/researcher of the 1970s and 1980s[7]—did uncover some very interesting findings, even if none quite transcended the "grandmother principle."

Some of the more important of these findings as they relate to school learning included:

Increased Instructional Time (or Time-on-Task)

Despite the obvious differences in settings, the classic learning principle that more instructional time (although classic learning researchers seldom labeled their presentation of nonsense syllables *instruction*) results in greater learning did indeed apply to the classroom. In its most elemental form, the more time that is allocated to teach a topic, the more students will learn.[8] In fact, the amount of instructional exposure is one of the strongest determinants of school learning yet discovered.[9]

Of course none of this would come as a surprise to anyone's grandmother. Neither would secondary evidence showing that children who are assigned homework (which, after all, translates to extra time-on-task) learn more than those who do not[10] or that those who attend summer school (which involves increased instructional time) learn more (or forget less) than those who do not.[11] Other similarly obvious manifestations of the relationship between instructional time and learning include the negative impact of school absences and even tardiness.[12]

Strangely, given its obvious importance, as far as I'm aware no one made a serious attempt to document the dose–response relationship between the amount of school instruction until the mid-1970s, when David Wiley and Annegret Harnischfeger[13] conducted a secondary analysis of data from 40 Detroit schools contained in the Equality of Educational Opportunity Survey. Defining the number of hours of schooling delivered to students in any given school, they used the following simple formula:

[# Hours of Instruction Delivered = Daily Attendance (which encompasses absences) x # Hours in the School Day x # days in the School Year]

They found huge discrepancies in the total number of hours of schooling in this one city, ranging from 710 to 1,150 hours per year. "Typical pupils in some schools receive 50% more schooling than pupils in other schools." Then, controlling for student characteristics as best they could, they found that "over a year's period … in schools where students receive 24% more schooling, they will increase their average gain in reading comprehension by two-thirds and their gains in mathematics and verbal skills by more than one-third" (p. 9). Needless to say, this finding reflects an *extremely* powerful relationship between the *amount* of school instruction and student learning.

Yet, as powerful a factor as the amount of instructional time is, historically it has not been found to be the most powerful determinant factor influencing school learning. That distinction belongs to a relationship that was probably recognized the first time children were ever grouped together in classrooms.

Individual Differences Between Children

Based upon a number of studies (primarily involving large test score databases), it has been estimated that from 40% to 60% of all the individual differences in later school achievement can be predicted as early as the fourth year of life. The best known of these studies was conducted by James Coleman, a sociologist whose 1966 report ("The Equality of Educational Opportunity") definitively demonstrated that *the most powerful determinants of success in school lies in what children bring to the schooling process, rather than what happens to them once they get there.*[14] This is also reflected by the fact that standardized tests administered to children at age three are strongly predictive of test scores obtained throughout their schooling experience.[15]

In a nutshell, what these studies demonstrate (and there are a plethora of them), involving different databases such as the National Longitudinal Survey of Youth and the National Assessment of Education Progress and different types of tests,[16] is that:

- The higher the parents' educational attainment and income level (which reduces to socioeconomic status), the higher the children's achievement.[17]
- Caucasian and Asian students perform significantly better on standardized tests and on just about every other indicator of schooling success than black and Hispanic students.[18] (Of course, race and ethnicity are also related to socioeconomic status.)
- Children from single-parent homes (and especially those in which the mother is very young) fare worse in school.[19] (This also is related to socioeconomic status and race, since 70% of black children are born to single mothers.)[20]

- Children with many siblings[21] do more poorly on standardized tests. The spacing of siblings (closer together is detrimental because of less time available for the parent to interact with any one child) and birth order are also important for the same reason.[22]
- Students who are the beneficiaries of a home-learning environment characterized by (a) plentiful reading material,[23] (b) procedures to restrict the type and amount of television viewing and video game playing,[24] and (c) parents who read to them when they were young achieve significantly higher than children who come from homes without these advantages.[25]
- Children who are actively taught the alphabet, the sounds letters make, words, numbers, number concepts, and even how to read prior to attending school obviously do better in school than do children who are not so taught.[26]

Historically, there has been a great deal of disagreement among educators and educational researchers over the question of why some children seem destined to succeed in school and others seem destined to fail. Some have seen these findings as irrefutably supportive of the heritability and preeminent importance of intelligence, aptitude, and/or ability, whereas others have visualized them as primarily environmentally determined. As will be discussed in Chapter 4, however, these findings possess a considerably more parsimonious explanation.

Instructional Methods

So far, we've only discussed one school-based *intervention* that has any positive effect upon school learning, and that is the amount of instruction delivered. Children who are given more instruction learn more than those who are given less. Surely a more mundane finding is difficult to envision.

Unfortunately, although researchers have evaluated just about every other factor imaginable, not much else appears to influence school learning. Every so often, however, someone comes along and recommends this or that instructional method—such as the use of visual aides, hands-on activities, certain types of discussion groups, discovery learning, educational games, or some other combination of bells and whistles—based upon the belief that his or her brainchild should produce superior learning.

Intuitively, this is quite appealing, for even our grandmothers would agree that the way in which children are taught ought to make a difference in how much they learn. And, at a tautologically absurd level, this is certainly true, such as delivering a lecture to non-Asian American students in Mandarin versus English.

But alas, whenever a sane innovative method is compared to the same amount of traditional classroom instruction, the result is always the same. No statistically significant difference. One method is just about as effective (or ineffective) as another *as long as the amount of instructional time is controlled.*

There are two important caveats to this statement, however: First, if the new approach involves teaching a different subject or a new set of skills to the exclusion of something else, then obviously students will learn more of the new subject (or set of skills) than will students who weren't taught it, *if* the test used to evaluate the new approach measures this new material. (This is a combination of classic time-on-task and common sense.) Also, if the new approach involves teaching prerequisite skills not taught via the traditional method, then the former will most likely be superior to the latter if (*and only if*) these skills are sufficiently useful (and, of course, the test is appropriate). The best example of this is the inclusion of a phonics component in reading instruction. If one group of students is taught to read phonetically by learning to sound out the syllables of words and another group is taught to read by learning words by sight (i.e., memorization), then even if instructional time is controlled, the students taught to decode the phonetic structure of words usually learn to read faster.[27] There is nothing that earthshaking about this phenomenon. It is comparable to saying that students who have mastered algebra will learn calculus faster than those who have not, because calculus employs algebraic constructions hence prior instruction in algebra translates to *additional* instruction in calculus. The second caveat involves interventions that increase the *relevance* of the instruction delivered to the learner because this has the effect of increasing *time on task* (which is the same thing as increasing instructional time). Examples involve not teaching content the learner already knows (which would obviously make the instruction irrelevant regardless of how much of it was delivered) and reducing classroom distractions (which would require more instructional time to produce the same degree of learning). Both strategies are enhanced by reducing class size and (most notably) by tutoring, but let's save these latter issues for later and use the remainder of this chapter to discuss the preeminent role of instructional time in determining the amount children learn in school.

Methods Versus Programs

The equivalence of different instructional methods should not be confused with different programs of instruction. Contemporary examples of the latter are listed in the Institute of Education Science's "What Works Clearinghouse." Usually, when such programs report positive results, a closer examination will determine that they (a) entail extra instructional time (in comparison to their control group) and/or (b) their content is more closely matched with the standardized tests used to assess student learning.

An excellent example of one of the high-quality trials appearing on the IES website is a study entitled *The Enhanced Reading Opportunities Study*[28] in which 34 high schools from ten districts were randomly assigned[29] to either receive the program or not. The program basically involved 225 minutes of literacy instruction *on top of* the students' regular ninth-grade language art classes (obviously a huge increase in instructional time). The experimental high schools were further randomly assigned to receive one of two different instructional methods. The results were that the *experimental program* resulted in significantly superior reading comprehension skills for those students who received it than for those who did not. However, there was no difference between the two instructional methods comprising the program itself (because both received the same amount of additional instructional time), although of course both were superior to the control group (because its students received significantly *less* instruction).

School and administrative restructuring

To a certain extent inspired by the *No Child Left Behind* (NCLB) legislation (which constituted a bizarre attempt to legislate *school learning*)[30], there have been a number of administrative (e.g. district wide reforms based upon corporate accountability models) and school restructuring (e.g., breaking up large urban high schools into smaller ones—primarily championed and funded by the Bill and Melinda Gates Foundation) initiatives in recent years. School districts have also experimented with outsourcing the management of their schools to for profit corporations as well as various school choice initiatives (most notably the charter school movement). In general the results emanating from evaluations of these interventions have been uniformly disappointing, although most of this research is so poorly controlled as to be scientifically meaningless[31]. Diane Ravitch, a well regarded educational policy expert, provides a thorough narrative review of this research in her very informative and readable book entitled *The Death and Life of the Great American School System* [32]. Once a vocal supporter of both NCLB and many of the accountability/school choice initiatives, Dr. Ravitch later changed her position while still managing to provide the most even handed historical perspective on these issues of which I'm familiar.

Aptitude-by-Treatment Interactions

Historically, the absence of research pointing to the superiority of any instructional methods over others was completely counterintuitive to many educators. There just *had* to be some instructional methods that would dramatically increase student learning in the schools! Surely, there were some methods of instruction superior to simply standing in front of a class and teaching! After all, don't we all have different learning *styles*? Don't some people prefer visual versus auditory presentations of information or more participatory methods, for example?

Well, we may have different learning styles, and some people may *prefer* one method of instruction over another, but this particular attribute (or preference) doesn't appear to affect learning one iota. Nowhere is this better illustrated than in the case of a well-known educational psychologist named Lee J. Cronbach, who in the late 1950s gave a stirring call to arms on the topic in his inaugural presidential address to the American Psychological Association.[33]

Dr. Cronbach advanced a deceptively simple (and intuitively attractive) hypothesis for explaining why nothing seemed to work better than anything else in the classroom. Turning the concept of learning *styles* on its side, he suggested that it was their ubiquitous *presence* and potency that explained why there seemed to be no difference between teaching methods (and presumably why most educational innovations didn't seem to work to advance learning).

Professor Cronbach hypothesized that, in a research study contrasting a new, well-conceived innovation such as Instructional Method X with an old standby such as Instructional Method Y, there would surely be a significant cadre of students (with, say Attribute A, whatever "A" happened to be) who would benefit from New Method X but who would actually learn *less* when taught by Traditional Method Y. Unfortunately, there would likewise be another cadre of students with, say, Attribute B, for whom the opposite would be true. They would learn more when taught by Traditional Method Y but less when taught by New Method X. Thus, when the two Methods were contrasted with one another in the same research study, the learning styles of the two types of students would cancel each other out, thereby disguising the fact that there really are very important differences between the methods.

Soon published in an article titled *"Two Disciplines of Scientific Psychology,"* this paper generated a great deal of excitement among educational researchers because it explained the frustrating plethora of studies resulting in "no statistically significant difference" that had characterized schooling research for decades. Dr. Cronbach went on to call for a research initiative designed specifically to identify those "aptitudes" (which included not only learning preferences but also such student characteristics as ability, gender, and ethnicity) that conspired to mask the effectiveness of the interventions designed by our best and brightest educators.

The proposed existence of these hypothesized "aptitude-by-treatment interactions" was especially attractive to schooling researchers, who were beginning to realize that they were members of a failed discipline in which absolutely nothing worked better than anything else to increase learning. (With the ubiquitous and powerful exception of increasing the amount of instruction delivered—but since everyone's grandmother already knew that more instruction was better than less instruction, this didn't count, and this relationship was often ignored.)

Yet, despite the hypothesis' promise, it had one small problem. No one could find these dueling attributes. Even worse, a thorough review of the research literature by Glenn Bracht, an educational researcher, conducted a few years after Professor Cronbach's clarion call, basically concluded that the techniques for identifying these effects "was often an afterthought rather than a carefully planned part of the experiment" and that "this approach has not been successful in finding meaningful disordinal[34] interactions" (p. 639). In other words, such effects were not factors in either schooling research or schooling practice in 1970, and alas nothing has intervened in the ensuing decades to change that conclusion.[35] Incredibly, Cronbach himself later acknowledged researchers' failure to find his cherished interactions but, undaunted, suggested the abandonment of statistics and science in favor of "intensive local observation" since "too narrow an identification with science ... has fixed our eyes upon an inappropriate goal."[36]

Fortunately, this tenacity in the face of overwhelming negative evidence has not harmed Lee J. Cronbach's scientific legacy, and he is remembered for more memorable achievements. As far as the science of schooling is concerned, however, the unfortunate bottom line is that research on "learning styles," like research contrasting different ways of teaching, has been an exercise in futility. Neither is a serious factor in classroom learning.

Another Caveat

Obviously, everyone knows that some types of students learn more (or more quickly) from instruction than others. It is therefore not impossible to find "ordinal" aptitude by treatment interactions involving differences in "ability level" (or amount of prior knowledge) in which, say, high-ability students learn more from one type of instruction (or all types of instruction) than do low-ability students. What is difficult (if not impossible) to find is a method of instruction that benefits one type of student but not another when both types of students have the necessary prerequisites for learning the content being taught.

Teacher Differences

But surely, schooling researchers reasoned, if individual differences among students constitute the most potent determinant of school learning, then individual differences in teachers must also be an important factor in classroom learning. Common sense would seem to tell us that this *should* be the case, since we've all experienced both good and bad teachers during our schooling careers, even though we're usually judging them on qualities other than their ability to elicit higher test scores. Perhaps one teacher seemed to particularly value us and/or our potentials. Or, perhaps some had a gift for enlivening their classes with humor or interesting asides or unwavering enthusiasm for an otherwise boring subject. So, although we all personally probably know what good teaching means to us personally, the sad truth is that educational researchers, despite myriad attempts, have been unable to consistently identify teachers who, year-in-and-year-out, produce superior *standardized test scores* than their peers.

There are several reasons for this difficulty. One is the questionable propriety of employing standardized tests primarily to rank order students on their knowledge of certain relatively ill-defined subject matter content followed by a subsequent *re-ranking* of teachers based upon the same data. (We'll discuss some of the deficiencies of standardized tests in more detail in Chapter 8.) Another problem is that test scores are influenced by so many factors other than teachers, such as differences in (a) children's home learning environments (which include direct parental instruction, parentally instilled expectations for achievement accompanied by incentives/disincentives far more effective than anything a teacher can bring to bear in a classroom, supervision of homework/study assignments) and (b) classroom ambiances (e.g., the need to constantly discipline disruptive students or the presence of extremely heterogeneous students with different instructional needs).

We also don't have a particularly strong theory for why two identically trained individuals with identical amounts of experience standing in front of identical classrooms and teaching the same topic for the same length of time *should* produce different results, unless one of the instructors:

- Had a communication deficit that prevented students from understanding him or her (which hopefully is quite rare among teachers) and/or
- Couldn't maintain sufficient discipline to ensure that his or her students were attending to the instruction (which is possible, but chances are that such a teacher would eventually either learn certain rudimentary class management skills or leave the profession).

Of course, given the causal relationship between instructional time and student learning, we would predict that if some instructors devoted a higher proportion of their classroom time to actual instruction than others, then their students would be expected to learn more. (And, as will be discussed shortly, there is indeed research indicating that major differences do exist among teachers with respect to how *much* time they actually devote to instruction.) We also know that if some instructors teach material more closely aligned with the end-of-year standardized test, then *their* students will perform better in those tests.

Unfortunately, until recently, there had been very little research to indicate whether teacher differences, if they exist, are consistent from year-to-year. (Obviously, even if we could identify teachers who are effective one year but *ineffective* the next, the information would avail us nothing.) And, although a limited amount of research has attempted to ascertain if teacher behaviors in general are stable across time (based upon the assumption that if teachers don't teach in a consistent manner from year-to-year, then their student learning probably won't be stable either), the results of this line of work have been generally negative.[37]

True, in the past there have been several studies that demonstrate modest teacher effects[38] upon student learning, but most of this work was fatally flawed because it didn't follow teachers longitudinally, nor did it adequately take the huge individual differences among students' propensities to learn into account. Some studies control for little more than the proportion of students in each school who receive federal lunch subsidies, arguing that once this is done, any systematic differences in test scores between *classrooms* must be due to teacher differences. After all, what else could it be?

Well, I'm sure that just about everyone can come up with a plethora of alternative explanations, such as students' past academic performance, the possibility that some teachers are systematically assigned children with poorer (or superior) educational prognoses, and so forth. But even those studies that do attempt to take these factors into consideration seldom attempted to assess the consistency of teacher performance. So, although some studies that have employed large student/teacher/school test score databases have shown that students taught by more-knowledgeable teachers (or teachers who are certified[39]) achieve higher test scores than those of less-qualified teachers, it is also true that suburban schools are able to attract better-qualified teachers than are impoverished inner-city districts.[40] And, assuming that achievement differences as dramatic as those that occur between children from, say, professional families and single-mother welfare recipients can be statistically subtracted out by simply controlling for factors such as racial mix or the proportion of students receiving free lunches borders on the absurd.

A truism, law, or educational fact of life is that no statistical procedure can make an apple an orange, nor can *anything* control for socioeconomic learning differences when it isn't the socioeconomic differences themselves that *cause* these learning differences. The real factors that *cause* childhood differences in learning, which just happen to be associated with socioeconomic factors (hence ethnicity and poverty), are children's home learning environments and their parents' behaviors.[41]

Now, obviously, no one really believes that *some* teachers aren't better than others, or that some teachers don't devote more class time to academic affairs than others, or aren't more conscientious in covering the curriculum, or don't have a better grasp of the subject matter they are charged with teaching, or can't explain their subject matter better than others. Our problem, as will be discussed in Chapter 8, has been that the huge sets of test scores of questionable validity (that is, that don't actually assess what is taught in any given classroom) have so much accompanying extraneous error (noise) associated with them that they aren't really appropriate for identifying teachers whose students perform consistently better or worse over time. This is not to say, however, that there haven't been some Herculean (and promising) efforts undertaken in this arena.

Value-Added Teacher Assessment

Most commonly associated with William B. Sanders and his colleagues (originally at the University of Tennessee and now at the SAS Institute), one such approach is predicated on the proposition that if enough data on individual students are available over time, then this information can be used to predict these students' test score *gains* in the future. It therefore follows that, if all of any given teacher's students' test score gains can be predicted based upon these students' past performance, then any discrepancies from these predictions represent that teacher's effectiveness-ineffectiveness for that particular year.

Called *value-added teacher assessment*, this approach uses sophisticated longitudinal statistical modeling procedures to generate predictions regarding students' test score gains for a given year. It then defines any observed classroom performance that turns out to be better than predicted on the end-of-year test as the *value added* by the teacher of said classroom. (Again, what else could it be?) This approach has resulted in some relatively promising findings, especially for mathematics, to a lesser extent for reading, but apparently not so much for other subjects. Before considering these findings in any detail, however, it is worth noting that the model attempts to simulate the situation in which:

- Students are randomly assigned to teachers (which would help to decrease the individual differences in students' propensity to learn between teachers' classes that occur when students are assigned on the *basis* of their likelihood to gain more or less highly on standard-ized tests—such as occurs when parents request that their children be assigned to a given teacher based upon that teacher's reputation *or* when a principal assigns students that he or she believes will pros-per more with one teacher than another *or* when students are grouped/tracked based upon their ability level);
- Students are tested twice per year, once at the beginning of the year and once at the end (because the learning and forgetting that goes on during the summer is not under the control of the next year's teacher but obviously affects how much children improve from the previous May's testing to the next May's testing—which in turn *is* used to judge that teacher's effectiveness);
- Subtract the two test scores for each teacher to get a measure of how much his or her students learned during the year;
- Repeat the entire process the next year;
- Compare each teachers' learning results across the two years after statistically controlling for as many factors not under the teachers' control as possible (such as the amount of instruction students' had previously received, and continued to receive, from their home learning environments).

Since these conditions are extremely difficult to implement (and informa-tion regarding children's actual home learning environment is nonexis-tent) in the real world of schooling, Sanders and colleagues have made a valiant attempt to do the best they can with what is available to them. Their results have generated a great deal of excitement outside education (both President Obama and Malcolm Gladwell are huge fans), but unfor-tunately, although the value added researchers' efforts are interpreted as showing that teacher effects are considerable in any given year, the results assessing the consistency of these effects over time are considerably less impressive.

In the largest analysis addressing the consistency of his effects of which I am aware, Sanders[42] compared 4906 teachers who remained in the same school three years in a row and who were categorized (using his value-added approach) as producing below average, average, and above average effects. I have taken the liberty of doing my own representation of those results in Table 1.1 below.

Altogether there were 941 teachers who were considered below average the first year, but less than half of these (404 or 43%) were judged to be below average the third year. (Data weren't presented for what happened during the second year.) And remarkably, 111 (or 12%) of these supposed below average teachers were actually judged to be above average in the third year while 45% moved up to the average category.

Of the 1,253 teachers judged to be above average the first year, 136 (or 11%) were actually *below* average the third year and 44% had regressed to the middle category. This left only 45% of original "high performing" teachers in the above average category both years.

Now think what would have happened if the below average teachers had all been dismissed and replaced based upon their first year performances. In 57% of the cases, the schools in question would have lost a teacher who would have performed at an average or above average level two years later. Similarly, if the high performing teachers been rewarded monetarily based upon their first year performance, in over half of the cases (55%) the schools would have wasted their money because these "high performers" had slipped back into mediocrity (or worse).

Table 1.1. The Value-Added Consistency of Teacher Performance

Teacher Performance	Below Average (Year 3)	Average (Year 3)	Above Average (Year 3)	Total of Year 1 Value-Added Categories
Below Average (Year 1)	**43%**	45%	12%	941 (100%)
Average (Year 1)	21%	**59%**	21%	3712 (100%)
Above Average (Year 1)	11%	44%	**45%**	1253 (100%)

To me, the bottom line here is that only in the case of average teachers did the value-added predictive scheme produce a consistency rate of over 50% (as indicated in the bolded percentages in Table 1.1). For below average and above average teachers the consistency of the technique was only 43% and 45% respectively. This level of consistency is much too low to base important policy decisions upon and it is too low to have any true practical implications for improving public school education.

Another large scale analysis involving the consistency of value-added teacher assessment was conducted using Chicago high school ninth-grade math scores and produced similarly discouraging results.[43] Here, only 33% of the teachers found to be in the lowest quarter of teaching effectiveness one year (based upon their students' predicted scores) were also found to be in the lowest quarter the following year (and 35% of this lowest group were actually judged to be *above average* the next year). And, using the same data base, while 41% of the teachers in the top quarter were able to repeat their performance the next year, 36% were found to be below average. Although these (and the previous) results were statistically significant, it is difficult to see how they possess any practical significance whatever. Certainly everyone would be exceedingly disappointed if we bused thousands of high-performing teachers into the inner city to increase learning there, only to discover that over a third performed below average once they got there—thereby validating Yogi Berra's observation that "prediction is very hard, especially about the future."

Still, even though I think everyone who cares about schooling research would love to have a method to predict which teachers will and will not facilitate salutary student learning, I'm afraid that value-added teacher assessment may not be quite what we're looking for. Allow me to illustrate via the following cautionary notes:

Cautionary Note #1. The most serious problem bedeviling the use of test data to evaluate teachers is the very real likelihood that students are purposefully assigned to certain teachers based upon their past test performance (such as honoring parental requests that their high-achieving children be placed with an unusually effective teacher, which in turn would help perpetuate a self-fulfilling prophesy). If this occurs with any frequency, it could completely invalidate the entire underpinnings of the technique. One researcher, Jesse Rothstein, actually attempted to test the effects of this potential nonequivalent student–teacher assignment process using as close a variant of Sanders' value-added approach as possible.[41] Incredibly, what he found was that the value-added *fifth*-grade teacher effectiveness scores also predicted the same students' *fourth*-grade teacher effectiveness scores quite nicely. Since students' fifth-grade teachers couldn't have possibly had a *causal* influence upon their fourth-grade teachers' effectiveness, something *had* to be very wrong here. Rothstein interpreted his results as indicating that there was something quite purposeful and consistent about the way students were assigned to teachers at the beginning of the year. Of course, another possibility is that there may be something very wrong with the value-added teacher evaluation model itself.

A similarly troubling finding from the Chicago high school analysis just discussed, of which Sanders was an author, was that the value-added effects for English teachers tended to predict their students' math teachers' effectiveness as well. This sounds suspiciously like a glitch of some sort in the predictive scheme itself, although, as is their wont, Sanders and his colleagues put a happy face on this finding, calling it a "robustness check"—whatever that means.

The real question, of course, is why should having an effective ninth-grade English teacher *cause* students to have an effective ninth-grade math teacher? (Naturally, we wouldn't be surprised if English test scores are correlated with math test scores, but the value-added model supposedly controls for this.) Or, stated another way: Why should what students learn in ninth-grade English have a *causal* effect upon what they learn in ninth-grade math? If this occurred in, say, third grade, we could hypothesize that the children's reading improvement helped them read their math textbooks better (or their standardized math test's word problems), but in general most ninth-grade English teachers don't teach basic reading skills or how to facilitate comprehension of math word problems. (Of course, there is no question that many ninth-grade students would benefit from such instruction.)

So, in the presence of nonrandom student assignment to teachers and these backward (Rothstein's work) and sideways (English teachers predicting math teachers' effectiveness) predictive findings, shouldn't we worry just a little about the circularity of the fact that teacher effectiveness and student improvement are based upon exactly the same data (student test scores)? Would it really be so bizarre to speculate about which causes which? Couldn't the students' performance also be conceptualized as at least partially causing some of their teachers to *appear* more effective (or ineffective) than they really were? To me, this makes more sense than students' fifth-grade teachers' performance "predicting" the same students' fourth-grade teachers' performance.

Cautionary Note #2. In effect, value-added teacher evaluations control what they can and then assume that everything that can't be predicted on the basis of previous test scores must be due to the teacher. (At present, we have no way to disaggregate classroom contextual effects from teacher effects.) This is a rather tenuous assumption, because undoubtedly classroom dynamics play into how much is learned in a classroom over an entire year. Perhaps, unbeknownst to the teacher (or outside of her or his control), bullying is occurring during recess, in the bathroom, or at lunch. Or, perhaps the classroom instruction itself is impeded by an unusually large number of disruptive influences, or the actual physical environment of the room itself is substandard for some reason.

As another example of the dangers of relegating everything that isn't controlled to teacher influences, the fact that tests are administered once a year by necessity assigns any summer learning losses due to forgetting (as is typical among students from depressed home learning environments) to the next year's teacher. This also relegates any new learning occurring over the summer (due to formal or informal summer instruction which is more typical of children from families of higher socioeconomic strata) to the next year's teacher. Perhaps we can eventually develop a method by which these problems can be statistically controlled (possibly by something as simple as testing students at the beginning of the year as well as in May), *but, in the meantime, it is almost 100% certain that uncontrolled home environmental variables overestimate the size of current value-added teacher effects.* It probably also explains value-added proponents' counterintuitive conclusion that teacher effects are more powerful than individual differences between children. (That is, they are ascribing a substantial portion of these differences between children to differences between teachers.)

Cautionary Note #3. There is a school of educational research, to which value-added proponents are charter members, that believes that, if enough data are available, all future occurrences can be predicted with extreme accuracy (and the effects of all previously occurring causal factors can be whisked away). The problem with most existing educational databases, however, is that they (a) are fraught with error, (b) contain a great deal of missing data due to student absences/family movements, and (c) lack key information on potentially important variables (because the databases were constructed for completely different purposes in the first place).

These limitations in our existing data almost surely *reduce* our ability to statistically control for what is far and away the most potent determinant of school learning: *individual differences among students* and therefore erroneously inflate the effects attributed to teachers. Thus, to the extent to which errors, lack of data, and unknown determinants of learning impede our ability to adjust for these differences, value-added teacher differences will be overestimated because teachers are credited with the outcomes they haven't affected (or with uncontrolled effects having nothing to do with teacher performance).

On the other hand, there is no question that value-added analysts have earnestly endeavored to produce the most accurate predictions for students' performance possible (based upon their past performance) and for this they deserve a great deal of credit. There are situations, however, in which statistical adjustment just can't solve the problems of unmeasured influences on learning. One involves comparing students enrolled (or the teachers who instruct them) in schools serving economically depressed families to those enrolled (or teaching) in schools serving economically/ educationally advantaged families. Disadvantaged students most likely will exhibit cumulatively decelerating achievement trajectories as a function of time and exposure to these nonconducive learning environments whereas, in contrast, advantaged students will exhibit increasingly propitious educational prognoses. There is no way that I know of to disaggregated teacher effects from these diametrically opposed learning trajectories because *they occur during the same time interval* and because they will be *more* pronounced each subsequent year than they were the year before.

With all of this said, sometime in the future, a value-added approach to estimating teacher effects may prove workable. Unfortunately, claims for its present validity, characterized by some of its proponents breathlessly positive claims[45] and reluctance to make their work sufficiently transparent to permit independent replication[46] has led at least one inveterate

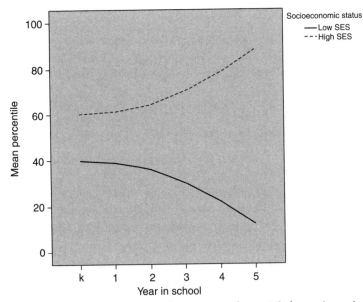

Figure 1.1 Natural Trajectories of Students from High vs. Low Learning-enriched Environments

champion of using student achievement to evaluate teaching performance (W. James Popham, a former president of the American Educational Research Association) to characterize this particular version of value-added teacher assessment as follows:

> There is an old saying that "data gathered with a rake should not be analyzed with a microscope." I think that in Tennessee the rake-collected data are being analyzed with a *mystery* microscope. (p. 270)[47]

So, although we may all believe it is possible (and wish it were already a reality) to evaluate teachers using existing standardized test scores, I'm afraid that value-added teacher assessment really isn't anywhere near ready for prime time. As it happens, however, in the chapters that follow, I will propose some strategies that could greatly increase teachers' ability to produce the learning gains we aspire for all of our children, while at the same time decreasing *differences* between teachers in their ability to do so. But first, let's see what classic research tells us about about what could *cause* some teachers to be more effective than others.

Beyond Value-Added Teacher Assessment

One of the problems with the value-added approach to teacher assessment, which is probably also one reason for its failure to identify teachers who are *consistently* effective or ineffective across time, is its black box approach to the entire process. In other words it employs a strictly statistical strategy for differentiating between teachers without attempting to explain *why* the students of some teachers seem to learn more than the students of other teachers.

As it happens, however, we already know *why*. The explanation is found in the truly seminal piece of educational research called the "Beginning Teacher Evaluation Study" which will be discussed in more detail in Chapter 2. Employing intensive, repeated observations of 25 second- and 25 fifth-grade classrooms, this study found that, on average, 2 hours and 15 minutes of the second-grade school day was devoted to academic activities (which were defined as instruction in reading, mathematics, science, and social studies), whereas 55 minutes was devoted to nonacademic activities (such as music and art), and 44 minutes was "wasted" on things such as waiting for assignments and conducting class business.

Taking math and reading as the two primary academic subjects of interest, the researchers found that, on average, the 25 second-grade teachers allocated 2 hours and 6 minutes per day to instruction. Their students were actually engaged in learning for 1 hour and 30 minutes (or 71% of the time). What was even more telling, however, was the fact that the top 10% (approximately) of the teachers allocated 50 minutes more to instruction than did the bottom 10%, and their students were actually engaged in learning these subjects for about the same amount of extra time (50 minutes).[48] Although this may not sound like a great deal, it means that, in these two crucial subjects, some children could receive 150 hours more instruction during a school year than other students. And, since the average amount of time actually allocated to teaching these subjects was 2 hours and 6 minutes, this means that some children received 71.4 days more instruction than others, or *a total of over 14 weeks of extra schooling*!

To put all of this in context, the investigators contrast two hypothetically average students, one of whom (Student A) receives a grand total of 4 minutes per day of relevant instruction and one (Student B) who receives

52 minutes. Since these students are average, they would start the year at the 50th percentile on the standardized tests, yet by midyear Student A would decline to the 39th percentile, while Student B would improve to the 66th percentile! The authors go on to justify the feasibility of their analyses as follows:

> It may appear that this range from 4 to 52 minutes per day is unrealistically large. However, these times actually occurred in the classes in the study. Furthermore, it is easy to image how either 4 to 52 minutes of reading instruction per day might come about. If 50 minutes of reading instruction per day is allocated to a student (Student A) who pays attention a third of the time, and one-fourth of the students' reading time is at a high level of success [these authors defined "a high level of success" as instruction administered at an appropriate level of difficulty], the student will experience only about 4 minutes of engaged reading at a high success level. Similarly, if 100 minutes per day is allocated to reading for a student (Student B) who pays attention 85 percent of the time, at a high level of success for almost two-thirds of that time, then she/he will experience 52 minutes of Academic Learning Time per day. (p. 23)[49]

So, the moral here is that *massive* differences exist in both the amount of instruction that different teachers deliver, as well as in the amount of *relevant* instruction students *receive*. (We've already mentioned some work[50] that found that the variability in the amount of instruction received by typical students on a school wide basis can be as much as 50%, which borders upon a criminal offense in my opinion.)

So while I haven't seen these studies even mentioned in the value-added literature, in my opinion they constitute the only theoretical rationale of which I am aware for why we *should* be able to differentiate teachers who produce more learning from those who produce less of it. And by simply monitoring classroom instruction by continuously recording it on digital cameras (assuming that provisions were made for constantly identifying opportunities for improvement and then providing sufficient professional development to show teachers how to teach more intensely) we could go a very long way toward either reducing teacher differences in performance or weeding out those teachers who *consistently* teach less. At the very least we could combine these data with value-added procedures, which in turn might improve the latter's present woeful ability to identify teacher differences that were consistent over time.

Teacher Training

Of course, it could be argued that it isn't even necessary to attempt to properly differentiate between good and bad teachers, given the exemplary training all of our teachers receive. Said another way, perhaps our teacher-preparatory institutions ensure that all of their graduates perform competently, hence negating the possibility of documenting learning production differences among teachers.

One of the first schooling experiments I ever conducted was, in fact, an indirect test of this proposition. My study was inspired by a very famous educational researcher at the time, W. James Popham (mentioned previously as a critic of value-added teacher assessment), who conducted a series of experiments that were designed to find a way to measure teaching proficiency but inadvertently found instead that *neither* teacher experience nor training had any effect upon student learning.[51]

The rationale for his studies was innocuous enough. Popham hypothesized that perhaps one reason we cannot differentiate exemplary teachers from abysmally ineffective ones (always defined, incidentally, by how much their students *learned*) was that our standardized tests simply weren't sensitive enough to measure teacher performance. Just as today, these large amorphous tests weren't that closely matched to the school curriculum, so commercial tests themselves didn't necessarily assess what teachers actually taught in their classrooms. How then could they be used to measure teaching performance? Especially since up to 60% of these test scores are due to individual differences in student backgrounds, thereby leaving only 40% to be explained by other factors (of which teacher differences may account for only a small percentage).

So, Popham decided to start from scratch and develop a series of *teaching performance tests*. First, he designed experimental units based upon discrete instructional objectives, which reflect small pieces of instruction that can be tested directly such as:

> *Sample Instructional Objective:* "Given any two single digit numbers, the student will be able to supply their sum."

Then, each instructional objective was accompanied by a test item that assessed its mastery:

Sample Test Item Assessing this Objective: 7 + 4 = ___.)

The use of instructional objectives and tests based upon them accomplished two crucial functions:

1. They ensured that the teachers knew exactly what they were expected to teach, and
2. The resulting tests assessed exactly what the teacher was expected to teach, nothing more and nothing less.

Thus, for our exceedingly simple illustrative instructional objective above (Popham used more complex ones in his studies involving high school students), there are exactly 100 (and only 100) test items that can be generated to assess the degree to which students mastered the objective (and presumably how well the teacher performed her or his job). Before advocating the use of his tests as a full-blown measure of teacher proficiency, however, Popham wisely decided to validate his approach via a technique called the "known-groups" approach.

The logic behind this technique involved finding two groups of teachers who were "known" to differ on the "thing" being assessed, having them teach the same instructional unit to a comparable classroom, and then seeing if the students taught by the two groups differed in the amount they learned. In this case, the "thing" was teacher proficiency in eliciting learning, so the first task was to find two groups of teachers: one of whom was known to be much more proficient than the other. But therein lay a classic Catch 22. How could anyone identify proficient versus nonproficient teachers if a test didn't yet exist that was capable of rank ordering instructional success?

No problem for Popham. He simply defined his proficient group as professionally trained, credentialed, experienced teachers and his nonproficient group as individuals who had never had any formal teacher training or teaching experience, such as housewives, electricians, and auto mechanics. (The housewives taught social studies, while the other two groups taught topics in their respective vocations.)

And, intuitively, how could anyone construct two more disparate groups of instructors than trained, experienced teachers versus untrained, inexperienced nonteachers? Thus, Popham had done everything he could to stack the experimental deck (which is appropriate in this instance) to ensure his obtaining huge learning differences between the two groups of students that these teachers and nonteachers taught. So, then this researcher did what all researchers must finally do. He ran the studies and analyzed the results.

While I don't know for sure, I suspect that Popham considered the outcome to be a slam dunk. After all, the experiments' sole purpose was simply to provide a gross validation of a very carefully constructed teacher proficiency examinations (which, in turn, were to be simply based upon how much students *learned* of what they had been taught). And it is worthwhile to note that Dr. Popham was and is one of our most renowned testing experts.

But as the Scottish poet Robert Burns warned us a couple of centuries ago, "The best-laid schemes o' mice an 'men gang (*often*) aft (*go*) agley (*astray*)." The tests functioned quite well for everything except the one purpose for which they were developed. They didn't differentiate between (a) trained, experienced teachers and (b) untrained, inexperienced nonteachers. The conclusion was obvious, if unstated at the time: perhaps (just perhaps) there *really wasn't any difference between trained, experienced teachers and untrained, inexperienced nonteachers as far as student learning is concerned.*

But, although the conclusion was obvious, it wasn't one that I was willing to accept at the time, even though this investigator had basically conducted three separate experiments and found the same thing in each. I was a graduate of a baccalaureate teacher preparatory program, after all, and although none of my courses ever taught me anything about how to teach reading, language arts, or science, for some reason (probably simple cognitive dissonance) I couldn't bring myself to connect the dots. I reasoned instead that the fault must lie in the way the studies had been conducted: one possibility being that it would be much easier to document an effect for teacher training at the elementary school level than in high school (where these particular studies took place). After all, elementary education graduates take many more education courses than do secondary education graduates.

So, being an inveterate skeptic, I set out—with my collaborator, Dr. William B. Moody (who was in charge of preparing elementary school mathematics teachers at the University of Delaware)—to prove Popham wrong and demonstrate that trained, experienced teachers were indeed better at eliciting student learning than were untrained, inexperienced nonteachers.[52] We designed an experimental elementary school curriculum based upon a set of very explicit instructional objectives that addressed a few number theory topics that we knew elementary students wouldn't have been already exposed to. We then developed a test based upon those objectives (and only those objectives) and located 15 accredited teachers who were willing to devote a week's instruction to them. We also located 15 undergraduate elementary school of education majors who had not yet enrolled in the College of Education course designed to teach them how to teach mathematics (and who had no formal teaching experience).

Each undergraduate was then randomly assigned to teach a comparable classroom within the same schools that housed the real teachers. (Unfortunately, we couldn't randomly assign the trained teachers because they didn't have the time to travel between schools, but we did make sure that they weren't assigned any of their regular students, since this could have conceivably influenced the results.) Both the undergraduates and the credentialed teachers taught the same instructional objectives for exactly the same amount of time for a week. And, at the end of the week's instruction, all of the elementary school students in all of the 30 classrooms were administered the same test based solely upon the instructional objectives that had been covered.

And, of course, the results were the same as Popham's! There was absolutely no difference, not even a trend toward a difference, between the amount the children learned in the 15 classrooms taught by experienced elementary school teachers and the amount the children learned in the 15 classrooms taught by inexperienced, untrained undergraduates. The conclusion seemed inescapable. Teacher training (and perhaps teaching experience) has no (or very little) effect upon student learning. Therefore, should we be surprised if it is extremely difficult to differentiate effective from ineffective teachers (or very effective from moderately effective teachers)?

As I'll discuss in Chapter 5, I even replicated these results later. By that point, I could no longer ignore what my data were telling me, as exemplified by the concluding paragraph I wrote in an editorial for the premiere educational policy journal (*Phi Delta Kappan*) of the time. A paragraph which also saves me the bother of explaining why I had to seek employment at somewhere other than a college of education:

> Teacher preparation as provided by colleges of education does not result in increased student achievement. The implications of this conclusion are equally inescapable. If the effect of an institution upon its primary purpose is not robust enough to be detected by existing measuring instruments, then the lives of men should not be much affected by its absence. Therefore, given limited educational resource allocations, should we not abandon teacher education?[53]

But, before I share a couple of the studies that completely changed my vision of how children *should* be educated in our schools, I think it would be informative to examine some alternative visions of how school learning can be improved. For the first of these visions, we will have to go back a few years in time to examine how one educational theorist used the research results we've just discussed to come up with a theory of school learning guaranteed to set anyone's teeth on edge who cares about the education of society's children. Research findings, incidentally, which might succinctly be summarized as follows:

> *When it comes to standardized test scores, be they achievement, aptitude, intelligence, or just about anything else, everything is related to everything else, and performance on one test at one point in a child's life predicts performance on another test at another point. When it comes to steps we can actually take to improve learning within the classroom setting (which involves everything from trying to improve teacher education to tailoring instructional methods to students' learning attributes), nothing seems to work except additional instruction.*

For a couple of opposing views, we'll then fast forward to a time after I had left education, and examine a few theories that were informed by some astonishing findings about the educational process that we've only briefly alluded to.

CHAPTER 2

Dueling Theories

If you think about it, our little whirlwind trip through the world of learning research results could be viewed as rather discouraging to anyone whose objective is to improve public school learning. This was especially the case in the late 1960s, when I enrolled as an educational doctoral student and began doing research. These were heady times, when cynicism was fashionable among the young, but when they truly believed that things could be changed for the better, even something as intractable as the public schools. After all, why would anyone go into education if they didn't think they could transform it to something that promoted, rather than impeded, the attainment of all of our children's ultimate potentials?

But there was at least one educational theorist who was exceedingly well grounded in the bottom-line research conclusions just reviewed and who was accordingly quite pessimistic about what could be done to improve the institution of schooling. Or, even what it was *capable* of accomplishing under the best of circumstances.

This individual's name was John Mortimer Stephens, and he was invited one winter day to the University of Delaware's College of Education to give a talk based upon his recent book, *The Process of Schooling.*[1] At the time, I was a huge admirer of Professor Stephens' theory of schooling and, to my surprise, he was also aware of my work, even though I was still a graduate student and had only recently begun publishing some of my experiments.

He consequently asked to see me on the day of his arrival, and the two of us wound up conversing for an hour or so in an empty office that had been temporarily designated for his use. Despite the obvious cultural and generational gaps separating us, we appeared to be completely in synch intellectually. He even acceded to my request to include in his lecture my favorite metaphor from his book, since I knew that few if any of the undergraduates who would be coerced into attending his talk would have read *The Process of Schooling*.

THEORY #1: THE CORNFIELDS OF LEARNING

This stereotypical 1940s/1950s, tweed-suited professor's theory, in fact, was about as cynical and nihilistic as anything any 1960s radical could have conceived. Perhaps this is what initially attracted me to it. Stephens published his book in 1967, but its first sentence is enough to elicit a sense of déjà vu from anyone with even a passing familiarity with what is going on in our schools today:

> The current and growing agitation about education and the schools has expressed itself in a demand for immediate reform and for an increase in efficiency. (p. 3)

How sad, then, that this discouraging commentary on the state of education is as relevant today as it was in 1967. How much sadder still that the even more discouraging prognosis for our schools emanating from Stephens' theory has proved so prophetic: that the most powerful determinant of schooling success among students remains their individual differences, which appear to be set in stone before those students ever arrive at school.

Further, since schools are almost perfectly segregated by this learning prognosis, the schools that serve students with lower propensities to learn will themselves be judged as less successful (as defined by standardized testing results) than are those schools that enroll students with higher learning propensities. This in turn requires parents with higher aspirations for their children's educations to exit one set of schools for the other as soon as possible if they have the economic means to do so—which encourages the more committed teachers and administrators to exit as well.

And, incredible as it may seem, to this day we remain absolutely impotent to do anything at all to arrest this vicious cycle, much less close the gap between "high" and "low" performing children and the schools they attend. The result? Our schools are arguably as racially segregated as they were in 1967—at least for African American children from lower socioeconomic families.

But, let's briefly look at J.M. Stephens' vision of the "process of schooling," if only to examine one defensible implication of the discouraging research results we've previously discussed. Early on in his book, Professor Stephens posited a fanciful parallel between the development of agriculture and the institutionalization of teaching (which was the metaphor that I requested he include in his lecture to the undergraduates). According to Stephens, the former had its genesis in some ancient peoples' custom of burying their dead along with a small store of wild grains to help tide them over on their journey into the afterlife. Since some of these seeds were inevitably spilled around the gravesite, observant precursors to our scientific community noted that the process often resulted in a small harvest a few months later. The conclusion was obvious: Burying a corpse caused grain to grow.

And, as history records (at least according to Stephens), the formulation of this brilliant conclusion turned out to be a giant leap forward for mankind. Once the tribal elders became convinced of the inference's veracity, each spring thereafter a corpse was planted and, sure enough, the grain grew. If corpses were not available through natural causes, society's growing dependence upon cereal products ensured that one would be supplied at the critical time. Fortunately, to the great relief of the unfortunates who were earmarked to rectify these deficits, Stephens tell us that:

> It was not until many years later that some bold radical questioned the value of this main feature of the process and found, after experimentation, that the planting would be almost as effective if there were no corpse at all. (p. 4)

For Stephens, the lesson here was obvious:

> It is easy to focus our attention on the conspicuous, dogmatic events that call for deliberate decisions. Conversely, it is natural to ignore the humble, ever-present forces that work consistently, independent of our concern. Seeds sprout and take root, and plants mature, with little attention from us. Corpses, on the other hand, call for deliberate and careful attention. (p. 4)

Professor Stephens went on to argue that children's learning was very similar to plants growing. Given naturally persisting conditions, seeds will germinate and grow; children will learn. Plant some seed in reasonably fertile soil and, assuming normal meteorological conditions, corn will result. Plant the seed in sand and no corn will grow, corpse or no corpse. Put children in front of an adult willing to talk about tribal rituals or geometry and learning will occur. Based upon this parable, Stephens concluded:

> If this theory should be true, we would be making a great mistake in regarding the management of schools as similar to the process of constructing a building or operating a factory. In these latter processes, deliberate decisions play a crucial part, and the enterprise advances or stands still in proportion to the amount of deliberate effort exerted. If we must use a metaphor or model in seeking to understand the process of schooling, we should look to agriculture rather than to the factory. In agriculture we do not start from scratch, and we do not direct our efforts to inert and passive materials. *We start, on the contrary, with a complex and ancient process, and we organize our efforts around what seeds, plants, and insects are likely to do anyway. Through an improved understanding of these organic processes we can almost revolutionize the output, but we do not supplant or ignore these older organic forces. We always work through them.* (p. 11)

Thus, unlike a factory forced to work with "inert and passive materials," the management of schools permitted a far more relaxed attitude, according to this elderly scholar. True, it might be possible to improve the output of schooling (i.e., learning) by understanding the forces involved, but probably not by much:

> One of the psychological phenomena to be explained is the remarkable constancy of educational results in the face of widely differing deliberate approaches. Every so often we adopt new approaches or new methodologies and place our reliance on new panaceas. At the very least we seem to chorus new slogans. Yet the academic growth within the classroom continues at about the same rate, stubbornly refusing to cooperate with the bright new dicta emanating from the conference room. (p. 9)

Why? Because the crop "once planted may undergo *some* development even while the farmer sleeps or loafs. No matter what he does, *some* of the aspects will remain constant."

As would any good academician, Stephens gave the generalizations resulting from these processes a name—the "theory of spontaneous schooling"—and went on to suggest that an acceptance of its attendant principles permitted a *"prescription for relaxation."* A few selected quotes illustrate this attitude quite nicely:

1. "In dealing with schooling, as in dealing with so many other vital processes, we are reminded that we can rely on powerful, pervasive forces, ready to do their work with only moderate deliberate direction from us. In dealing with crucial problems, of course, the most convincing reassurance comes from the awareness of the built-in machinery (i.e., children's natural propensity to learn in the presence of *instruction*) that can be depended upon to take care of matters." (p. 132)
2. "In respect to the curriculum (i.e., *what* is taught)... the primitive forces will continue to produce schooling, whether accompanied by a valid rationale, by a phony rationale, or by no rationale at all." (p. 134)
3. "After setting up the primitive school, our community is seen as going blithely on its way and leaving the school to manage its own affairs. The community, of course, provides the necessary support, both physical and moral. But there is no suggestion that it goes in for the frantic cooperating between home and school that is so often advocated at present." (p. 135)

Undoubtedly, it was this laissez-faire attitude toward schooling, coupled with Stephens' understandable reliance upon the type of schooling research available to him in those days (which tended to be quite poorly controlled), that ultimately prevented his work from having any long-term, serious impact. For, although Stephens' conclusions were indeed correctly based upon the preponderance of the scientific evidence available in those days, he did not appear to understand that research conducted based upon assuming that the classroom model of delivering instruction is some law of nature that can never be changed actually precludes researchers from ever finding anything of true significance. (I'll discuss this more fully in Chapter 5, where I contrast the science of "what could be" versus "what is.") He also chose not to bother himself with the wasteland of urban schooling in any detail, probably because he believed there was very little that could be done about it.

But, although Professor Stephens' interpretation of the evidence may have been flawed, it has been said that in science the best fate to which any scientist can aspire is to perform work important enough for those who come later to make the effort necessary to disprove it. So, I like to think— if the choice were his, based upon our meeting lo so many years ago— that Professor Stephens might well have selected that young man to be the one to perform this coup de grâce. Unfortunately, several people beat me to it.

THEORY #2: EVERYBODY CAN

Although not unaware of research findings emanating from the statistical mining of large test score databases, J.M. Stephens based his view of schooling primarily upon the work of interventionists who actually went into the schools and manipulated various aspects of the instructional process (such as different instructional methods) in order to observe their effects upon learning. He was, of course, fully aware of Coleman's seminal conclusions, in 1966, that the most powerful determinants of success in school lie in what children bring to the schooling process, rather than in what happens to them once they're enrolled.[2] Or, that of other researchers whose work preceded the Coleman report, such as John Kemp,[3] who, in 1955, wrote the following:

> To estimate the general academic performance that will occur in a given school, ask first about the general intellectual level of the children and the social and economic background of the parents . . . . *This information will account for almost 60% of all the differences that will be found from school to school.* (p. 50)

The theorist who may have been most influenced by this genre of work, however, was Professor Benjamin S. Bloom, of the University of Chicago, who had a storied career as an educational theorist, researcher, and taxonomist of instructional objectives. Completing his most influential work a decade or so after Stephens' book, Professor Bloom had a more lasting impact upon the field and remains highly regarded (if ignored) to this day.

The evidence-based components of Bloom's theory[4] were largely, although not exclusively, grounded on the analysis of test scores, but its conceptual underpinnings were heavily influenced by a researcher/theorist named John Carroll and his concept of "mastery learning."[5] Carroll believed that one of the classroom model's greatest failures lay in its propensity (some would say its inherent *necessity*) to allow teachers to administer as much instruction on a topic as they had time for (or personally considered to be sufficient) and then to move on to the next unit. If an unknown proportion of the class had not learned the unit's most important concepts before the next unit was sprung on them, what of it? Someone had to make an executive decision and balance the need of faster learners against those of their slower counterparts.

For Carroll and Bloom, the alternative was as obvious as the draconian consequences of this "teach and move on" approach: Provide students with individualized instruction on a topic or unit they learned (or "mastered") it—*then* move on. This might mean that some students would master a topic in one 50-minute class period (in which case *they* would move on to the next topic) while it might take others a week, but the final result would be that everyone would wind up learning what they needed to know.

The alternative, since much of the schooling curriculum is sequential (i.e., learning one topic is prerequisite for learning another), is that students who do not master prerequisite concepts become increasingly and utterly lost as their teachers progress through the curriculum. In fact, the instructional process reaches a point at which children must be segregated according to their mastery of a subject, or at some point a majority of the class will either:

- Be incapable of understanding *anything* that is being taught, or
- Have already mastered everything that is being taught.

In either case, instruction becomes totally irrelevant for a sizable portion of any given classroom.

True, conscientious teachers have always done the best they could to take previous learning into consideration by tailoring their instruction to the needs of individual students. They do this via the use of special materials that different students can work on individually at their desks and via small-group instruction involving students at different levels of accomplishment.

In many classrooms, however, teachers do not have good data on exactly which aspects of an instructional unit any given student has mastered. And, although all teachers administer tests of their own making to assess learning, only those tests that make appropriate use of explicit instructional objectives[6] are sensitive enough to indicate mastery of a unit of instruction.

Trimmed to its core, the mastery learning concept involved assessing exactly what students had learned from a unit of instruction and reteaching those who did not demonstrate mastery until they did. Implicit in this approach was the belief that just about everyone in a typical classroom could learn everything in the curriculum; it just might take longer because they hadn't mastered the prerequisite knowledge and skills. There was also some evidence from laboratory-type studies that, once this prerequisite knowledge was obtained, *slower students began to pick up speed and master the learning objectives quicker.*

In presenting his theory of schooling (or school learning), Bloom stated this position more explicitly than anyone else in education of whom I'm aware. As an example, speaking of the "middle 95% of students where *equality of outcomes* is a realistic possibility," Bloom made the following prediction that probably best encapsulates his view of the potential of schooling:

> Essentially, it is that what any person in the world can learn, almost all persons can learn *if* provided with appropriate prior and current conditions of learning. While there will be some special exceptions to this, the theory provides an optimistic picture of what education can do for humans. It holds out the possibility that favorable conditions of school learning can be developed which will enable all humans to attain the *best* that any humans have already attained. (p. 7)

Bloom went on to argue that, although he acknowledged the huge individual differences in students that Coleman and others had found (and that he himself found in his voluminous analyses of test scores), educators in his day (and I would argue today as well) were using the existence of this phenomenon inappropriately:

> Individual differences in learners are invoked to explain and account for individual differences in learning and as a rationalization for the differential opportunities for further learning to be provided by the schools and the communities that support them. (p. 8)

He further believed that test scores should be tools to inform instruction, and he eschewed the use of tests to make self-fulfilling prophecies:

> A judgment is made about the learner and only rarely is a judgment made about the teaching or the previous preparation of the learner. These judgments about the learner by the parents, teachers, and the schools are effective in convincing the learner that he is different from other learners and that he can learn better or that he can learn less well than others of the same age or school level. Having convinced the student and themselves, both the students and the significant adults in his life act accordingly.

Bloom therefore developed a theory of school learning in which the student's learning outcomes for any discrete instructional experience were dependent upon two student characteristics and one instructional characteristic. The only two student characteristics of merit in Bloom's theory were (a) "cognitive entry behaviors" (comprised of a student's prior instruction, whether it took place in the home or in previous school instruction), and (b) "affective entry characteristics" (comprised primarily of students' attitudes toward learning, which Bloom considered to be largely based upon their interpretation of their personal prior learning experiences and the messages delivered by "the significant adults in their lives"). The single instructional input was termed the "quality of instruction" and primarily involved ensuring that the student had mastered all necessary prerequisites for the impending instructional episode and (of course) that *enough* instruction was administered until the student achieved mastery of the content.

But, as important as instructional quality was, Bloom believed—based upon the evidence we've already discussed—that it was dwarfed in importance by what the students brought to the learning environment:

> We doubt that the Quality of Instruction can overcome the effect of the lack of prerequisite cognitive entry behaviors unless the instruction is directly related to remedying these deficiencies or unless the nature of a learning task is sufficiently altered to make it appropriate for students in terms of the entry behaviors they bring to the task. In other words, the lack of the necessary prerequisite cognitive entry behaviors for a particular learning task should make it *impossible* for the student to master the learning task requirements no matter how good the quality of instruction for that task. (p. 109)

And this, I believe, was Bloom's seminal theoretical contribution to our understanding of school learning. Central to this thesis, however, was his acknowledgment that some students learn the same material much faster than others (perhaps requiring from one-fifth to one-sixth as much time).[7] He argued, however, that this learning time was quite malleable[8] and, indeed, Lorin Anderson, one of his doctoral students at the University of Chicago, demonstrated that with practice, testing, and remedial tutoring, *the time needed to learn decreases quickly with repeated experiences.* In Anderson's words:

> Two major conclusions can be derived from this study. First, the amount of necessary time-on-task-to-criterion can be altered by an effective teaching–learning strategy such as mastery learning. Second, a relatively heterogeneous group of students can become quite homogeneous in the amount of time-on-task they require to learn a particular learning task after mastering a series of preparatory tasks. This would imply that if equality of learning outcomes is a desired goal in certain instances in education, it can be achieved by designing learning situations that allow for inequalities in the characteristics that students bring to the learning situation. If, on the other hand, students are presented with a learning situation in which all are given an equal amount of elapsed time and instructional help, the results would be unequal learning outcomes. (pp. 232-233)[9]

Of course, no one has ever demonstrated that individual differences in learning time will ever disappear completely, but so what? This simply means that some individuals will have to spend more time studying (or schools will have to spend more time teaching them); everyone's grandmother knows that.

THEORY #3: EVERY TEACHER CAN

Another conceptualization of school learning, which is basically an extension of both Carroll and Bloom, is sometimes referred to as Academic Learning Time (ALT). It was born in a previously mentioned study known as the *Beginning Teacher Evaluation Study,*[10] which both validated much of Bloom's theory but generated some fascinating findings that were potentially more germane to everyday classroom instruction than Bloom and his students' laboratory work.

The study itself involved the careful observation of a sample of 261 second- and fifth-grade students. The targeted students were purposefully selected based upon their being in the midranges of ability (to partially control for that 40%–60% difference in student achievement that has been mentioned so many times previously) and were observed in their classrooms for one complete day per week for 20 weeks (i.e., from October to May). Three types of classrooms were also purposefully chosen, but this time to ensure as wide a range as possible of classroom practices: specifically classes where student achievement in math and reading were exceptionally high, average, and exceptionally low.

The observations were made by trained field workers who recorded the amount of time teachers allocated to their instruction, the students' engagement rates, and the degree to which the instruction assigned to individual students was appropriate (i.e., could be performed with a reasonable degree of success). The major analyses of these data assessed relationships between (1) the amount of ALT and student achievement and (2) selected teaching behaviors and student achievement. The results of most interest to us here were:

- *"The amount of time that teachers allocate to instruction in a particular curriculum content area is positively associated with student learning in that content area" (p. 15).* A secondary, but very interesting finding, involved the huge differences found among teachers with respect to the time actually allocated for instruction. As one example, "in the fifth grade some classes received less than 1,000 minutes of instruction in reading comprehension (projected) for the school year (about 10 minutes per day). This figure can be contrasted with classes where the average student was allocated almost 5,000 minutes of instruction related to comprehension during the school year (about 50 minutes per day)" (p. 16). Is it really surprising, therefore, that instructional time of these magnitudes is related to school learning?
- *"The teacher's prescription of appropriate tasks is related to student achievement and student success rate" (p. 16).* Here, the classroom observers rated how reasonable the difficulty of the instruction was for the particular students to whom it was delivered (i.e., whether it was likely to be too challenging or not challenging enough). This, of course, can also be conceptualized as an indicator of instructional

relevance (which we'll return to later), since instruction on topics that have already been learned (or which students do not have sufficient prior knowledge to master) is time wasted.

- *"The teacher's accuracy in diagnosing student skill levels is related to student achievement and Academic Learning Time"* (p. 19). Here, the teachers were asked to predict how their students would do on selected test items included in the tests used for the study. Not surprisingly, students whose teachers' predictions were more accurate learned more since we would expect those teachers who were more aware of their students' instructional needs to assign more appropriate (or *relevant*) learning tasks á la the previous finding.
- *"The percentage of instructional time during which the student received feedback was positively related to student engagement rate and to achievement"* (p. 20). This relates directly to the two preceding findings. In other words: How can a teacher prescribe appropriate tasks if he or she can't diagnose students' skill levels? And how can he or she do either if he or she doesn't observe the students' work closely enough to provide meaningful feedback?
- *"Teacher emphasis on academic goals is positively associated with student learning"* (p. 21). The investigators explained this as follows: "Classes judged to have high emphasis on academic performance typically showed high levels of achievement. These classes were not necessarily 'cold' or unconcerned with student feelings. They did, however, emphasize the importance of school learning. In contrast, some classes were primarily oriented toward affective outcomes, such as student attitudes and feelings. In these classes, less time was allocated to academic instruction, student engagement rates were lower, students were more likely to be given low success tasks, and student achievement was therefore lower."

From my perspective, this was an exemplary schooling study with truly exciting findings that not only supported Carroll and Boom's work, but which informed a credible schooling theory. It is hardly the only study of its kind that provided very similar results, however. One of my favorites, called the Instructional Dimensions Study[11], was published in the same year as the Beginning Teacher Evaluation Study and involved an in-depth examination of a whopping 400 classrooms selected from 100 different schools. Some of its authors' conclusions (William Cooley and

Gaea Leinhardt) resonate over the decades and make one wonder why anyone bothers to do educational research in the first place, since we are all doomed to be ignored in the end. Conclusions such as:

- "The most pronounced trend in these data, the importance of opportunity to learn (which was defined in terms of percentage of students on task and whether what was taught overlapped with what was tested), suggests that the most useful thing to do for children with underdeveloped reading and mathematics skills in the primary grades is to provide more direct instruction in these areas.... It seems clear that what gets taught is a more important consideration than how it's taught" (p. 22).
- "When certain ends are met, such as regular assessment of student mastery and attention to individual student needs, the question isn't how it's done, but that it is done in some fashion" (p. 22).
- "The results support the idea that instruction should emphasize the cognitive rather than the managerial. When teachers are forced—by overly complex programs, poor class discipline, or poor general organization—to focus on classroom management, they do so at the expense of direct instruction. This contention is supported, in this study, by consistently negative relationships between the number of management statements and the quality of instruction" (p. 23).
- Or, finally (see Chapter 8, which discusses the need to replace our obsolete testing system), "there is a danger of attributing instructional effectiveness to specific programs or ways of teaching when it is really a matter of the curriculum content being a good fit to the particular achievement test that happened to be selected" (p. 23).

And there were many other voices repeating these identical messages, such as Jere Brophy's summing up of two decades of this genre of research:

Students achieve more when their teachers emphasize academic objectives in establishing expectations and allocating time, use effective management strategies to ensure that academic learning time is maximized, pace students through the curriculum briskly but in small steps that allow high rates of success, and adapt curriculum materials based on their knowledge of students' characteristics. (p. 1069)[12]

Ultimately, however, the ALT paradigm (and the studies that supported it) seems to have had little impact upon actual classroom practice. And I think the reason is obvious. Like Bloom's theory before it, too much dependence was placed upon teacher behavior.

In other words, what if teachers themselves *choose* not to engage in those practices that promote student learning (as was obviously the case for a significant proportion of the teachers involved in both the Beginning Teacher Evaluation and the Instructional Dimensions Studies)? Or, what if the teacher was simply not *capable* of engaging in these behaviors because of the constraints inherent in the woefully obsolete classroom model?

The bottom line (as will be discussed in Chapter 5) is always the same. If we cannot "teacher proof" our children's instruction, it is impossible to improve learning on any consistent basis because too many teachers will either choose not to change the practices that they have become comfortable with or have no idea how to do so even if they choose to.[13] In reality, this is completely understandable because it is patently unrealistic to expect every teacher to perform all the tasks required, say, by the ALT or Bloom's model without providing them with the necessary infrastructure to do so. And the explication of exactly what that infrastructure needs to be is the subject of Chapter 6 as well as much of the second half of this book.

Classroom management is an extremely complex and demanding task. So, although the last two schooling theories presented (Benjamin Bloom's and the ALT paradigm) are largely correct, most teachers (even the most conscientious ones) cannot possibly perform all of the recommended tasks unaided within a typical 50-minute classroom period. I have personally observed both my parents attempting to prepare to do some variant of these individualization recommendations night after night for their following day's instruction, but it is very close to an impossible task and nothing short of a machine can do it accurately for an entire classroom for an entire school year. So, the sole reason why none of these models of classroom instruction had any real chance of implementation wasn't teacher noncompliance; it was a lack of technological capability that doomed them to the trash bin of educational history. And both factors are why J.M. Stephens' theory has proved to be correct for all of these years—just for the wrong reasons.

Fortunately, I had access to a source of evidence (and especially a *method of collecting this evidence*) that was not seriously considered by any of these theorists, and it is this evidence that will serve as the basis for a somewhat different view of the schooling process, one that happens to be very much closer to Professor Bloom's and the ALT researchers' position (as well as to John Carroll's) than to Professor Stephens'. Before discussing this evidence and the lessons its collection are capable of teaching us, however, I think it might be constructive to take a cursory look at the disparate philosophical views of the schooling process that modern educational thinkers have espoused.

CHAPTER 3

Dueling Political Perspectives

Modern educational policy, if based upon empirical evidence at all, tends to be almost exclusively informed by macro-level analyses of huge standardized test score databases. For our purposes, these data aren't particularly useful, since standardized tests are not measures of *classroom* learning per se. Instead, they measure learning resulting from all others sources of instruction as well, most notably the home learning environment. Still, these test scores do define what is considered by most people to be the number-one issue in American education: the racial/cultural/socioeconomic gap in school test performance that is present on the first day of preschool and persists until the final day of high school.

And, since discussions involving race, culture, and wealth are almost always politically motivated, I have arbitrarily chosen three candidates to represent the U.S. political spectrum on this issue, here labeled tongue-in-cheek as the "Demented Right," the "Naïve Left," and the "Almost Ready for Prime Time Center." All of these candidates address the following question:

> What is the genesis (and the solution) to the huge test score discrepancies characterizing schools serving inner-city African American/Hispanic children versus those serving suburban Caucasian/Asian children?

Each of the disparate answers to this question is represented by a book, which, in order of publication are (1) *The Bell Curve: Intelligence and Class Structure in American Life* (1994), by Richard J. Herrnstein and Charles Murray[1]; (2) *No Excuses: Closing the Racial Gap in Learning* (2003), by

Abigail and Stephan Thernstrom[2]; and (3) *The Shame of the Nation: The Restoration of Apartheid Schooling in America* (2005), by Jonathan Kozol.[3]

THE DEMENTED RIGHT

I think it is safe to say that Richard Herrnstein, a now-deceased Harvard psychologist, and Charles Murray, a recently deceased fellow at the American Enterprise Institute, would have proudly consider themselves members of the political far right. Their view of schooling also bears certain superficial similarities to Stephens' "Prescription for Relaxation," in the sense that they conclude that there is little or nothing that can be done to improve the public schools (as least as far as *racial* disparities in test scores are concerned).

They arrive at this conclusion from a perspective that is drastically different from that of Stephens, however, since they basically ascribed to the genetic determinism view of race and intelligence held by so many pioneers of intelligence testing. This position begins with the assumptions that:

- Intelligence tests are absolutely infallible gold standard assessments of human intellectual potential.
- Intelligence itself is associated with all things good (such as success in school, admission to high-prestige colleges, later employer ratings of productivity, and law-abiding behavior).
- Intelligence is just about 100% genetically determined based upon such unimpeachable research as (1) the administration of an intelligence test to a group of South African copper miners during the apartheid era, and (2) surveys of "experts" regarding what proportion of intelligence they *believe* to be genetic.

It was, therefore, no great logical stretch for Herrnstein and Murray, like their predecessors, to infer that since African Americans score lower on intelligence tests than Caucasians, then obviously they would be expected to benefit less from the schooling process. And while I personally find it extremely doubtful that many of *The Bell Curve*'s buyers actually read the entire 800-page tome, or seriously perused its 1,000+ citations (collected by five research assistants and many largely irrelevant to the case being made), the book's theoretical rationale was disarmingly simple and appealing to a large audience.

Now, of course, this is not a new educational or psychological position. One of its strongest proponents, the British educational psychologist Cyril Burt, felt so strongly about the heritable inevitability of intelligence that he apparently was moved to fabricate IQ data on nonexistent twins supposedly separated at birth.[4] Perhaps secretly embarrassed by what became known as the "Burt Affair," Herrnstein and Murray correspondingly took great pains to assure their readers that the accusations against Burt, however well-documented, amounted to little more than character assassination of a truly outstanding scholar despite his admittedly annoying habit of employing fictitious co-authors for his (fake) research studies (not to mention his citing of fictitious reviewers who unanimously heaped lavish praise upon his books). Similar defenses were mounted for such outstanding scholars as physicist William Shockley and psychologist Arthur Jensen to counter the racist/eugenicist slurs leveled against them.

However, simply because a position fits the construct that a more liberal audience might choose to label as *racist* doesn't mean that it can't constitute a serious theory of schooling. Some variant of this position is, I believe, the *prevalent* paradigm through which our intellectual elite still views the public schools.

Among the more interesting implications the authors derive from their philosophical orientation is that, since there is nothing the schools can do to reduce racial testing disparities, we should cease throwing good money after bad in the futile attempt to improve the performance of the genetically inferior and instead:

- Redirect more of our resources toward fostering the education of our intellectual elite and,
- Make immigration standards more stringent (since Hispanic children also perform worse than Caucasians on just about all types of standardized tests).

THE NAÏVE LEFT

Best known for his book, *Death at an Early Age*,[5] in which he describes his first year of teaching in the Boston public schools, Jonathan Kozol was active in the civil rights movement and remains dedicated to issues involving social justice. He has written a number of books, but in my opinion *The Shame of the Nation: The Restoration of Apartheid Schooling in America*, published in 2005, best exemplifies his view of the schooling process.

At the risk of oversimplification, Kozol's position appears to be that the most effective way to end racial disparities in school learning is to reduce concomitant disparities in school spending and school learning environments. Fostering civility and respect toward students, Kozol believes, is much more effective than the militaristic learning atmosphere advocated by some packaged systems designed to increase discipline and motivation in inner-city schools. As suggested in his book's title, he also rigorously opposes the current de facto racial segregation of our public schools.

He seems to believe that if we can make inner-city schools more like their suburban counterparts, then their test scores will be more similar as well. Schools that stress "back to basics" curricula are contraindicated and, in his view, also ultimately racist.

Kozol doesn't review much research evidence per se, preferring to cite observational and anecdotal examples of schools that serve African American students with optimally civil learning environments and that apparently produce better than average testing results. Unfortunately, he offers little in the way of concrete interventions capable of improving the learning output of inner-city schools. Although most people would agree that equitable funding, racial integration, and increased civility should all be integral components of any educational system, Kozol's—like most of Herrnstein's and Murray's arguments—are more of a political position than a theoretical view of the schooling process itself.

THE ALMOST READY FOR PRIME TIME CENTER

Abigail and Stephen Thernstrom, both fellows at the Manhattan Institute, share Herrnstein and Murray's ties to the think-tank culture, but the argument they espouse in *No Excuses: Closing the Racial Gap in Learning* probably owes more to the James Coleman's view of the educational process than to anyone else's. Coleman's genre of research, as you'll recall, was based upon large-scale, nonexperimental data that suggested it was the student's family (especially socioeconomic status as reflected by parental education, occupation, income, and race) that accounts for the vast majority of the variability in educational achievement—dwarfing any contribution made by the schools.

The Thernstroms conceptualize these factors in terms of culture, which they define as a sort of "tool kit" of skills provided by students' families (not unlike Bloom's "affective entry characteristics"). From this viewpoint, test performance can be improved for poor performing subgroups by changing the culturally accepted tolerance for substandard school performance.

Occasionally the Thernstroms appear to be flirting with advancing an actual theory of schooling, by which both school achievement *and* failure can be understood, without resorting either to the right's cherished black box of genetic intelligence or to the left's "all you need is money" refrains. Like Kozol, they provide glimpses of what they consider to be exemplary schools, but their favorites tend to possess the very characteristics that Kozol eschews: schools that stress discipline, motivational slogans, physical mannerisms, "back to basics" curricula, and uniforms. But in the end, they too wind up largely ignoring the prime determinant of learning (instructional time), and in so doing wind up simply rearranging the proverbial deck chairs on our schooling Titanic for perhaps the thousandth time. (In the Thernstroms' defense, however, many of the schools that they prefer also stress more hours of classroom instruction.)

The Thernstroms' take on racial disparities in test performance also has an interesting time-on-task twist, however. After demonstrating that the difference in the Asian American versus white American testing gap is almost as large as the difference in the testing gap between white Americans versus African Americans, the authors explain this phenomenon via survey results indicating that "Asian American youths study a lot more and spend fewer of their after school hours on sports or part-time jobs" (p. 94). This is, of course, completely in sync with what everyone's grandmother knows—that more instruction does result in more learning, a fact that the Thernstroms very succinctly sum up as:

> The children of immigrants are typically beating the competition because they are the true descendants of Benjamin Franklin. These American newcomers are the group that has most intensely embraced the traditional American work ethic. (p. 95)

This evocation of Benjamin Franklin is interesting, since he supported the institution of slavery for much of his life.[6] To his credit, however, he later changed his mind on this issue, and it would be particularly ironic if this change occurred following his observation of a black school in Philadelphia, in which he judged the students to be learning at the same rate as their white counterparts. Of course, this observation would have long preceded the development of standardized achievement tests, so who knows if he would have arrived at a similar conclusion today? Or, even if the school he described could have any counterpart in today's inner-city Philadelphia?

Recognizing student cultural backgrounds as important determinants of schooling success, the Thernstroms attribute part of African American children's failures to their lack of anything like the millennia-long literate cultural history that, say, Chinese immigrants had upon their arrival here. The Thernstoms also believe, partly as a consequence of this, that black students aren't pushed nearly as hard to succeed by their parents as are Asian or white students, presumably because of cultural differences in expectations and work ethics. They support this view with data from the National Educational Longitudinal Study:

> Black students who believed that they were working just as hard as they could "almost every day" reported doing 3.9 hours of home-work per week. Whites who made the same claim put in 5.4 hours, nearly 40% more. Asian Americans averaged 7.5 hours, about 40% more time than whites and nearly twice as much as blacks. (p. 145)

Although this certainly has the time-on-task or increased instructional time implications endorsed by John Carroll, Benjamin Bloom, and the Academic Learning Time (ALT) researchers, I don't think these relationships were the Thernstoms' primary interest, since they argued earlier that an important reason for the poor performance in school among black students is "that disproportionately large numbers of black children find it hard to adjust to the demand of a well-ordered classroom" (p. 137). This difficulty, they believe, has its roots in a cultural approach to learning that must be changed in order to reduce the racial gap in test learning.

Their solution appears to be a sort of "tough love" approach, if you will, in which the message to students from educationally impoverished home environments is, in effect, that it's a shame that (a) you started out behind due to circumstances that weren't your fault; (b) your ancestors were forced to immigrate here, enslaved, and deprived of education by law in many parts of the country; and (c) once freed, multiple generations of your family were subjected to the most atrocious educational conditions conceivable. However, there's nothing anyone can do about any of those circumstances now. You're just going to have to pull yourself up by your own bootstraps. You're going to have to take the schooling process seriously, because disruptive behaviors, parental noninvolvement, and noncompliance with school policies (including homework) just won't be tolerated. There are, in other words, "No Excuses" for failure.

Unfortunately, there is no empirical evidence that shouting slogans in class or wearing neatly pressed uniforms will have any effect upon learning unless the amount of instruction is somehow increased. However, it is conceivable that these strategies could result in children paying more attention to the instruction they do receive (thereby making it more relevant) or provide incentives for more conscientious completion of homework assignments. Otherwise, the Thernstroms' position is simply the other side of Kozol's coin. Neither produces a tangible prescription for providing the massive increase in relevant instructional time necessary to deal with current racial/socioeconomic disparities in test scores. (With this said, however, although I'm sure they wouldn't consider this particularly flattering, my own solution offered for the racial disparity in school achievement bears a remarkable similarity with the Thernstroms' viewpoint.)

NEEDED: A COMPREHENSIVE PRESCRIPTION FOR INCREASING ALL SCHOOL LEARNING

The reason for visiting our theorists in the previous chapter and our three sets of educational commentators in this chapter is not to advance a strategy to reduce racial disparities in test scores, but to provide a context for a theory that I hope will be capable of serving as a roadmap for maximizing the amount of learning produced by the schooling process for *everyone*. Still, if the research on aptitude-by-treatment interactions has shown us anything, it is the difficulty of finding an intervention that will be more effective for some groups than for others. The flip side of this message, however, is that if one of the three views of the schooling process just discussed had been capable of showing us how to improve the learning output in one *type* of school, most likely the approach would work for all of the rest as well.

Unfortunately, none of these three positions comes close to proposing a change in the schooling process that is capable of affecting learning in any dramatic way. And, unlike the three theories discussed in Chapter 2, none of the three possessed any true scientific backing.

As for our theories of schooling, it pains me to conclude that J.M. Stephens' prescription for relaxation (which I once actually admired until I understood that the research upon which it was based was fatally flawed) seems downright demented today. Benjamin S. Bloom's theory, on the other hand, is largely on target, but it isn't quite parsimonious enough, and it isn't particularly helpful without some translation to actual schooling practice. The ALT theory is similarly on target, but no one has yet figured out how to implement its implications.

As it happens, however, after my brief visit with J.M. Stephens, but before either Bloom's work or the Beginning Teachers Evaluation Study was published, I had the opportunity to conduct a program of schooling research that fortuitously taught me the types of changes that would need to be made in classroom practices before any substantive increases in school learning could ever be effected—theoretically driven or not. These previous lessons resulted in a total of four schooling and five testing principles whose adoption, in combination with a theory capable of comprehensively predicting the conditions under which school learning occurs, have the potential of *inexorably increasing the amount of learning produced by the schooling process.*

So, what I'd like to do now is present the most comprehensive and parsimonious theory of school learning yet developed. It encompasses (and is consistent with) all of the research discussed so far, as well as some equally important work that will be presented in the next two chapters that specifically supports this new theory. And, of course, it also rests solidly on the shoulders of such giants as John Carroll, Benjamin Bloom, and, yes, even J.M. Stephens.

CHAPTER 4

The Theory of Relevant Instructional Time

We've now considered both the evidence surrounding the determinants of school success *prior* to enrollment and the factors influencing learning *within* the classroom. We've also visited three credible theories, two of which are positioned on opposite polls of the continuum regarding the potential for improving the amount of learning produced by schooling process: J. M. Stephens, who argued that, *Nothing can be done!* And Benjamin S. Bloom, who argued that *95% of all students can learn any topic that any of their peers are capable of mastering under the correct conditions.* (Conditions, it will be remembered, that basically boiled down to ensuring that students (1) have mastered necessary prerequisite knowledge, (2) are administered all the high-quality instruction they require, and (3) possess the prerequisite attitudinal/motivational characteristics to take advantage of this instruction.)

I remain troubled, however, by both theories' lack of explicit implications for how day-to-day classroom learning can be increased. True, the ALT theory, positioned in between these two extremes, based as it is upon actual observations of high achieving vs. low achieving classrooms does provide us with some hints in this regard. I believe, however, that a more practical, succinct, and causally explicit theory can be developed from which a more productive mode of instruction could be derived. Furthermore, I believe we now have all of the evidence we need, as well as the perspective and the context, to do just that: to develop a succinct, parsimonious theory regarding what truly determines classroom learning.

So, let's do it! For contextual purposes, let's adopt a simple industrial production model to describe the learning process: We have a single raw material (*students*), a single production process (*instruction*), and a single product (*learning*). If we then couple this model with the past research we've discussed, we have an extremely rigorous scientific basis for the following three generalizations about the determinants of school learning:

- *Determinant #1*: Increased relevant instructional time (but precious little else) increases learning (à la classic learning theory if nothing else).
- *Determinant #2*: Some children arrive at school with large individual differences with respect their propensity to learn (à la the Coleman report, Bloom's analyses, and a multitude of other studies before and since).
- *Determinant #3*: No obvious interventions exist that can alter these individual differences in propensity to learn once children enter school (e.g., the absence of aptitude-by-treatment interactions), but *all* children's learning increases in the presence of increased relevant instructional time.

So, if we wanted to start out with a very succinct theory, we might come up with something like this:

All school learning is explained in terms of exactly two factors: students' propensities to learn and the amount of relevant instructional time provided to each individual student.

Or, for a slightly more verbose version that includes the absence of aptitude-by-treatment interactions:

Given the same amount of relevant instruction, some students will learn more than others because they have a greater propensity to learn. With increased relevant instructional time, all students will learn more, but those with a greater propensity will continue to learn more than those with a lesser propensity to learn.

Now, the problem with theories like these, if their authors are lucky and anyone even notices them, is that they won't get past go with the scientists who will eventually look at them. Scientists can be very, very irritating, nit-picking individuals. Almost immediately, one of them will inevitably demand an explicit definition of two terms: *"relevant"* and "*propensity to learn.*" And the type of definitions demanded will not be found in any dictionary. They will be the sort that requires information on how the scientific concepts underlying the terms can be measured and what conditions can be manipulated to influence these measurements.

Although irritating, this demand is quite reasonable because the more explicit the language making up a theory, the more explicit will be the predictions derived from the theory itself. And the more explicit the predictions made, the more easily the theory itself is to refute.

Often, very broadly defined terms in a theory provide so much wiggle room that the theory itself can never be tested, and a theory that cannot be tested is worthless.[1] Said another way, any disclaimers contained in a theory must be examined closely to ensure they aren't so exhaustive that the theory itself winds up being trivial. And nothing should be further from our goal here, for ultimately our theory should be capable of providing a very explicit roadmap regarding how classroom instruction can be changed to increase learning. The good news is that we have only two such terms here that need to be defined in this way (let's simply assume that everyone knows what learning is). The bad news is that we'll have to provide some examples to explicitly illustrate what we do and do not mean by said terms.

DEFINITION #1: RELEVANT INSTRUCTION

First, the use of the "*relevance*" disclaimer is absolutely necessary because there are obviously circumstances under which no amount of instruction will produce any learning at all. I've already provided a purposefully absurd example of this in the form of instruction being delivered in a language unfamiliar to the learner, but even the classic learning total-time hypothesis eluded to earlier involving paired-associate learning (which is infinitely more controlled than classroom learning) found it necessary to include a relevance-like disclaimer that is quite apropos to its use here.[2]

But, in classroom learning, "relevance" is an unavoidably broad concept. To illustrate what is and is *not* meant by "relevant instruction," let's consider the following scenario:

Assume the existence of two comparable classrooms (i.e., comparable with respect to the ability levels of the students and the skill of the teachers) that were taught the same instructional unit using the same pedagogical approach. Classroom A, however, received 30 minutes of instruction, while Classroom B received 60 minutes. Given our three determinants of school learning just advanced, we would predict the following results:

- The students in Classroom B would learn more than the students in Classroom A because they received more instruction. (Not twice as much, perhaps, but we do know that Classroom B students should learn *more*.)[3]
- Some students (whose identity we could predict based upon such things as previous test scores or their parents' educational attainment) would learn more than others in both Classroom A *and* Classroom B.[4] (We've called this "propensity to learn," which we'll explicitly define shortly.)
- The identity of these children with greater and lesser propensities to learn will generally remain constant over time (given what we know about aptitude-by-treatment interactions and the voluminous research involving longitudinal test scores).[5]

Now, let's look at the concept of "relevance" within the context of these two classrooms. The easiest way to define the term is to describe the conditions under which the learning occurring in Classroom B would *not* exceed the learning occurring in Classroom A (or the difference would not be as great as expected). Consider, therefore, the following scenarios:

- A large proportion of the students in both classrooms already know the instructional content. In a typical classroom, the teacher very seldom has the time or expertise to ascertain who does and does not know a particular topic or its component parts. Thus, the instruction will be relevant only to those students who have not mastered the topic; for those who have already learned it, the instruction will be *irrelevant*. A huge advantage of the use of instructional tests based upon explicit objectives (remember Popham's work) is their ability to facilitate (a) the identification of subject matter that has already been mastered by almost everyone and hence does not need to be taught, and (b) the individualization of instruction (which by definition increases its relevance).
- The instructional content is too *difficult* for a large proportion of the students. This can occur if these students have not mastered

prerequisite concepts. An obvious example is if these students' reading level is below that at which their textbooks (or other instructional materials) have been written.

- The classrooms are too disruptive for students to attend to the instruction. If students can't hear (or concentrate on) instruction, it will not result in learning and therefore will not be relevant.
- The two teachers involved aren't exactly clear about what they are supposed to teach, hence they teach content that was not mandated and is not contained on the tests used to evaluate either learning or teaching. (Another advantage of explicit instructional objectives and tests keyed to them.)
- The teachers do not conscientiously teach the appropriate content (e.g., through laziness, a tendency to digress or teach other content, lack of sufficient knowledge about the particular content to teach it, and so on).
- The instruction is diluted by the teachers' reliance upon time-consuming games or hands-on activities that are inefficient as compared to direct instruction.
- The test used to assess the amount learned is not explicitly based upon the instructional content and nothing but that content. (All commercial tests pretty much fall into this category). Tests that do not assess learning are a huge problem for schools, and their use makes classroom instruction even more inefficient and ineffective.

And, of course, all of this assumes that the extra instructional time available in Classroom B is actually devoted to instruction and isn't given over to noninstructional time-wasting activities.[6] Defined more explicitly, then, *relevant instruction is instruction that can be understood, attended to, and involves topics that have not already been learned and that are mandated by the curriculum (which assumes the existence of tests that match the curriculum as well).*[7]

DEFINITION #2: PROPENSITY TO LEARN

This term basically refers to the research indicating that up to 60% of the individual differences in school-age standardized test scores can be predicted by preschool factors existing among children as young as age three. On one level, the term might simply be seen as a more politically correct synonym for "ability," or "intelligence," or any number of other attributes that some educators and psychologists seem to have an inborn propensity of their own to reify based upon their fervent belief in test scores.

On another level, however, any theory of schooling must come to terms with the fact that all cognitive tests (whether they are ostensibly designed to measure intelligence, aptitude, achievement, or learning) tend to correlate quite substantially with one another. Said another way, test scores obtained on students at one point in time tend to predict test scores obtained on the same students at all other points in time as well. The question is: *Why does this occur*? Is it because

- All of these tests are measuring the same "thing" (e.g., intelligence)? Or,
- These tests don't necessarily measure the same "thing," but *something* is influencing all of these test scores?

This is a crucial, crucial distinction because, if the first explanation is correct, Herrnstein and Murray (and to a large extent J.M. Stephens as well) may be correct in simply concluding that there are severe limitations upon what we can expect from our schools. Some children may simply be genetically programmed to succeed and some to fail based upon their IQs, and that's that. But, if the second explanation is true, the implications for our purposes here will depend upon the answer to one simple question: *What is this "thing" that influences so many cognitive test scores?*

Obviously, this is another crucial question, because if the unknown entity is some stable, immutable attribute similar to what intelligence is reputed to be, then we are right back to where we started. If, on the other hand, this thing that is capable of influencing children's test scores over time is amenable to change, then the implications for school-based instruction would be radically different. Regardless of the "thing's" etiology, however, no serious theory of schooling can ignore the fact that children who perform well on tests on the first day of school are generally the same children who perform well on tests on their final day of school. Many of these same children will also do well on college entrance tests, graduate-professional school entrance tests, and so on, ad nauseam.

Under these circumstances, how are we going to define "propensity to learn"? If we can't explain exactly what this phenomenon is—or if it turns out to be something we can't do anything about—our theory is a bust.

- *What is this thing then?*
- *Why is it so potent?*
- *And why is it so strongly related to learning?*

One hint involves the indisputable fact that it shows up more prominently in certain families than in others; hence, a reasonable guess is that it is something that is genetically determined (such as intelligence, cognitive ability, or aptitude are hypothesized to be). But, if we don't come up with something more explicit than this, all we're doing is substituting one unhelpful term for another. What we are in desperate need of is a theory-building *deus de machina* of some sort, and fortunately, I've been holding one—a trusted advisor—in reserve.

William of Occam, a 14th-century Catholic monk, probably couldn't have designed an educational experiment if his life depended upon it, but he had a true gift for enabling scientists to cut through the morass of terms, preconceptions, and unnecessary theoretical assumptions that endemically conspire to cloud their thought. For his trouble, he was excommunicated, but he had already counseled his 14th-century colleagues that *"What is done with fewer assumptions is done in vain with more."* And this simple advice, the "parsimony principle," proved so powerful that it has reached out over the centuries ever since to counsel scientists who find themselves faced with two hypotheses, both possessing equally insufficient evidence bases: *"Always choose the one requiring the fewest unproved assumptions."*

Since we're facing a similar dilemma, let's imagine how this edict might be applied to our problem. There is no question that William would have been quite disdainful of our use of the term "propensity to learn." True, he wouldn't have had a clue about the existence of genes and chromosomes, but he would have surmised, even in his day, that many traits (good and bad) were hereditary. He would simply have used different language to describe the fact, such as "Like father like son," or "The apple doesn't fall far from the tree."

William, as a scholarly monk, would have most likely known all he needed to know to ensure that his novices learned to read and speak Latin fluently. Chances are that if one of his students encountered difficulty with a subject, such as learning certain grammatical constructions, he would have simply been given extra tutoring or required to study longer. William, in other words, would have no need for a concept such as "propensity to learn," counseling us instead that coining a term for something we really know nothing about is simply a disguised *assumption*—if not immediately, then as soon as we get comfortable with the term and forget how little we truly know about what it was named for.

And, if he lived today, he would scoff at any intimation that this unknown factor was hereditary, especially if the specific genes that regulate learning itself hadn't been identified. This would certainly be recognized as an unnecessary assumption. Or, once genes *were* identified, if the conditions under which they are expressed weren't documented, then another assumption would be substituted. And to conclude that any or all of this (assumed) hereditary process constituted the *only* path to learning would yield still another.

I think William would counsel us that assumptions such as these are nothing but unnecessary place holders, vague disclaimers, and resource-consuming middle men. And, if he were privy to the evidence we've discussed to this point, he would argue that the only causal relationships we have that aren't based on unfounded assumptions are that instruction begets learning, tests assess learning, and *therefore instruction begets test scores*. Thus, the only causal factor that doesn't require an unnecessary assumption to explain why children who score higher on tests at age three tend to be the same children who score higher on tests at age ten is *their instructional histories.*

To illustrate, let's review a sampling of the preschool characteristics of children and their families that are related to later schooling success (temporarily ignoring the fact that, to a large extent, we define schooling success on the basis of inappropriate test scores):

- The parents' education level
- The family's income
- The family's racial/cultural background
- Single- versus two-parent families
- Family size
- The mother's age (being extremely young versus of "normal" age)
- The child's birth weight

The first two factors are computationally collapsed into that single variable, socioeconomic status, for which the evidence of a link with later schooling success is sometimes found to be actually stronger than that for intelligence.[8] The next four factors are related to socioeconomic status, although both (a) single- versus two-parent families and (b) family size have instructional components associated with them. (Namely, the presence of two parents in the household means that there are two potential instructors available rather than one, and a large family means that there is less instructional time available for any one child.) The final two factors are also related to the family's socioeconomic status, although they have additional educational risk factors associated with them (e.g., children severely underweight at birth are more likely to experience organic developmental problems, and infants born to teenagers are more likely to be underweight).

But let's concentrate on the principal variable we're left with here—parents' socioeconomic status. Our immediate task should be to identify a theoretically justifiable causal link between it and school learning (since our ultimate goal is to find an acceptable *causal* alternative for our assumption-laden "propensity to learn" place holder). William of Occam, if he had had access to the research that we do, would immediately recognize that we already have a *behavioral* causal link between socioeconomic status and school achievement, and hence he would conclude that it is absurd to invent an *assumed*, invisible, or latent cause! Behavior is something we can observe directly, unlike intelligence, aptitude, propensity to learn, and/or ability.

We'll discuss the identify of this behavioral link shortly, but first let's examine another principle that I think is derivable from William of Occam's parsimony principle, which is that the act of simply *naming something really doesn't cause it to spring into existence*. We have names for many things (ghosts, extraterrestrial aliens, vampires, extrasensory perception) that simply don't exist. By the same token, constructing a test to assess an attribute such as "intelligence," *naming* the resulting hodgepodge of items or tasks that make up this measure an "intelligence test," and then assuming that (a) the name reflects reality *and* (b) the test fits all of our personal beliefs/biases about the meaning of intelligence all constitute an inferential leap large enough to make William of Occam turn over in his crypt.

As an example, consider the following series of *assumptions*, none of which has any evidence base and some of which are dead wrong:

- Intelligence (for which we could substitute ability, aptitude, or propensity to learn) is not amenable to behavioral manipulations such as instruction, thus

- If we construct a test composed of myriad, seemingly unrelated cognitive tasks (such as remembering a random series of numbers) that aren't taught in school, then the resulting test measures intelligence (or one of our substitute terms), then
- Since intelligence can't be taught, intelligence test scores are also impervious to instruction, therefore
- Intelligence must be heritable since it has to come from somewhere (and since parents who score highly on all types of tests, including intelligence tests, tend to have children who also score highly on all types of tests, including intelligence tests), ergo
- Since the tests that measure intelligence are related to the types of tests that measure school performance, attributes such as intelligence and ability and propensity to learn not only exist, but imply two additional bogus schooling assumptions as well:
  * Bogus Assumption #1: Intelligence, ability, and propensity to learn bear a direct causal relationship to school performance.
  * *Bogus Assumption #2:* These attributes are *not* associated with any *other* causal paths to school learning.

The first of these assumptions is difficult to test for two reasons. First, an attribute such as intelligence can't be directly observed; hence, we can't bring any observational evidence to bear on the issue. Second, the most satisfying method of demonstrating that a relationship is causal in nature is to experimentally manipulate the presumed cause (intelligence) and see if this manipulation results in changes in the presumed effect (learning). But, since many intelligence aficionados argue that by definition intelligence can't be manipulated, any investigator who claims to have done so obviously must (also by definition) have manipulated something other than intelligence.

Of course, a Catch 22 such as this is quite transparent, and something all serious theorists should avoid, but even if a definitive trial could be designed to disprove Bogus Assumption #1, the process would require years and a great deal of money to complete. (As will be discussed in Chapter 8, there has already been a considerable amount of research showing that instruction is causally related to performance on intelligence tests.) It is also doubtful, given the ingrained beliefs of much of the educational and psychological professions, that funding for such an experiment could ever be obtained.

The second bogus inference (that intelligence, ability, and/or propensity to learn are not associated with one or more other causal paths to school learning) is a bit easier to test. There is one rival candidate that we can actually observe and that has been causally linked to school test performance—thereby casting serious doubt upon the need to test the first assumption anyway. Let us, therefore, consider this evidence piece by piece, this time making no assumptions, but relying upon validated research findings:

- Children from families with higher socioeconomic status (i.e., whose parents have higher educational attainment and higher-paying jobs, and which place more value upon education) arrive at school with better test scores and higher propensities to learn.
- The most powerful educational intervention (i.e., something we can directly manipulate) known to man involves increased relevant instructional time.
- Not coincidentally, higher socioeconomic families also provide their children with massive doses of extra language experience before those children ever walk through the school's front door.

In fact, one of the most impressive and labor-intensive studies in the history of education, performed by researchers Todd Risley and Betty Hart,[9] involved meticulously measuring both the amount of time that parents talked to their children and the quality of that linguistic interaction. The study consisted of observing children from 42 families, beginning when the children were around the age of one and continuing for the next two-and-a-half years. Dividing the families into professional, working-class, and welfare socioeconomic classifications, these investigators estimated that, in an average year, the total parental communication to professional-class children was a mind boggling 11 million words as compared to 6 million for the working-class families and 3 million for the welfare families. The complexity of this speech (e.g., vocabulary, grammar) and the proportion of encouraging phrases ("You're so smart!") versus negative tones/imperatives (e.g. "Don't do that!") varied similarly. Not surprisingly, these massive communication differences (which have been documented by other researchers[10] but never this painstakingly) were better predictors of later language development and intelligence than either socioeconomic status or race. And what, after all, are these massive doses of extra (and higher-quality) language experience if not extra instruction?

- Other studies[11] have shown that children from higher socioeconomic status families arrive at that proverbial schoolhouse door, having been:
    - Exposed to books
    - Read to
    - The beneficiaries of informal instructional activities, such as dinner table conversations surrounding intellectual topics
    - Required to watch educational television programs (often with a parent present) instead of escapist entertainment
    - Provided with the opportunity to visit museums (and other education-related institutions, such as science centers and aquariums)
    - Provided the opportunity to travel to other areas of the country/world on educationally enriched vacations
    - Exposed to a constant barrage of varied vocabulary
    - Expected to express themselves in grammatically complete sentences
    - Expected to achieve highly in school
    - Taught the alphabet (as well as to recognize an impressive repertoire of words)
    - Taught the types of content that will be taught in school (thereby receiving practice in *attending* to instruction—not to mention listening to the millions of extra words spoken to them, as documented by Risley and Hart—all of which is probably related to what teachers refer to as a student's attention span)
    - Exposed to elementary number concepts
    - Taught to actually read

Obviously, then, when these children are tested on the very content upon which they have received instruction, they will achieve higher test scores than will children from lower socioeconomic status families (of whom a disproportionate number happen to be African American and of Hispanic descent) who have *not* been the beneficiaries of these thousands and thousands of extra hours of instruction.

- Although it is true that the amount of instructional time made available to children has been shown to vary from classroom to classroom, there is no evidence to suggest that this factor is strongly related to the amount of nonschooling instruction children receive. *Therefore, there is no possibility that this initial testing advantage due to prior instructional histories will decrease as children progress through the schooling process.* In fact, the differential advantage of the higher socioeconomic status students should increase because they will continue to be exposed to extra-school instruction from their home environment. (Ergo, the children who perform well on tests prior to, and at the beginning of, school will continue to perform well on tests throughout the schooling process.)

- There is really no necessity, therefore, for hypothesizing a separate noninstructional, genetic, causal factor for these huge individual differences in later schooling success. This is especially true since socioeconomic status and race (which are correlated with one another) are themselves so strongly related to the availability of extra-school instruction. And, since performance on all cognitive test scores tap learning *of one sort of another,* and since learning *only* occurs in the presence of instruction (broadly defined), all of these tests tend to be related to one another because of their common tie with the *amount of instruction received.* (Those children who receive more instruction will therefore score better on all subsequent cognitive tests regardless of what the testing companies decide to name their tests and regardless of any of their claims to the contrary.)

Why bother then, at least from an educational perspective, to even assume the existence of attributes such as intelligence or propensity to learn, much less an underlying mechanism between them and test scores? Why assume anything? Why not simply go with what we *know*? Increased instructional time produces increased learning, which in turn increases test scores.

The causal factor is therefore the *amount of instructional time received.* The only reason that intelligence, ability, and/or propensity to learn *seem* to be constant (or immutable) is because once children receive instruction, the advantages of that instruction are constant (and are largely immutable) in comparison to what is seen in children who never receive it. And, to further cloud the issue, the same children who receive extra instruction in the home prior to school also continue to receive it after school has begun via (a) help with homework, (b) parental or professional tutoring when needed, and (c) all the other advantages listed above that go along with membership in an enriched home learning environment.

I think it is understandable why we have so long embraced other explanations to explain why some children thrive so much better in an institution devoted to delivering instruction. The extra instruction (and tolerance for receiving it, which goes under the rubric of longer "attention spans"—both preschool and after school commences) largely occurs in private, out of educators' sight, and is therefore relatively invisible.

So, with all this in mind, I don't believe there is any question as to how William of Occam would apply his relentless razor to a theory that posited an as-yet unobserved heritable attribute to explain why the same children who exhibit superior performance on tests prior to (or at the onset of) schooling continue to maintain that advantage on later tests. Or, why these children happen to be found far more frequently in families comprised of parents with histories of high test scores. Personally I like to think that even if William hadn't decided to share his intellectual epiphany with us we'd have come to the same conclusion in the end.

But William did advance his parsimony principle, so we must credit him for facilitating our movement to a single-factor theory. For it makes no sense whatever to posit previous test performance as a causal factor in subsequent test performance when both are *caused* by instruction. To posit attributes such as propensity to learn and intelligence as causal factors in test performance is tantamount to positing test performance as the cause of test performance. The causal factor in *learning* always boils down to instruction—whether it takes place in the home or in the school.

Thus, we can move our theory of school learning to a single-factor iteration by reducing it to:

All school learning is explained in terms of the amount of relevant instructional time provided to a student.

This version of the theory explains why some students learn more in school and why some schools perform better than others. It explains why some races and ethnic groups do the same. It explains why nothing seems to work better than anything else in the classroom when instructional time remains constant. And, it explains why John Mortimer Stephens was almost totally wrong and Benjamin S. Bloom was almost totally correct.

From a schooling perspective, however, explaining why individual learning differences occur is not as important as predicting what actions can be taken to increase *all* children's learning, and that is our true purpose here. This is a mission of the utmost importance, and all the evidence discussed so far supports the following more action-oriented (and final) iteration of our theory:

The only way schools can increase learning is to increase the amount of relevant instructional time delivered.

CHAPTER 5

The Science of What Could Be

Theories are informed by research and, if they are successful, possess important implications for how scientists and academicians go about their business. My case was a little unusual, because the method I was forced to employ to conduct my research ultimately proved as important as the results themselves: perhaps even more so because it demonstrated what we would have to change about classroom instruction if we ever hoped to substantively increase how much children actually learned in school.

Prior to my meeting with J.M. Stephens, I never considered testing the effects of schooling innovations anywhere but within the public school environment. After all, how else could I be sure that my findings would translate to actual classroom practice? Following that meeting, but completely independent of it, I never really considered conducting research in the public schools *without* drastically altering the classroom environment because otherwise, I came to realize, this chaotic, learning-unfriendly environment would overwhelm any innovation I aspired to test and doom it to failure.

Before this proverbial light bulb flash, if I wanted to compare a new instructional strategy with usual practice (or trained teachers with untrained teacher or experienced teachers with nonexperienced teachers) I would assign students (or classrooms) to either receive my pet strategy/ intervention/innovation (let's just call it Method A) or an appropriate comparison/control condition (Method B). I would then assiduously step aside and let the teachers do their thing for a few weeks before testing their students to see if those exposed to Method A learned more than those exposed to Method B.

In other words, I conducted research like 98% of my contemporaries, predecessors, and successors (although today educational researchers are more likely to randomly assign entire classrooms instead of individual students). The teacher training study discussed in Chapter 1 was of this genre (others involved testing the extent to which probability instruction transferred to students' everyday life experiences[1] and the effectiveness of activity-oriented mathematics instruction[2]). And, on one level, the logic of experiments like this made (and make) perfect sense because everyone knew how chaotic the classroom environment was, thus this chaos had to be factored into the study design. Otherwise, no matter how impressive the experimental results were, the innovation would fall flat on its face the first time someone tried it out in the public schools. The educational researchers in the late 1960s and early 1970s even had an expression for this phenomenon: *Everything turns to [fecal material] in the public schools.*

Thus, no matter how much sense (logically or theoretically) the innovation made, once the research data were analyzed, the answer was *always* the same if instructional time was held constant: *no significant difference* between Method A and Method B. A reframe that became so common that it was awarded its own acronym: NSD.

And, of course, it was this refrain, this omnipresent failure to find statistically significant differences, upon which Stephens based his theory, because, with a few exceptions, everyone seemed to always find the same thing: *Nothing works better in the public school classroom than anything else.*

But sometime after my meeting with Professor Stephens (although again, independently of it) I was fortuitously introduced to a different approach to conducting schooling research. My first experience with this genre of research was an experiment that Joe Jenkins, my mentor, requested my help in running. Joe (now at the University of Washington) published a ton of research in those days, a lot of it involving the effects of different types of incentives on educational performance in a special-education laboratory classroom housed in the University of Delaware School of Education Building.

I personally had no interest in this type of research because my passion was learning, not performance, and I was too dense to see that what Joe was trying to manipulate by increasing his students' performance was *time on task*—which is the same thing as instructional time. And, of course,

everyone, including their grandmothers, knew that this is the most important determinant of school learning that can be directly manipulated.
I was also turned off by the artificial nature of Joe's experimental classroom. After all, it contained only about 12 students, had a full-time teacher
and usually at least one teaching assistants/tutor. It was, in other words,
nothing more than a laboratory classroom, specifically designed to facilitate *learning* rather than to mirror a "real" public school classroom. How
absurd!

Of course, Joe's experiments also seldom resulted in an NSD, but for
some unexplained reason I never made the connection between that and
the fact that there was little or no chaos in his laboratory classroom. The
study he had in mind (and guaranteed me would be published anywhere
we sent it, would be heavily cited, and would "make a difference"—an
important incentive in the heady days of the late 1960s and early 1970s)
involved the first carefully controlled laboratory test of which I'm aware
of the theory behind phonics instruction. (Everybody's grandmother knew
that phonics instruction provided children with a huge advantage in learning to read, but the evidence supporting this obvious fact left a lot to be
desired.)

Although I didn't entirely buy his sales pitch, Joe was (and is) very
good at both conducting and publishing research, so I figured I had nothing to lose except a great deal of my time. But time is cheap in youth, and
I also owed him big time for teaching me more about conducting
well-controlled, definitive experiments than all of my doctoral courses
combined.

What Joe wanted to do in this particular study was to demonstrate that
learning letter sounds would transfer to actually learning to read better
than would learning letter names. As mentioned earlier, preschool knowledge of letter names had long been know to be associated with later
schooling success but then so had the presence of books in the household,
and there was no real theoretical reason to explain how either one would
facilitate learning to read. After all, the simple presence of the written
word in the home environment couldn't seep into children through osmo-
sis, and we don't use the letter *names* in actual reading.

Joe's logic was that if we could demonstrate that knowledge of the
sounds the letters represented in different words enabled children to learn
the words themselves quicker than simply knowing the names ascribed
to the same letters, then that would be a good first step in proving the

worth of phonics. So, without going into excruciating detail, the study involved randomly assigning first-grade students to two groups. One group was taught letter names one-at-a-time in an administrator's office; the other group was taught letter sounds in the same way in the same office by the same person (yours truly).

There was a slight catch with this study, however. Because the school served suburban, upper-middle-class families, we couldn't employ regular letters. These families routinely sent their children to school knowing their letters, and often also able to recognize more actual words than the average inner-city student learns during a full year of school.

Joe got around this inconvenience by using completely new symbols for the letters that would be taught (and, of course, the words which were made up of these letters). Otherwise, we would have had to journey to inner-city Wilmington to find children who had not been the beneficiaries of parental (or other preschool) instruction in initial reading skills.

As soon as each child had mastered this little lesson (taught via flash cards similar to the time-honored paired-associate tasks of classic learning theory), each child in both groups was then presented (always individually) a list of words composed solely of the letters that had just been taught. For example, if the short "a" vowel sound and the consonant sound for "t" had been taught in the first half of the lesson for the letter sound group, the word "at" would have comprised one of the words to be learned in the second half. (Naturally only the names for the same two letters would have initially been taught to the other group but its participants would still have been charged with learning the word "at.")

Neither of us was particularly interested in reading instruction per se, but I had personally become quite annoyed at one of the professors in the college of education continuing to assertively advise educators not to teach phonics in the pubic schools, and instead recommending a "language experience" approach to teaching reading in which young children dictated stories that the teacher then transcribed, in order to subsequently use to teach them to read. (How a teacher could do this individually for 35 or 40 students wasn't clear, but the technique attracted a number of academic followers for a brief period of time.)

So, I don't know what Joe's motivations were, but part of mine was to help pay off my mentoring debt to him and to demonstrate how bogus this reading "expert's" efforts were. I have since come to believe that this sort of professional behavior is one reason why the knowledge base for education does not advance linearly, as it does for sciences such as biology and physics. Education simply moves in cycles, in which teachers, say, use phonics for a decade or so, then are trained or encouraged to use something else. Then someone like Rudolf Flesch (*Why Johnny Can't Read*)[3] comes along, shows how absurd these countermeasures are, and educators are forced kicking and screaming to go back to the drawing board. Once the issue has dissipated a bit, someone like our colleague at Delaware then pronounces phonics to be worthless, and so the cycle repeats itself.

But back to this decades-old research study. Naturally, as Joe had predicted (and certainly as Rudolf Flesch *would* have predicted) we obtained statistically significant results. The children who had been taught letter sounds were able to learn to read words comprised of those sounds much quicker than were the children who were taught only the letter names that *spelled* the words.

And, although I grew exceedingly tired of tutoring children to recognize nonsense letters day-in, day-out in the assistant principal's office, I did leave that experience with an abiding appreciation for this artificial experimental paradigm that permitted us to (a) so very carefully control all the factors extraneous to the issue of interest, (b) identify topics that none of our experimental participants had been taught, and (c) teach these students so effectively and efficiently. I also left with a sense of wonder at how extremely effective tutoring was. To have achieved the degree of learning necessary to demonstrate differences between our two groups in a chaotic classroom setting, we would have probably needed to supply these first-graders with a week's worth of instruction. Perhaps more, since some children complete their first year of schooling learning less than a word a *week*.

So, on one level, it is difficult to imagine a learning study conducted in a more artificial setting. The subject matter was completely nonsensical, and the method used to teach it (tutoring) was about as far removed from actual classroom practice as it is possible to get. Thus, it could be legitimately argued that this experiment had zero applicability to first-grade reading instruction, and the peer reviewers of our study ultimately made that very statement when we submitted it for publication, thereby forcing Joe (because I refused) to replicate the original experiment by talking his wife into tutoring a different group of children employing conventional symbols for the letters before it was published in the *American Educational Research Journal*.[4]

But, within these seemingly legitimate experimental limitations also lay one of the greatest limitations (and the most daunting problem) of classroom instruction itself: the necessity of simultaneously teaching two types of students:

- *Type A Students* who have already mastered the content presented to the class because they have had previous exposure to it (often outside of the classroom, as a function of their home learning environments) or had been taught prerequisite concepts (therefore enabling them to learn faster than their peers from less-enriched learning environments).
- *Type B Students* who have varying degrees of difficulty mastering the content because they have not had access to these prior learning experiences.

Our study, however, depended upon *everyone* (even Type B Students) in both groups learning all of the letter names and/or sounds, otherwise how could we expect to demonstrate that knowing letter sounds facilitated learning to read words? So, how did we get around this? We simply tutored everyone until as many as possible had learned what they needed to learn, á la Benjamin Bloom's and John Carroll's mastery learning. Of equal importance, our study also depended upon Type A Students *not* already knowing all of the letter sounds, names, and words before the experiment began – which of course they couldn't since they had never been exposed to the symbols employed. (This is a radical concept in classroom instruction, because a certain portion of the class almost always knows what is being taught; which, of course, means that the instruction is irrelevant to them.)

Suffice it to say that after this experience, I never again employed "real" teachers in "real" classrooms conducting business as usual. After all, I reasoned, it wasn't my fault that everything turned to excrement in public school classrooms.

It was, in other words, the classroom model that needed to be changed, not the science of learning.

In the final analysis, what did it matter anyway if the laboratory model didn't have a great deal of applicability to the everyday realities of classroom instruction? The worthless NSD study after worthless NSD study conducted within this reality most definitely did not demonstrate that nothing *could* work better if the classroom environment was made more conducive to learning.

In retrospect, I regret that it took me over half of my brief schooling research career to appreciate this simple fact, but there is no point crying over decades-old spilled milk. I'm not even sure when I first came to this obvious conclusion, at least on a conscious level. But surely it couldn't have been completely coincidental that my very next study was a laboratory-type experiment investigating what "could be" rather than "what is" (or what passes for "typical classroom conditions"). In fact, this particular study directly compared classroom instruction to the most efficient learning environment ever discovered.

THE FIRST TUTORING STUDY

Tutoring is as old as mankind and undoubtedly the first instructional model ever employed. For millennia, it was the model of choice for the rich and powerful of the earth, surely long before Aristotle reputably served as Alexander's tutor.

Although not quite in this distinguished historical strata, as far as I can ascertain, I had the distinction of conducting the first carefully controlled randomized trial in which tutoring was directly compared to classroom instruction.[5] And, as I said, it was also my first foray into the science of what *could* be, after becoming so enamored with the laboratory model during the course of running Joe Jenkins' phonics experiments.

The experiment itself, like the phonics study before it, was published in the premier educational research journal of its time (the *American Educational Research Journal*).[6] It was basically designed to demonstrate not only how effective tutoring as an instructional medium was, but how much *more* effective it was than regular classroom teaching. And, while I realize that no one is likely to share my enthusiasm for this study, it was by far my favorite of the scores of experiments I conducted and ultimately the one that has the most direct implications for showing us why we need to abandon classroom instruction as we know it.

Although the experiment was primarily designed to contrast tutoring with regular classroom instruction, I simultaneously tested two additional hypotheses that should be familiar by now (and that also have important implications for our purposes here).

The first of these subsidiary hypotheses was related to the aptitude-by-treatment issue. Previous to this study, many educators would have hypothesized that even if tutoring proved to be more effective than classroom instruction, this effect would probably be due to its success with low- rather than high-ability students. (Of course, Glen Bracht's previously mentioned review of the aptitude-by-treatment interactions tacitly predicted that this wouldn't happen, but I wanted to get my study published, and I certainly couldn't count on journal reviewers being familiar with Bracht's work.)

The second factor will also sound familiar by now. I knew that policy-oriented individuals would almost certainly point out, regardless of the results, that we simply couldn't afford to employ "trained" teachers' to tutor children. Thus, I reasoned that if I could show that untrained teachers could administer tutoring as effectively as trained ones, I would partially answer these concerns. Naturally, like the aptitude-by-treatment comparison, I knew ahead of time that teacher training would have no effect whatever (based upon the previously discussed work by Popham's, as well as my own).

I always tried to replicate my more important findings, however, both to increase their credibility within the scientific community and to assure *myself* of their validity. Thus, in this experiment I compared (a) elementary education undergraduates who had received course work in teaching mathematics *and* who had completed most of their required practice teaching internship with (b) elementary education undergraduates who had received no such coursework (and, of course, who had not yet received any formal practice teaching experience).[7]

I hate to think how much this trial would have cost if it had been funded today by the U.S. Department of Education, but conducting research was a lot simpler for me. I had no need of funds to conduct my research because I had access to everything I needed:

- A key to the room that housed the mimeograph machine that allowed me to clandestinely access it at night to duplicate the experimental materials. (Alas, the Xerox machine was off limits and jealously guarded by a human pit bull.)
- A car of ancient and questionable lineage, which was perfectly capable of transporting me to and from the local schools.
- And, most crucial of all, I had Professor William B. Moody (originally my undergraduate advisor but by now a full-fledged collaborator)

to create the instructional objectives, the test based upon them, and possessive of the charisma/contacts to carry off the whole affair. (The latter entailed talking a district mathematics supervisor, three principals, and 20 classroom teachers into engaging in a few hours of orderly chaos, not to mention selling a gaggle of undergraduates on the notion that this experiment represented an unparalleled opportunity for them to get some truly unique teaching experience—plus, of course, to participate in what I had modestly named The Super Study.)

Despite the amount of persuasion involved, the major problem with pulling the study off (which ultimately turned out to be exceedingly fortuitous) was the fact that the three schools involved in this study understandably didn't feel comfortable tying up a great deal of classroom time for a hare-brained experiment such as this. Fortunately, Joe Jenkins' phonics experiment had prepared me for this, because I had learned just how much it is possible to teach students in a very brief amount of time if it is done intensively in a laboratory setting.

From a practical perspective, however, this meant that for the study to be carried out an extremely *sensitive* test would be needed; a test capable of detecting statistically significant learning gains *within* a single class period. From the perspective of the standardized testing industry, such a task would have been judged as patently impossible. Standardized mathematics achievement tests are not constructed either to be sensitive to change or to assess classroom learning. Instead, they are constructed to consistently rank order students based upon their mathematical ability, mathematical aptitude, and overall grasp of mathematical concepts *regardless of when or where* all of this was learned—in school or somewhere else. That is why we used one of them to identify students with differing mathematics ability levels and, as will be discussed in Chapter 8, why one of the first implications our theory of schooling will be to replace these monstrosities with something that actually assesses school-based *learning*.

But, back to the experiment, where I was faced with the seemingly impossible task of not just designing an instructional unit that could be sensibly taught within a single class period, but also a test on that unit that could be administered within the same class period and still leave enough time (which turned out to be 30 minutes) to allow instruction to take place. A test capable of not simply documenting learning gains after

30 minutes of instruction *but being sensitive enough to detect differences between two instructional methods within a 20 minute time period!* The only way that either task could be accomplished was if: (a) one of the instructional methods was extremely effective, (b) the other was extremely ineffective, and (c) a most remarkable test was available to document the learning effects of this intervention.

Fortunately, all of these conditions were met. The power of the intervention or the impotence of the control weren't in question, since I was contrasting the most efficient learning environment known to man to the obsolete classroom model (one of the most inefficient learning systems conceivable).[8] The task remained, however, of developing something that didn't exist: a test sensitive enough to detect learning differences accruing after only a few minutes of instruction. Fortunately for me (and I sincerely hope for some future generation of students), I had the most gifted item writer in existence, in the person of Bill Moody, who accepted the challenge to develop an experimental test possessing a number of characteristics that will become integral to our discussion of the absurd (and also obsolete) testing industry:

- *The test would have to be extremely sensitive to change.* In other words, unlike a standardized test constructor, we didn't care anything about the test's psychometric properties involving psychometric blabber such as reliability, validity, and a host of other terms. We didn't care whether or not individuals', schools' (or states') performances could be consistently rank ordered on the basis of our test scores. We didn't care what else our test's scores were related to or what they predicted. We couldn't have cared less what our test "looked" like because we didn't have to sell it to anyone—nor did we need to convince an administrator to stake his or her professional career on its results.
- *The test would have to assess everything taught within our brief, golden 30-minute instructional period and absolutely nothing else.* This was done quite simply. All of our "teachers" were provided with eight extremely explicit instructional objectives, along with sample test items for each that reflected what their students would be tested on. (I'll provide an example of one of these instructional objectives and the items built upon them in Chapter 7.) Thus, all of the teachers knew exactly what they were to teach, and they were

told to attempt to cover everything in their 30-minute class period (or tutoring interval). The test itself was comprised of 16 items, two explicitly assessing each objective. This extremely transparent test construction process was diametrically opposed to a typical standardized elementary school mathematics test whose purpose is to rank order children, schools, school districts, and entire states on *something* at the end of a school year that can be demonstrated to be stable, so that the company's marketing department can sell it. Said another way, the primary characteristic strived for by standardized tests is the ability to rank large numbers of heterogeneous students stably (or consistently) *irrespective* of the vicissitudes of local curricula or cultural differences. The purpose of our test was to document *classroom* learning, a concern only tangential to a commercial standardized test.

- The test would need to be brief enough to be administered within a 5-10 minute time period because we hadn't been allotted sufficient time for a longer test. (We had pre-tested the students a few days earlier to ensure that the vast majority hadn't been introduced to exponents.) Consider, for example, what would have happened if a substantial portion of the elementary school students exposed to our 30 minute instructional interval already knew what was going to be taught and therefore could answer most of the test items correctly before the experiment even began. Obviously, a test based upon such items would be worthless if our experimental subjects didn't have any room for positive *change*, regardless of how powerful the intervention was.

Oddly, in actual classroom practice, just as in standardized test construction, no one seems overly concerned if a large proportion of any given class may already know the content being taught. But then, eliciting classroom learning has nothing like the urgency with which I approached the conduct of my research, where failure meant months of wasted planning; worse yet, failure meant that the opportunity to do more research of this magnitude would most likely never present itself again. Jonas Salk once said that "the reward for doing good work is the opportunity to do more," and that is an opportunity that no scientist takes lightly because the statement very definitely has a converse.

In any event, the experiment went off without a single hitch.

AND THE RESULTS WERE:

As everyone's grandmother could have predicted, tutoring was significantly more effective than classroom instruction when time, teacher differences, student abilities, and the curriculum were all rigorously controlled. And, not coincidentally, because without them these intuitively obvious results could not have been documented, the instructional unit and the test functioned *beautifully*.

And as far as our two auxiliary hypotheses were concerned:

- As expected (and as Popham would have predicted by this point in time), students taught by "trained" undergraduates with some formal teaching experience learned no more than students taught by untrained undergraduates with no formal teaching experience.
- And, as I at least expected, and as Bracht did predict á la his aptitude-by-treatment work, there was not even a suggestion of a trend for one ability level to profit more from tutoring than another.

Said another way, tutoring was the quintessentially optimal learning environment for everyone, irrespective of "ability level." Naturally high-ability students learned more in the experiment than medium-ability students, who in turn learned more than low-ability ones. But this was constant in both the tutoring and the classroom instruction groups, and consonant with what standardized tests are designed to do (and do well, incidentally): rank order students consistently and predict performance on other tests—even ours.

A Small Caveat: Teacher Training Versus Teaching Experience

One aspect of this study that bothered me at the time was that neither Popham's work nor ours was designed to definitively separate teacher experience from teacher training. A critic could have criticized us both for combined these two characteristics, since in reality none of our teachers were that experienced in teaching the specific instructional objectives we employed.

In an attempt to separate experience from training experimentally, our next study involved having undergraduates repeatedly teach the same unit to different elementary school students. What we found was that there was a statistically significant improvement in children's learning between the first and second time our teachers taught the unit, but not anytime thereafter.[9] As always, I replicated the study and found the same effect. (Some researchers have found similar effects in the educational world of "what is," with the largest effect for teacher experience occurring during teachers' first year (i.e., the first time they teach a set of objectives or topics) and very quickly disappearing thereafter.[10]

A FOLLOW-UP STUDY

After this, I was on a roll. I was completely enamored with my laboratory model of doing research, since I could control the classroom environment rather than allow it to control me. *I had, in other words, completed my transition from the science of what is to the science of what could be.*

And, although there is no need to go into excruciating detail on this work, I probably should at least mention my replication of the tutoring study. The second time around we (Bill Moody and I, this time with Joe Jenkins as a collaborator) not only compared tutoring to classroom instruction again, but added *small-group instruction* to the mix (i.e., one instructor teaching two students, and one instructor teaching five students).

We would have preferred to compare class sizes from one to say, 40, in increments of five students each to more precisely ascertain the minimum number of students that had to be subtracted from a typical public school classroom to realize significant learning gains. Unfortunately, a few disadvantages are associated with conducting research at a zero funding level (if sneaking into the mimeograph room after hours to steal paper doesn't count), so instead we started at the other end and assessed how soon the tutoring (i.e., one-to-one instruction) effect would dissipate.

As always, we carefully controlled for (nonexistent) teacher differences in (a) learning elicitation (by having the same instructors teach different class sizes), (b) what was taught, and (c) how intensively it was taught. We also ensured that there were no behavioral problems or down time in any of the class sizes.

The results came out exactly as anticipated once again.[11] Tutoring was more effective than both classroom and small-group instruction. The 1:2 and 1:5 ratios were, however, also significantly superior to classroom instruction, but significantly inferior to 1:1 tutoring. There was no statistically significant difference between the 1:2 and 1:5 groups, but there probably would have been if we had had more teachers available. However, in examining the learning projection depicted in Figure 5.1 it appeared that once the teacher–student ratio begins to approach our average 1:23 figure, the class size advantages would become smaller. How much smaller it is difficult to say because our data just didn't extend this far, plus even class sizes of 23 would be considered small in some schools.

From my perspective, the truly important finding in all of this wasn't that tutoring was superior to classroom instruction, that it was also superior to small-group instruction, or even that small-group instruction was superior to classroom instruction. The truly astonishing finding here was the sheer *size* of the learning effect. Keeping in mind that teacher, student, and curricular differences were carefully controlled in these studies, students who were tutored learned 50% more than their counterparts in a classroom setting within a 30-minute instructional interval.

But I would guess that even this 50% figure itself is misleading because the classroom instruction employed in this study undoubtedly produced

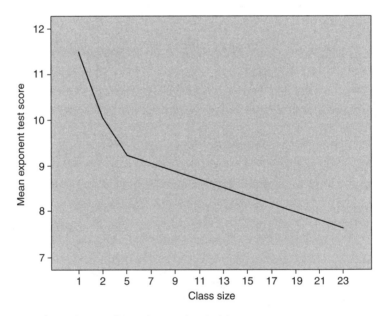

Figure 5.1 Class Size and Mathematics Achievement

more learning than occurs in routine everyday schooling practice for the following reasons:

- There were few if any discipline problems in *any* of these classrooms, partly because of the unique nature of the experiment and the curriculum, and partly because of the amount of adult observation occurring. (Bill and I obviously had to supervise our experiments carefully to make sure the protocol was being followed.) Under everyday schooling conditions, there would typically be considerably more distractions occurring within a classroom setting than occurred within our study.
- There were no unmotivated, burned out, or noncompliant teachers in our classrooms. There was no union interference, no one with tenure, no one intent on doing his or her own thing. We employed only undergraduate volunteers who wanted to be involved and, as I said, we supervised them to make sure they were actually teaching the prescribed curriculum (and only that curriculum).
- The purpose of our classroom instruction was to produce as much *total* learning from the class as a whole as possible. We therefore included more instructional objectives than we thought any significant number of students could master to avoid creating a ceiling to our learning effect. Perhaps this "jam-packed-hurried" instruction wasn't an optimal learning experience for some individual students, but I wasn't interested in translating my findings to everyday schooling practice. My job in these experiments was to produce as much learning as quickly as possible from the classroom as a whole in order to ascertain what *could* be. And, indeed, the total amount of learning (i.e., in both the classroom instructional group and the tutoring group) was quite impressive. The students learned, on average, over five of the eight exponent objectives within the 30-minute instructional period. Although I have no data on it, I doubt seriously if this much learning hardly ever occurs in an entire day of instruction in a typical classroom.

A Large-scale Replication of the Class Size Study

The study just described was designed as both a replication and extension of the tutoring study. Unfortunately, the class size study was simply too difficult for us to perform again, but as things turned out, a very large (and apparently well-designed) field trial was conducted a decade or so after I left education. This new study used our definition of large classes (ranging from 22 to 25 students), but defined their small class size as ranging from 13 to 17. This study, one of the most ambitious randomized trials in the history of schooling research, also found a substantial learning effect for the smaller classrooms. Sometimes referred to as the Tennessee Class Size Study,[12] it spanned a four-year time interval (K–3) and followed its students' performance for several years after they returned to regular-sized classes.

As would surprise no one's grandmother, this study also found that students do indeed learn more in small classes than in large ones. Further, this initial increased learning effect persisted,[13] but what appeared to be a surprising initial aptitude by treatment interaction (reflected by students from inner-city schools seeming to profit more from small classes than their suburban counterparts) soon dissipated over time—suggesting that the effect might have been a statistical fluke endemic to subgroup analyses, which often simply involves continuing to analyze the data over and over again until *something* is found.[14]

A MORE MODERN EXAMPLE OF THE "IS" VERSUS "COULD BE" DICHOTOMY

The Tennessee Class Size Trial was basically an example of a large-scale study that fell somewhere between the *"what could be"* and *"what is"* research continuum. Its authors didn't attempt to control what went on in the classroom to the extent that I liked to do, but they at least exerted as much control over the implementation of the innovation as is possible in this type of research.

A more typical example of the science of what is (and the type of trials funded by the Institute of Education Sciences, U.S. Department of Education) involved the evaluation of a number of computerized software instructional programs to ascertain their effects on learning, as compared to "conventional" classroom instruction.[15]

At the end of the day, after contrasting classrooms with access to one of 16 reading and mathematics software products to conventional classroom instruction (on standardized achievement tests, of course), the results were predictably negative (i.e., NSD). Despite employing 132 schools and 439 teachers, the investigators found that students in the classrooms without access to computerized instruction learned just as much (or just as little) as the students in classrooms with access thereto.

From my perspective, this study was doomed to find "no significant differences" from the beginning because its design allowed the *classroom teachers* to decide the extent to which the educational software would be used. And surprise, surprise: the average teacher decided to employ the software for an average of a whopping five minutes out of each 50-minute class period. (Note that this is really worse than it sounds, because five minutes was the *average*, meaning that probably half of the teachers used the instructional software for *less* than five minutes).

If instructional time (or time on task) is as important a determinant of learning as classic learning theory suggests, what a monumental waste of taxpayers' money this $14,000,000+ study was! And from a scientific perspective, shouldn't the important question here involve the concept of what *could be*? Or, at least, shouldn't an attempt be made to address a "what is" question under *reasonable* learning conditions?

When confronted with criticisms of this ridiculous decision, the lead investigator of the study was quoted as replying: "We felt pretty confident that 10% of use reflects the sound judgment of the teacher about how often and for what kinds of instructional modules they wanted to use technology."[16] But what this study truly investigated was how much teachers *would* use the technology if left to their own devises.

Ignoring how ridiculous this is when applied to research designed to ascertain the worth or learning potential of computerized instruction, the study itself illustrates a basic dichotomy that faces education research in general. It may be true that this study is fine for answering the question of whether or not computerized instruction (adjunctive to regular classroom instruction) will result in improved test scores under normal classroom conditions, but is it really necessary to accept the inevitability of the current classroom model? Should we be content with allowing teachers and administrators this much discretion, not just in a research study, but in the schooling process itself? Or, more vulgarly rephrased, should we *accept* the inevitability of everything turning to excrement in the public schools?

I think it is obvious that if *we* do, *it* will. Now, granted, my research could be (and often was) criticized because I completely avoided the necessity of dealing with:

- The madness of a classroom environment (or even coordinating candy sales)
- Student misbehavior
- Teachers (both committed and uncommitted) who have been acculturated (often because there are no other options) to "doing their own thing"
- Absenteeism
- Student-peer cultures that actually place a *negative* value upon learning
- The myriad macro and micro political realities that relate to everyday schooling practices

But forget my research. This book isn't about research, it is about classroom instruction, and anyone seriously interested in increasing classroom *learning* must deal with this environmental milieu and its most disconcerting characteristic implication. Within the constraints of our current classroom model:

> A modern-day Socrates could engage only a certain proportion of the students in any classroom at any one point in time. No matter what a teacher does, no matter how skillful he or she is, at any point in time, some students will not be attending to what is going on and some students who are attending still won't process the content being taught.

I began this book by discussing research for three crucial reasons. First, I am a scientist so I consider any theory or hypothesis advanced in the absence of evidence to be irrelevant. Second, I considered the method by which I conducted my research to serve as an excellent metaphor for illustrating the possibility of viewing school learning through a lens other than our current obsolete classroom model—for if we consider (as almost everyone does) this model as fixed, then we currently have no answer for substantively improving school learning, much less reducing the cultural disparities fostered by this very system.

But third and most importantly, learning is learning, so what is true of research targeted at testing instructional innovations designed to increase learning is true of everyday classroom instruction, which is also targeted at producing learning: both find it difficult to overcome those extraneous factors that compete for students' attentions.

Is it any surprise, then, that a typical classroom environment, coupled with these huge and intractable individual differences between children, continue to overwhelm our best attempts at increasing school learning? Even if an innovation is clearly superior to traditional classroom instruction, documenting this superiority by simply looking at end-of-year standardized test results is the equivalent of a physicist attempting to measure the difference between the speeds of two subatomic particles using a stop watch. And *this* in turn is the true genesis (as well as the true meaning) of the sanitized adage of what everything turns to in the classroom that I have probably already repeated too many times—so, instead of repeating myself, allow me to summarize that adage into two equivalent principles: one for research and one for schooling practice.

- *Research Principle #1*: It is exceedingly difficult to document the superiority of an educational intervention in a classroom setting simply because the setting itself will overwhelm the effects of the intervention.

But in effect, each time a teacher presents a topic to a classroom of students for the first time, she is conducting an educational experiment of her own design because she does not know exactly what the outcome of her instruction will be. Hence, our first principle of schooling, which is destined to become the founding principle of the book itself:

- *Schooling Principle #1*: It is exceedingly difficult to improve learning in a typical classroom setting simply because this setting will overwhelm the attempt itself.

But, far from being a pessimistic conclusion, this principle is actually an empowering manifesto. To illustrate, let's return to the first and most effective of all learning models and consider what it has to teach us about educating our young.

CHAPTER 6

The Theoretical Importance of Tutoring and the Learning Laboratory

Like most experiments, the tutoring study generated at least as many questions as it answered. The most intriguing of these was:

- Why is tutoring so effective?

Or, for anyone who prefers their glass half empty:

- *Why is classroom instruction so ineffective?*

Of course, we've already hinted at the answer to the second question, which also suggests the answer to one of the most pressing issues facing our society:

- *Why is it so difficult to increase school learning?*

I believe it is the tutoring paradigm, the first and most effective yet developed, that holds the key to answering this latter question and, in the process, to revolutionizing school learning. Let us therefore take a look at why tutoring is so much more effective than traditional classroom instruction.

WHY TUTORING WORKS

There are two explanations for why tutoring is so effective. One is bio-logical, in which the answer to everything is: it's genetic. The other is purely educational in nature, but probably explains why the relevant genes evolved in the first place.

Biological Explanation

Teaching and learning are crucial to some species' survival, probably largely dependent upon the organism's brain size. Learning, teacher-based or otherwise, is not as important to many species (although biologists are revising earlier beliefs that it is irrelevant) whose survival behaviors seem to be genetically hardwired (e.g., insects). For other animals, such as mam-mals, however, the infant must be cared for by one or both parents as its brain develops and the instruction that occurs while this is happening becomes a crucial survival strategy. Predator species are, perhaps with some hardwired help, taught to hunt. Prey species are correspondingly taught to frustrate these efforts. The larger the brain, and the more com-plex its circuitry, the more a species depends upon instruction (often deliv-ered by the mother or other adults, such as aunts), and the longer the young's dependency upon its mother and family/pod/herd/pride.

Humans are at the upper end of this dependency continuum with respect to both brain size and complexity, which makes teaching and learning the most crucial of survival activities. Not coincidentally, humans are normally not born in litters, but one at a time, which means that we have most likely been programmed to be maximally sensitive to the inher-ent advantages of one-on-one instruction.

Although purely speculative on my part, I would guess that this is not completely true for mammalian predators (such as members of the various cat families). They learn by observing their parents in classrooms (litters) of usually less than five, where they can practice crucial behaviors among themselves through play. Perhaps their specialized learning needs are even facilitated in class sizes such as these due to sibling modeling behav-ior. Or, perhaps it was the other way around, with the sibling behaviors developing only after the optimal litter sizes had been naturally selected based upon other criteria. Humans, however, along with most of the larger herbivorous mammals, are typically born one per pregnancy with twins being fairly rare and—at least until recently—with any larger "litter" sizes seldom surviving infancy.

Educational Explanation

For an educator, tutoring (as opposed to classroom instruction) maximizes relevant time on task (think classic learning theory). Relevancy is a crucial concept in both instruction and the time spent on it because we all know that the amount of time we devote to tasks is not necessarily created equal. Instead, the quality of the time spent depends upon the conditions under which a particular task is performed or practiced. Sometimes we are more alert, sometimes we purposefully work harder, and sometimes we are simply more productive for reasons that aren't entirely clear to us at the time. We can, in other words, accomplish more in the same amount of time.

The same is true for children receiving instruction. Not only do students who receive more instruction learn more than do students who receive less: Students' whose instruction is more relevant learn more than do students whose instruction is less relevant—in effect increasing their instructional time. Therefore, a child tutored for an hour effectively receives considerably more instruction than a child taught in a classroom setting for an hour. How does this occur? Let us count the ways:

1. *A tutor can efficiently ascertain exactly what the tutee has and has not learned.* While it is possible, and extremely desirable, for a teacher to assess what his or her students know prior to beginning an instructional episode, it is seldom practical to do this for an entire class, partly because it so disruptive and time consuming. (And, as we'll discuss in Chapter 8, commercial tests are not constructed to inform instruction or to even assess it, hence no useful, preexisting data exist at the individual lesson level.) In a tutoring session, on the other hand, it is quite easy to ascertain which components of a lesson the individual tutee has and has not mastered either by direct questioning (or sometimes by simple eye contact). This constant feedback permits the tutor to immediately change course and tailor the presentation directly to that student's individual needs, thereby making the instruction more *relevant*.[1] The tutor can also ascertain when the tutee hasn't quite grasped a specific concept and correspondingly

explain it again. Or, conversely, when it is obvious that the tutee has learned something, the tutor can immediately move on to the next concept. Teachers attempt to achieve feedback on classroom learning, but generally must rely upon sampling one or two students at a time, hoping that the selected students represent the class as a whole. Of course, this isn't particularly likely since in any given classroom some students will already know the content, some will not, and some will even lack a sufficient knowledge base to benefit from the level of instruction being administered. In a typical classroom setting, then, instruction will always be irrelevant to some students no matter how skillful the teacher or how hard he or she attempts to individualize instruction. In a tutoring session, however, instruction can always be made relevant to the individual tutee, assuming the tutor has a sufficient knowledge of the subject matter and is not linguistically challenged.

2. *There are fewer learning disruptions in a tutoring session.* Time spent on noninstructional activities, such as maintaining discipline, is greatly reduced in a tutoring session because the teacher is in such close proximity to the tutee that there are fewer opportunities for counterproductive behavior. It is actually rather difficult for tutored children to misbehave since they have no audience nor are they distracted by other misbehaving students. Similarly, content-related questions asked by other students (but which are irrelevant to the tutee) simply do not occur in the tutoring paradigm and hence do not consume precious instructional time. And the same applies to teacher-directed questions: In a tutoring setting, these questions are always directed at the tutee, hence are more relevant and not disruptive of the instructional process.

3. *The tutee's attention can be focused exclusively on the instruction.* Sitting directly across from the student, a tutor can immediately ascertain when the tutee's attention begins to waver or daydreaming commences. The tutor can then seamlessly refocus the tutee's attention. In a classroom setting, this is counterproductive because it is disruptive to other students' learning to constantly bring daydreaming students back online.

4. *Because the instruction is so personalized, the student is more likely to attend to it.* We all appreciate personal attention, especially from someone we respect or who is in a position of authority.

Therefore, tutoring has a built-in incentive in the form of a respected individual observing one's performance in a one-on-one setting accompanied by approbation and/or constructive feedback.

TOWARD A LEARNING LABORATORY TUTORIAL MODEL

Obviously, we can't afford to supply every child in America with a personal tutor. After all, economy of size, the lack of instructional manpower, and efficiency is why we adopted our present inefficient mode of instruction in the first place.

However, I would argue that that was then and this is *now*. What is so different, after all, between high-quality computerized instruction and the tutoring model just described? Aren't they both one-one-one teaching?

Is it really so difficult to reconceptualize our standard image of a single teacher standing in front of 35 students to a group of students sitting in front of computer monitors (or preferably iPad type devices embedded in their desk tops) equipped with earphones? Now each student is busy working on extremely specific learning objectives whose instruction is delivered via software designed specifically and solely to ensure mastery[2] of those objectives. Instruction is tailored to each student's needs, as determined by individualized testing (which is also solely objective based). Rather than occurring only at year's end, this testing goes on constantly throughout the school day to determine (a) which instructional objectives from the day's lesson each student has and has not mastered and (b) which instructional objectives he or she will need to be taught next.

At the rear of the room, on a raised platform, sits a learning technician with several monitors on her desk capable of providing split-screen views of all the individual monitors at any given point in time. Her raised seat is also positioned to provide visual contact with each student and bring any misbehaving students back on task (which can be done individually through the headphones without disrupting the entire class). Perhaps the room is even equipped with cameras to facilitate this process and to provide an early-warning system of potentially disruptive behavior (or other forms of noncompliance) to a centralized observation deck for the school as a whole. Each student's computer has software that facilitates constant monitoring by the learning technician, such as automatic notification when responses aren't keyed in (or screens changed) within a given period of time.

Students are encouraged to ask the technician for any pertinent directions or help, either via their headsets or by instant messaging, but no communication (oral or digital) is permitted between students unless it constitutes a planned part of the lesson. (The latter is designed to reduce disruptive behavior, which can further be minimized by changing desk configurations or the judicious placement of visual blocks between desks as needed.) An aide could also always be present to facilitate student learning by answering questions or delivering brief in-person tutorials. If these resources prove insufficient, a backup online "help desk" could be available for the school as a whole, to answer student queries and possibly schedule small-group in-person sessions for students experiencing difficulties with the same objectives. Peer tutors could also be employed to deliver similar remedial help after school.

Because the entire year's curriculum (indeed, the entire elementary school curriculum) would be broken down into discrete instructional objectives (which are small bits of learning material such as learning a particular letter sound, consonant blend, or math fact), all students' individual progress on these objectives would be saved in a database to which they, their parents, the learning technician, and school administrators have access. All students would progress at their own rate, and no one would be held back due to the progress of the overall class. By the same token, no one would be forced to move on to subject matter for which they hadn't mastered the necessary prerequisites. Furthermore, students would no longer be required to wait up to six months to be assigned to special-education classes, since everyone would already be receiving optimal instruction on what hadn't been mastered, regardless of learning rates or previous instructional histories. (Thus, the special-education ranks would be greatly reduced, but never eliminated because some children's needs will probably always be too great for even this type of learning environment to ameliorate.)

Every aspect of instruction could be transparent and easily accessible. All objectives, lessons (which may be a single objective or a cluster of them), and sample tests could also be available on a website to permit parents (or their designees, such as for-profit tutoring services) to provide extra-school opportunities for children to (a) progress faster, (b) receive instruction on enrichment topics, or (c) obtain remedial instruction at home. And, as previously mentioned, remedial in-school help (in the form of small-group instruction or tutoring) would also be available for students experiencing more difficulty than usual mastering an objective or set of objectives.

The basic mode of instruction in this approach would be test, teach, retest, teach again if necessary, and retest again until an objective is mastered. Review assessments and instruction would also be periodically administered to address forgetting (and ameliorated by targeted reteaching when necessary).

Full-scale comprehensive tests would be based solely upon the instructional objectives taught and would be administered at the beginning *and* end of the school year. The actual items and specific instructional objectives included on these tests, however, would not be available to anyone (students, parents, or school personnel) prior to their administration, although sample items addressing *each* instructional objective would be shared with all interested parties. Of course, these comprehensive tests could not include all of the objectives taught during the course of an entire year (because of their sheer number), nor would all students have necessarily progressed far enough in the curriculum to have been exposed to each and every instructional objective (due to individual differences in learning speed or the amount of extra-school instruction received). But even the process (e.g. randomly or stratified by difficulty or importance) by which objectives are chosen for the comprehensive tests would be totally transparent.

Rather than being primarily designed to rank order students, as current standardized tests are, these tests would be designed to provide estimates of the number or percent of instructional objectives mastered at any given grade level. In addition, the *difference* between the beginning and the end-of-year comprehensive tests could be used to more validly evaluate individual learning laboratories, schools, school districts, and states, if desired. The results of these evaluations would be largely anticlimactic, however, because the tests themselves would be redundant with the cumulative individual assessments children receive each day—being comprised as they are of parallel (but not identical) items perfectly reflecting the curriculum.

Although most instruction would be individually computer-based, didactic group lessons would still be delivered for certain topics, both to vary day-to-day routines and because they may prove to be more effective for certain content. The same holds for class discussion and lectures, although DVDs and the internet would be used much more frequently, due to the convenience of having a computer sitting on every desk. Existing forms of digital communication (blogs, Twitter, Facebook, and modalities that will continuously develop) might even be adapted for purely educational purposes.

Regardless of the specific instructional methods employed, however, the heart and soul of this model would consist of (a) an explicitly detailed curriculum, (b) the availability of computerized instructional materials to teach every concept covered in the curriculum, (c) transparent tests designed to assess this curriculum and only this curriculum and, potentially most importantly of all (especially for reducing learning disparities due to previous instructional time), (d) the online availability of all of this material to enable students, parents, or their designees to engage in as much additional self-study or instructional time as they choose at the time of their choosing. All of this is, I believe, one of the logical implications of our theory of school learning:

> *All school learning is explained in terms of the amount of relevant instructional time provided to an individual.*

Or its equivalent:

> *The only way schools can increase learning is to increase the amount of relevant instructional time delivered.*

Although I'm sure teachers won't initially agree, I also see the implementation of a system such as this as providing the desperately needed infrastructure both for them and their students to excel within the schooling environment. It should, for example, provide the opportunity for creative specialization within the profession. In other words, unlike such mundane and basically meaningless categories as "master" or "staff" teachers that have been implemented in some settings, especially dynamic teachers periodically could deliver lectures or talks on various topics to entire classrooms or even larger audiences—making DVDs of their more successful lectures to be incorporated into the learning laboratory model itself. Teachers with a special gift for presenting content in novel, interesting ways could work with computer programmers to prepare instructional modules for various instructional objectives or units thereof. And, although no one can predict the future, I would guess that eventually almost every phase of the schooling experience will possess some computerized instructional components: student–teacher discussions boards, for example, or time-saving virtual field trips.

But, returning to the learning laboratory where discrete reading, mathematics, and writing instructional objectives are taught, wouldn't such a setting at least *simulate* all of the above-mentioned conditions that make tutoring such an effective learning medium? Let's review them once again from this perspective:

- *Couldn't the learning technician (or the computer program itself) ascertain exactly what the tutee had or had not learned?* One of the huge advantages of computerized instruction is its potential to quickly administer brief quizzes anytime (i.e., beginning, middle, and/or end of an instructional session).[3] Students already knowing a particular lesson would be taught the next lesson (in a predetermined sequence) that they haven't mastered. Students knowing certain individual components of a lesson would be taught only those components that they didn't know. And students would *always* receive as much instruction as they needed.[4] It is criminal that teaching students only what is relevant to them and providing them with as much instructional time as they personally need to learn constitutes a radical concept in education—especially since we currently have the capability of programming a computer to use adaptive testing, to score short answer tests (as opposed to relying on multiple-choice items which facilitate guessing), and to tailor instructional content to individual students' needs. Wouldn't this simulate what a tutor does, ensuring that instruction is always *relevant* for all students?[5]
- *Wouldn't there be fewer learning disruptions in a computerized system such as this?* Certainly there would be less time spent on maintaining discipline in such a setting, where each student has a monitor staring him or her in the face upon which a task is displayed specifically tailored for his or her learning needs. It would also be difficult to talk to one's neighbors, given the presence of earphones designed to block out extraneous noise and to communicate oral components of the lesson displayed on the student's monitor. Of equal importance, time-wasting, time-honored (and often irritating) traditional classroom practices such as listening to other classmates ask irrelevant questions about the lesson (at least irrelevant to that proportion of the class that already knows the answer) would be eliminated. Also eliminated would be the practice of teacher queries delivered to random students (or downtime while the teacher

chooses among a sea of upraised arms). True, some theorists such as Barbara Rogoff (who herself was influenced by Lev Vygotsky's work conducted over a half century earlier)[6] will object that the social aspects of learning will be minimized in such a setting (and even the suggestion of such a setting ignores these factors). I would argue, on the other hand, that most of the social interactions that go on in the current classroom setting are detrimental to learning anyway. I would also suggest that whenever human beings are organized around a common activity, social interactions will inevitably arise. My hope is simply that they will not be as counterproductive as most of the ones taking place in the current classroom setting.

- *Wouldn't a learning laboratory simulate a tutor's ability to focus students' attention exclusively upon instruction?* True, there is no tutor sitting directly across from the student, but there is a computer screen upon which the student's tasks are displayed, which requires direct responses from the student, and upon which immediate feedback is provided. It is worth repeating that this screen would be directly in the learning technician's line of sight and could be displayed on his or her monitor with a click of a mouse, perhaps along with those of several others via split-screen imaging. The learning technician could also ascertain when anyone's attention begins to waver or daydreaming commences by the lack of electronic responses to the interactive instructional software. The technician could then ascertain if the student didn't understand something or simply needed to have his or her attention refocused (both of which could be done via personal oral communication using the earphones or by simply going over to the student's desk). Most importantly, all of this could be done without disrupting anyone else in the laboratory. Of course, it could be argued that the learning technician, by the nature of her or his role, will have less of a formative impact upon children than does the current teacher's role. I would suggest that this doesn't have to be true, but if is, it too isn't necessarily a bad thing. Haven't we all had about as many teachers who had negative as positive affective impacts upon us?

- *Wouldn't this instruction, tailored as it is to students' needs, be almost as personalized as occurs in the tutoring model?* I'm not suggesting that the computerized instruction envisioned here could possibly be as effective as instruction administered one-on-one by a competent adult tutor. Tutoring is the most effective instructional medium ever developed (actually it most likely wasn't developed at all but *evolved*). I'm simply suggesting that, with work and creativity, we could make computerized instruction a close second. It may even prove to have a few advantages of its own, such as the speed with which it can test students and the capability it provides to automatically track and record their personal progress. Decisions can also be made automatically and nonarbitrarily regarding which objectives need to be taught next, somewhat like the different levels of a video game, in which the successful completion of each stage is not only rewarding in and of itself, but also brings with it the built-in challenges of the next level. Also, like a video game, students will become very adept at negotiating this type of instruction through extensive practice using the same icons and standardized procedures.[7]

Interestingly, Benjamin Bloom once wrote a paper entitled "The 2 Sigma Problem: The Search for Methods of Group Instruction as Effective as One-to-One Tutoring,"[8] in which he announced a personal goal of trying to find an instructional strategy (or combination of strategies) that could match the power of tutoring. (The "two sigma" phrase in his title reflected his belief that tutoring was two standard deviations above regular classroom instruction in learning effectiveness.[9]) In so doing, he devised a "top ten" list of powerful educational variables in which instructional time (i.e., added to regular classroom instruction) was actually ranked below tutoring. Alas, Professor Bloom failed in his quest to find anything as effective as tutoring, probably because the task was impossible, perhaps because he was 71 years of age when he announced his intentions, perhaps because personal computers and their software were nowhere nearly as sophisticated in 1984 as they are today.

So again, I have no delusions that computerized instruction can ever be as effective a learning medium as human tutoring, with the latter's accompanying social, perceptual, oral communicative, and authoritative advantages. I do believe, however, that we can very effectively simulate tutorial instruction digitally with close human monitoring and supplementation. I also believe that this medium, coupled with the additional instructional time it is capable of freeing up, can easily bag Benjamin Bloom's two sigma quarry.

Even once developed, the learning laboratory model may never completely replace classroom instruction, but its existence will certainly make classroom instruction *less* obsolete. (If nothing else, its testing and record-keeping capabilities will make teachers far more effective in the production and management of learning.) There are so many options and permutations of such a system that I despair of enumerating them all, but the learning laboratory could function as a remedial, accelerated, supplementary, alternative, or shadow (i.e., to facilitate students "catching up" following absences or allowing them to receive instruction during extended illnesses) teaching option.

The bottom line here is that movement toward some variant of this system is nothing short of a technological imperative and will occur as inevitably as pay phones have given over to cell phones. In many ways the infrastructure for this revolution has already begun to be developed by small progressive companies such as *Headsprout.com*, which has developed excellent initial reading, reading comprehension, and mathematics computerized instruction which is marketed to both schools and families. Its system also has the capability of tracking individual student, classroom, school, and district performance on the achievement of specific objectives.[10] Likewise, serviceable student computers capable of accessing such software can also be obtained for around $100 per student, but somehow we must find a way to increase the implementation of these innovations.

It would be a tragedy if we continue to squander our children's potentials until this movement occurs naturally, however, but fortunately it turns out that two key components (the explicit specification of the curriculum and tests based upon this specification) required for its implementation would also improve learning anywhere: even in our obsolete classrooms.

This is because schools, be they comprised of classrooms or learning laboratories, are basically designed to provide instruction. Instruction, which we stereotypically tend to conceptualize in terms of a teacher delivering a didactic lecture to a classroom, is in turn, comprised of three components:

- The curriculum (or what is taught),
- The delivery of that curriculum (or mode by which it is presented—far and away the most important characteristic of which is providing the amount of time students need to learn what is being taught), and
- The assessment of the extent to which the curriculum is mastered.

The learning laboratory model primarily (and profoundly) differs from its classroom counterpart in terms of the individualized mode by which instruction is delivered and the capability it provides for the delivery of additional instruction outside of the schooling paradigm. The current classroom model also places formidable constraints upon how much we can actually increase the quantity of instruction delivered in school and especially how much additional learning we can expect to be generated as a result.

Fortuitously, however, both the curricular and assessment components of instruction can be greatly improved within the system we currently have via the adoption of a single strategy: the specification of what should be taught in terms of small, unambiguous bits of information, such as instructional objectives, or some medium with a similar degree of specificity. Although these extremely specific instructional specifications are useful in day-to-day classroom instruction, they are absolutely essential for (a) replacing current standardized tests with measures of school-based learning and (b) the extensive programming that will eventually be required for our learning laboratory, regardless of whether it replaces, supplements, or shadows the current classroom model. So let's hold testing for later and now take a quick look at the curriculum in general and the potential of instructional objectives for helping to ensure that everyone is on the same page with respect to delivering it.

CHAPTER 7

Demystifying the Curriculum

The curriculum is the beginning point of the school learning process because instruction can't commence until someone decides what should be taught. This decision, in turn, is influenced by the goals held for education by various stakeholders. All too often, however, these groups have little evidence regarding which specific subject matter content is most appropriate for the achievement of their expectations for the end result of schooling.

Since our primary emphasis is the elementary school, much of the curriculum is divided into large general topic areas considered to be comprised of the basic essentials for effective employment, citizenship, societal functioning, and further education. Historically, the elementary school curriculum was defined popularly as the "3-R's" and these remain the instructional emphasis of the very early grades. Increasingly, however, even elementary instruction is becoming more diverse, except perhaps in those schools whose students routinely rank the lowest on standardized achievement tests.

The contents of the curriculum are influenced from myriad directions, some of which are:

- State boards of education (or curriculum committees convened by them)
- High school and college curricular prerequisites that suggest what should be taught earlier via a sort of trickle-down process
- Lobbying by special interests groups (e.g., professional groups, politicians, religious denominations)

- High-stake test constructors, whose items can become de facto curricula because schools are judged based upon their students performance thereon
- Textbook authors and publishers, because textbooks themselves also have the potential of becoming a de facto curriculum
- School districts and individual schools that decide what should be emphasized at what else's expense
- Tradition, or what has been taught in the past
- Individual teachers, who sometimes don't fully understand what they should teach and sometimes simply teach what they think is most important, what they most enjoy, or what they are most comfortable with

In recent years, the advent of state educational standards has made curricula slightly more transparent and helped to ensure that teachers and school administrators understand what their students are expected to be taught, at least in general terms. These standards also help to guide the writing of textbooks and test construction, rather than the other way around. Regardless of the process by which the curriculum is determined, however, it ultimately defines both instruction and learning (which we infer from testing). This concept is so very, very important in the optimization of school learning that it deserves the status of our second schooling principle:

- *Schooling Principle #2*: Both instruction and testing should be exclusively based upon a meaningful, explicitly defined (such as via the use of instructional objectives) curriculum and nothing else.

In present day practice, instruction tends to be more closely keyed to the curriculum than testing, but even the most conscientious teachers cannot be perfectly compliant in this regard unless the curriculum is communicated to them in sufficient detail. As previously discussed, far and away the most precise and exhaustive method of defining what should be taught (and therefore what should be tested) involves the use of instructional objectives.

If I were forced to name the single most important determinant of the success of my laboratory approach to conducting my own schooling research, it would surely be the decision to base both instruction and testing on explicit, discrete instructional objectives. For my research studies, this was integral because it permitted me to optimize the amount of learning occurring within a single class period. But what is classroom instruction, after all, if it isn't a succession of individual class periods? Should we not therefore attempt to optimize the learning in each of our children's class periods throughout their schooling experience?

Certainly, in my sojourns into the scientific world of what *could* be, I found it absolutely necessary to ensure that:

- The curriculum for my 30-minute instructional window was completely and exhaustively defined, so that
- Instruction could concentrate *solely* upon this curriculum, so that
- The test would be able to capture *all* of the learning that occurred as a result of this instruction and *nothing else*.

I personally cannot conceive of how any of these conditions could have been met without the use of instructional *objectives or a similarly explicit means* of communicating exactly what teachers are expected to teach and learners are expected to learn. But, before discussing how all of this translates to classroom instruction, let's examine exactly what instructional objectives are.

INSTRUCTIONAL OBJECTIVES

Because they are so central to laboratory-based instruction and testing, I should probably define what is meant by an instructional objective. The best work on writing them probably remains Robert Mager's book, *Preparing Instructional Objectives*, which is still available at amazon.com.[1]

One of the most important, and paradoxical, characteristics of instructional objectives is that they don't describe instruction itself. They only very, very explicitly describe the intended *outcome* of instruction in terms of the types of learning behaviors expected of students as a direct result of instruction. These descriptions do not employ verbs such "to know" or "to understand" or "to appreciate." Instead, they use action-oriented verbs with testable implications, such as "identify," "write," "recognize," "apply," and "solve."

Their purpose is to communicate exactly what students will be tested upon following instruction, which is why their successful use *requires* (not just permits) the instructor (or the computer software) to teach the test. If written and employed correctly, their presence ensures that everyone involved in the instructional process (teachers, students, test constructors, administrators, and parents) is on the same page with respect to exactly what is to be taught, studied, and tested.

There is some disagreement regarding how detailed instructional objectives should be. I personally lean toward each objective reflecting an extremely small bit of instruction, but this isn't carved in stone anywhere. However, since instructional objectives are designed to explicitly describe the outcomes of instruction, it is necessary that an example of *every* type of test item or other performance indicator upon which students will be assessed be specified. Teacher (or test constructor) practices such as "surprising" or "tricking" students via the inclusion of unexpected test items is completely antithetical to the philosophy behind the use of instructional objectives and tests built upon them. Such practices are tantamount to disguising the curriculum, of keeping secret both what is being taught and why it is being taught. Perhaps educators who engage in such practices do so because they wish to ensure that what is taught can be applied to other arenas, but if this is one of the purposes of teaching a particular topic or unit, then those applications should also be translated to instructional objectives and taught themselves. (Solving mathematical word problems is one of many examples of this.)

In my own research, I went one step further than Bob Mager suggested. In working with both inexperienced and untrained as well as trained and experienced teachers I soon discovered that one can't assume that all teachers necessarily understand the content they are charged with teaching. I also found that many who do understand the topic area still appreciate very brief reviews of the rationales (i.e., the "why" of the objectives) for the contents of their lessons. Some even shared an age-appropriate version of some of this background information with their students.[2]

What I believe is ultimately absolutely necessary, therefore, is that the elementary school curriculum should be translated into some completely transparent method that is:

- As explicit as possible
- Limited to as restricted (small) pieces of instruction as practical
- Accompanied by sample test items upon which the students will be assessed
- Accompanied by brief subject matter background designed specifically to ensure a minimally necessary level of content knowledge on the part of the teacher

Now, I realize that this sounds like a great deal of information, especially since some individual class periods could be comprised of multiple objectives and entire units of instruction would be comprised by even more of them. However, there is no need for the materials accompanying these objectives to be particularly voluminous, as witnessed by the following example that we actually used in our class size study involving exponents.

> *Example of a mathematical instructional objective*: Rename a number to the "zero power" as 1.

Then, to make absolutely certain the teachers knew how the students would be tested, we provided some sample items. (I definitely don't recommend showing teachers the exact items that will be appear on the final test, but the exact formats should be shared.) Why, after all, shouldn't teachers know precisely what they are expected to teach? And why would we not want students to know precisely what they are expected to learn?

> *Sample Items*:
>
>   (1) $3^0 =$ ____ .
>   (2) If $142^x = 1$, what is the exponent "x" equal to? ____

Bill Moody and I preferred to use open-ended questions to eliminate guessing, but multiple-choice tests could have been constructed just as easily:

>   (1) $3^0 =$ ____ .
>   a. 0
>   b. 3
>   c. 1
>   d. 30
>
>   (2) If $142^x = 1$, what is the exponent "x" equal to? ____
>   a. 1
>   b. 142
>   c. 1/142
>   d. 0

Sample Rationale/Subject Matter Content: By definition, $x^0 = 1$ for any whole number ≥ 0. For example: $3^0 = 1$; $20^0 = 1$. It is defined this way to be consistent with other definitions and properties involving exponents. As only one example, consider the objective in which students are expected to rename the product of two numbers with like bases as the common base with an exponent equal to the sum of the two exponents. That is, $x^4 * x^5 = x^{4+5} = x^9$. This means that $x^4 * x^0 = x^{4+0} = x^4$, which is consistent, since any number times 1 is equal to that number (i.e., $2 * 1 = 1$ and $x^4 * 1 = x^4$). In mathematics, the operations and definitions used in one system of numbers (such as whole numbers) must be consistent with all of the others (such as exponents or rational numbers), otherwise mathematics itself would be inconsistent.

Or, translated to the teaching of reading, a typical beginning instructional objective might take the following form:

Example of an initial reading instructional objective: Recognize the five most commonly occurring words in the English language [the, to, and, he, and a].

Sample Items: This simple objective can be assessed in a surprising number of ways. Individually, either in person by a teacher/aide or via a headset to a learning technician:

(1) Read these words to me:
   the
   of
   and
   to
   a

(2) Alternately, the student could be orally instructed (either via computer or in person) to mark the box (either via mouse or paper-and-pencil) that spells "to":
   ☐ the
   ☐ of

☐ and
☐ to
☐ a

Or at a slightly more advanced level:

(3) Select the word that best fits the blank:

I go _____ school.

☐ the
☐ of
☐ and
☐ to
☐ a

For an objective such as this, we can assume teachers know the necessary content, but it still doesn't hurt to apprise them of the rationale for teaching the objective in the first place.

Educational Rationale: While phonetic word-attack skills are an integral part of initial reading instruction, students should also possess a repertoire of words that can be immediately recognized on sight. It has been estimated that the original Dolch list of 200 words represents 60% of the reading vocabulary found in any given nontechnical text, children's or adult's. Sight recognition of the members of this list, many of which cannot be sounded out phonetically, therefore constitutes a major step toward independent reading.

In our research, in addition to providing our teachers with this extremely prescriptive curriculum, we impressed upon them the importance of administering as much instruction as possible within their golden 30-minute class period. And since we couldn't assume that all of them would comply, we warned them that Bill would pop into the classrooms to observe them occasionally.

Now, of course, it could be argued that practicing teachers wouldn't put up with such treatment. Teachers consider themselves professionals after all, and many of them cherish their professional prerogative to use their professional judgment liberally. (In research, one consequence of this attitude is illustrated in the computer software trial mentioned earlier, in which many of the teachers decided to implement the computerized instructional intervention for five minutes or less per class.) Teachers also have unions to protect them from controlling behaviors such as these, a fact of institutional life that Bill and I didn't have to deal with. But professional practices do change. Physicians no longer bleed their patients, and their practices are no worse for it (and probably a lot less messy). The same would be true for teachers I think. Taking away the less effective practices now required by the obsolete classroom paradigm and replacing them with strategies that do work would ultimately have a liberating effect upon the profession.

Of course, when I was conducting my learning laboratory genre research, I certainly never conceptualized anything I did as tampering with the teacher's role or prerogatives. I simply knew that I could not possibly afford to allow the classroom teacher to make any decisions regarding *what* should be taught, how *much* instructional time should be allocated to teaching it, or at what *level* (defined by the sample test items) it should be taught. Said another way, a completely unintended byproduct of the type of research that I conducted wound up being *the disenfranchisement of teachers from the instructional decision-making process.* Or, viewed from another perspective, this approach provided the teacher with the tools he or she needed to maximize learning, thereby freeing him or her from the necessity of making imperfectly informed instructional decisions.

And this elimination of an entire layer of classroom-level decision making also constitutes one of the greatest advantages of the learning laboratory approach to instruction proposed in the last chapter. That is *the degree to which it would make curricular and instructional decisions on the part of individual educators (be they teachers, building principles, or curriculum supervisors) not only unnecessary, but contraindicated.* This isn't to say that brief didactic or one-on-one explanations for the content being learned wouldn't often be required to facilitate understanding of a topic. Or be necessary to compensate for inadequacies in the digital instruction available.

But, regardless of whether we migrate to the learning laboratory or retain the obsolete classroom, the existence of an extremely explicit, transparent, and exhaustive method of defining the curriculum—and tests derived solely based upon that curriculum—constitutes the first step in this migration away from idiosyncratic decision making, whether involving what to teach or how long to teach it. Certainly, I fully realize that many teachers react viscerally against this level of specificity and reject such a voluminous list of teaching topics. And perhaps they are correct in disliking the instructional objective *format*, but it is absolutely necessary that *everything* that needs to be taught be communicated, and that the tests we use to evaluate how much learning occurs be based on this content and nothing else. And if computers are used for nothing else, perhaps they can be used to store, organize, and make these objectives instantaneously accessible to teachers within the classroom. Perhaps this, in and of itself, would make them less daunting.

Standards Versus Objectives

To a certain extent, the public schools have been moving toward more explicitness in specifying what needs to be taught for some time now. Every state now has curriculum standards that their students are expected to meet, and many list these on their websites. For those that don't, there are websites[3] that list curriculum standards for every grade level and every state in the country.

In some cases, certain standards could actually double as instructional objectives (actually, semantically, a standard is an instructional objective of sorts), but generally speaking most state standards are so inclusive that they need to be broken down into a plethora of discrete instructional objectives (or instructional topics/units or possible test items). One way to conceptualize the difference between standards and objectives is that the latter can often be mastered in a matter of minutes or at most a few class periods, whereas many standards require much longer periods of time to achieve. Even subdividing standards into "benchmarks" (which provide a bit more specificity) does not sufficiently truly delineate what needs to be taught and learned.

Thus, a state that considered it important to introduce exponents into the elementary curriculum might write a standard worded something like:

Each student should be familiar with exponential notation.

Or, as an example of some that are actually in use:

(1) Understands the exponentiation of rational numbers and root extraction.
(2) Uses a variety of operations (e.g., raising to a power, taking a root, taking a logarithm) on expressions containing real numbers.

Now, all of these standards could technically encompass all ten of the instructional objectives we used in the tutoring and class size studies. However, if a standard *was* meant to encompass all ten of our instructional objectives (undoubtedly these are meant to include many other instructional objectives as well), and if all eight were not specified in some manner, there is little possibility that *all* teachers will cover the full set. There are, in fact, so many instructional objectives that could be encompassed by these standards that the end-of-year standardized test employed may not at all reflect what most teachers covered in class.

This is problematic from several perspectives. First, in these days of accountability based primarily upon test scores, any learning that occurs but is untested is in effect learning that never occurred at all: like the proverbial tree falling unheard in the forest. Or, from a slightly different perspective, if the test contains items that few teachers (or few teachers of, say, inner-city students) cover, then the test is *biased* toward those students (almost always those serving higher economic status families) who are privy to such coverage.

So, the exact format in which the curriculum is specified is not important. We can use instructional objectives, sample test items, or simple specific lists of topics as long as the entire breadth and depth of the desired learning is communicated. And, although curriculum standards don't do this, they could be very useful as organizational categories under which complete sets of instructional objectives could be stored.

Types of Instructional Objectives

The instructional objective examples provided earlier may give the impression that the technique itself is primarily useful for teaching and assessing factual (or "rote") knowledge, rather than the more complex learning outcomes that we eventually aspire to help children acquire. Nothing could be further from the truth, because anything that can be taught can be expressed as an instructional objective.

Benjamin Bloom's best known contribution to the field of education in fact wasn't his schooling research/theory mentioned earlier, but his much-earlier stint as editor[4] of a taxonomy of educational objectives that is still in use over a half a century later. This seminal work has, however, been updated in a somewhat more accessible form by Lorin Anderson (mentioned earlier as one of Bloom's impressive students) and David Krathwohl (one of the authors of the original taxonomy), along with six other contributors.[5] These authors first categorize knowledge as:

- *Factual*: Which they define as "the basic elements students must know to be acquainted with a discipline or solve problems in it," and which subsume most of the examples I've provided.
- *Conceptual*: Defined in terms of knowledge of classifications, categories, principles, generalizations, and theories (among other things).
- *Procedural*: "How to do something, methods of inquiry, and criteria for using skills, algorithms, techniques, and methods," which would hopefully lead to application, creativity, and transfer.
- *Metacognitive*: Knowing about knowing, which I will leave alone because I'm not 100% clear about this category's relevance to elementary school instruction.[6]

Perhaps more illustrative of the wide range of complexity that instructional objectives are capable of capturing (hence, we are capable of teaching children in school) is what Anderson et al. define as *cognitive processes* (which are quite close, but not identical to Bloom's original taxonomy):

- Remember: Which includes *recognizing* and *recalling*
- *Understand*: Interpreting, exemplifying, classifying, summarizing, inferring, comparing, and explaining
- *Apply*: Which, among other things, involves determining in which situations something fits some principle (*implementing*)
- *Analyze*: Which involves *differentiating* and *organizing* among other things
- *Evaluate*: Which involves skills such as critical thinking
- *Create*: Which involves *generating*, *planning*, and *producing* something

From a time-on-task perspective, these different types of objectives require different amounts of instruction to master, with the first three at least being hierarchical in nature. Said another way, generally speaking, it takes children longer to *understand* something (which is synonymous with comprehension) than it takes them to learn facts (remember), and it takes more time to teach them to learn to apply knowledge (which is another facet of transfer of learning) than it does to teach them to understand it.[7]

A SUMMARY OF THE CURRICULUM-BASED ADVANTAGES OF EXTREME SPECIFICITY AND COMPREHENSIVENESS

Admittedly, translating the entire elementary school's curriculum in this way would necessitate a huge (albeit finite) number of instructional objectives, and it would only constitute a beginning step in our migration away from the obsolete classroom model. In truth, however, a large proportion of the task has already been accomplished by state boards of education, untold thousands of teacher workshops, textbook writers, and (as just discussed) by the development of many of our curriculum standards. Regardless of how we go about this objective-based translation of the curriculum, its realization would move us a great deal closer to our ideal of a room full of students sitting in front of their monitors, receiving relevant individualized instruction rather than sitting in a classroom squandering their childhoods.

To summarize, then, some of the primary advantages of the exclusive use of instructional objectives (or some viable alternative) include:

1. *Their ability to communicate both what is to be taught and how this instruction will be evaluated.* There is nothing vague about an instructional objective accompanied by sample items to ensure that everyone involved in the instructional process knows exactly what is to be taught, studied, assigned as homework, and ultimately tested.

2. *These accompanying sample items in turn can be used to assess mastery of the curriculum and also both allow and encourage teachers to teach to the test.* While this may sound antithetic to principled instructional practice, in this paradigm, the test *is* the curriculum (or a representative sample thereof), which is by definition what teachers *should* teach. In any event, teaching the test is what many teachers in "low performing" schools are encouraged to do anyway.

The trouble is that, as long as test construction remains a carefully guarded black box designed to prohibit teachers from knowing precisely what their students will be tested upon, such teaching involves a great deal of counterproductive guess-work. There is absolutely no reason for this. Standardized achievement tests should transparently reflect the instructional objectives that define the curriculum. In fact, one would hope that teachers and schools would be able to construct equivalent tests of their own, based upon these instructional objectives.

3. *Properly constructed instructional objectives would also allow parents, researchers, administrators, and tutoring services to track children's progress, administer supplementary instruction, and predict final test performance.* Why, after all, shouldn't everyone interested in facilitating school learning have access to such information? Indeed, I wouldn't be surprised if the availability of this option didn't generate a plethora of for-profit enterprises, such as assessment companies that periodically could test children on behalf of their parents during the course of the year, to both track their learning progress and predict how well they will perform on the end-of-year test. And, of course, tutoring companies (or individuals, such as college students who wish to supplement their income) could provide additional instructional time targeted at specific content not yet mastered.

4. *For those parents who do employ tutoring services, the use of instructional objectives would make their services more cost effective.* Currently, many of these services require (or strongly suggest) a fixed number of initial, largely irrelevant sessions given over to noninstructional window-dressing prior to getting down to the business of serious instruction. The use of freely available instructional objectives should allow these companies to use their students' time more efficiently (and, if not, allow parents to supervise these services more closely).

5. *As mentioned in the preceding section, instructional objectives can be used to guide and assess instruction at any level of complexity, not simply at the basic/factual level.* Reading comprehension, for example, can quite easily be specified in terms of discrete instructional objectives, as can critical thinking, novel applications of facts, creativity, and even the generation of new principles from known

facts. Once again, anything that can be taught can be (and should be) translated into an instructional objective.

6. *The existence of such an explicit and detailed description of the curriculum would provide a very real opportunity for anyone (students, families, or community organizations) who wished to remediate an individual student's learning deficits by supplying extra instruction.* (Recall that our time-on-task hypothesis predicts that extra instruction is the *only* way a student who is "behind" his or her peers can catch up.) This can be achieved via tutoring (parental, school-supplied, or privately paid), extra classes, or self-study. Knowing exactly which instructional objectives have already been taught in school but not mastered, however, makes all of these options dramatically more efficient and, of course, having computer software available to do the "tutoring" would greatly facilitate matters.

7. *The reduction of broad subject matter swaths (as presented in textbooks) to small, discrete bits of information would furthermore greatly facilitate the development of computerized instruction.* The use of a standardized instructional objective format would be a godsend for computer programmers.

8. *Once available, digital instruction could be available online, so that any student or parent could access it to reinforce what was being taught in school or to prepare the student for upcoming instruction.* It might even be advantageous for schools and teachers to post schedules of which objectives were to be taught at what points in time to facilitate this process.

9. *Instructional objectives would make teacher training far more efficient (and perhaps even more effective than no training at all for the first time in its history).* Prospective teachers could be given practice in teaching representative objectives within the actual schooling environment. In fact, perhaps perspective teachers could spend a full year engaging in small-group instruction (or tutoring) within the public school environment as part of their degree requirements.[8] This could occur at the expense of otherwise ineffective courses and would actually enhance the learning of both the elementary student beneficiaries (due to the incremental learning effects of class sizes of five or less) while prospective teachers would gain experience teaching along with familiarity with the curriculum. The remainder of the elementary teacher preparatory curriculum could involve ensuring

that prospective teachers actually knew subject matter background represented by the instructional objectives they would be charged with teaching. (Hopefully in somewhat more depth than their future students would be taught.)

10. *The existence of instructional objectives would ultimately save preparation time on the part of the teacher since the blueprint for each day's lesson would be defined in terms of a discrete number of preselected objectives.* Conscientious teachers currently expend an enormous amount of time preparing lessons (partly due to their need to individualize their instruction to the unique needs of their students), even after they have spent years teaching the same grade level. Over time, however, instructional techniques and instructional options relating to the teaching of each objective would begin to build up and could be cataloged on a single website by an organization interested in supporting school learning.

11. *Sole reliance upon instructional objectives would have the potential to completely revolutionize grading.* Tests and marking period grades could be based upon the number of objectives achieved (perhaps weighted by individual differences in the average amount of time required to learn certain objectives). This, in turn, would potentially reduce pressures on teachers to inflate their grades and would make it possible for grades assigned in different settings to be comparable.

12. *Finally, instructional objectives could provide a framework by which the curriculum could be constantly evaluated for relevancy (which translates to the ultimate utility of what is being taught).* This is a key, and generally neglected, aspect of instruction and contains two components: ensuring (a) that necessary topics are taught and (b) that unnecessary topics are *not* taught.

A Final Observation on Instructional Objectives

Admittedly, very little I have said will dispel many educators' visceral objections to the specificity with which I advocate defining the curriculum and the resulting prescriptive nature of the educational model resulting from it. I realize that I cannot change any educator's mind for whom the philosophical approaches of John Dewey or progressive education in general holds sway or more modern (and to me completely inexplicable) conceptions of school learning as exemplified by a quote from the revised taxonomy just discussed (of all places):

> *In instructional settings, learners are assumed to construct their own meaning based on their prior knowledge, their current cognitive and metacognitive activity, and the opportunities and constraints they are afforded in the setting, including the information available to them. (p. 28)*

Recognizing my own limitations in these regards, all I can say in my own defense is that I am interesting in elementary school *learning*. I am interested in basic things like teaching children to read or to understand mathematical concepts or to string a few grammatically correct sentences together—areas of endeavor in which mastery of the learning content is important and the meaning that the learner "constructs" is irrelevant (and probably detrimental) unless it involves reading, performing the indicated mathematical tasks, and writing grammatically correct sentences.

I would argue, however, that mastery of very specific concepts are often prerequisites of more complex endeavors, and this step-by-step, objective-by-objective approach to instruction and learning is ultimately exceedingly effective. While I'm not a big believer in parables, I do think it is worth repeating one from a truly important book by Clayton Christensen, Curtis Johnson, and Michael Horn entitled *Disrupting Class: How Disruptive Innovation Will Change the Way the World Learns*. Using an industrial example contrasting Chrysler (which has just gone pretty much belly-up in our recent recession and requested bailout money as it did once before) and Toyota (which at that time, prior to its decision to prioritize profits over its customers' safety, was arguably the world's most successful automaker), these authors illustrate the advantages of both mastery learning and instructional objectives via a setting that I personally wouldn't have thought of.

The setting in question is an automotive assembly line where, say attaching brake drums in a "reasonably competent fashion" (or even in an 85% correct manner) is completely unacceptable, as is any alternative "*meaning* the learning brings to the task." At Chrysler, the time for someone on the assembly line to learn a task was fixed and, as would be expected, the results were quite variable, with some employees learning to perform the tasks and some not learning. At Toyota, employees were given all the time they needed to thoroughly learn their "objectives," and the results were that *everyone* learned to perform the necessary operations (which were basically a set of instructional objectives conceptually no different from what we've been discussing, although surely they weren't conceptualized or written as such—nor did they need to be).

The philosophy behind Toyota's teaching approach (and mastery learning and the Learning Laboratory) is perfectly illustrated by the following instructions: "There are the seven steps (read seven instructional objectives) required to install this seat successfully. You don't have the privilege of learning Step 2 until you've demonstrated mastery of Step 1. If you master Step 1 in a minute, you can begin learning Step 2 in a minute from now. If Step 1 takes you an hour, you can begin learning Step 2 in an hour from now" (p. 110).[9]

CURRICULUM EVALUATION

Regardless of how it is specified, taught, or evaluated, the curriculum is arguably the most neglected component of the schooling process. It has crucial and obvious implications with respect to increasing relevant instructional time, however, because:

> To the extent that any of the subject matter we teach students is irrelevant, then the instruction devoted to that subject matter is irrelevant. This, in turn, means that the amount of instructional time devoted to these irrelevances commensurately reduces the total amount of relevant instructional time delivered.

And, if there is one message I aspire to deliver in this book, it is that there is nothing more precious in education than the limited time we have to prepare the next generation for whatever lies ahead of them. Instructional time is simply something we cannot afford to squander.

Now, I realize that educators do superficially evaluate the elementary school curriculum, but they are constrained by (a) limited knowledge of societal needs, (b) practical concerns regarding the contents of the standardized tests upon which schools are evaluated, and (c) constraints placed upon them by special-interest groups (filtered through school board members and legislators). As I see it, there are three (and only three) reasons to include a topic in the curriculum and these are its demonstrative:

- *Utility* for future job, civic, social, or evolutionary/familial functioning,

- *Prerequisite necessity* for learning a more advanced topic (that is in turn itself demonstratively useful for one of these levels of functioning),
- *Documented consensus agreement* on aesthetic or quality-of-life benefits.

The most direct and efficient way to evaluate the utility of the curriculum according to these diverse criteria is to engage the best and brightest minds in our society in a *continuous* and *critical* evaluation of what we teach our children. The groups selected to provide this feedback should be as inclusive as possible, including at a minimum elementary/middle school/ high school teachers, mathematicians, engineers, economists, scientists, writers, public servants, employers, college professors, students (high school, undergraduate, and graduate), artists, and both employers and employees from as many sectors of the economy as possible. I italicize "continuous" here because new knowledge and new jobs are constantly being added, while old ones become obsolete; I emphasize the word "critical" because we have a tendency to accept traditional topics that we were taught in school as possessive of some sort of extrinsic merit or, even worse, embrace a mind set involving, "If I had to suffer through it, then so should the next generation."

Perhaps the most practical approach to this task would be to begin with online committees who would review the entire set of instructional objectives available for each subject in each grade level via a two-step process. Step 1, since it is always easier to add topics than to delete them, would involve identifying obvious candidates for *deletion*. Only after this was accomplished, would the second step (adding new content) be undertaken.

Each objective and each topic area could be rated by the respondents based upon their unique perspective regarding how necessary mastery is/ was in (1) the discharge of their jobs, (2) learning subsequent material that was necessary for this purpose, or (3) contributing to their personal quality of life through leisure time activities or personal-social-societal-familial responsibilities.

The biggest challenge these evaluators would face is the recognition that, just because a topic has been taught for a century, and just because they were required to learn it, doesn't necessarily mean that it should be inflicted upon the next generation. Only after the deletion process has been completed would new topics (or new instructional objectives within topics) be suggested. Each would be justified based upon the same process used for deletion.

Since the deletion of irrelevant content is most directly applicable to our schooling theory (because it will free-up additional relevant instructional time that could be redistributed elsewhere), allow me to present some examples of obvious candidates that currently consume enormous amounts of instructional time:

Example #1: Fractions

Most people not familiar with the elementary school curriculum would be shocked at the inordinate amount of time we spend teaching children how to add, subtract, multiply, and divide fractions. I would guess, however, that very few of these same people would question the need for such instruction—primarily because we aren't accustomed to questioning what our children are taught, as long as we were taught the same thing.

I would argue, on the other hand, that the only real function a fraction serves in society (or the study of more complex mathematics for that matter) entails a sort of linguistic estimation device, such as:

- *Question*: "How many came to your class reunion?"
- *Answer*: "A fourth – maybe a third of the class."

And that's about all the utility there is for this particular notation system. Even here, percentages or decimals (which are already part of the curriculum) are more useful for communication purposes:

- Alternative answer: "Oh, maybe 25% to 30% of the class max."

Even though it is a curricular staple, there is no known reason why an elementary school child should *ever* be taught to add, subtract, multiply, or divide fractions. And then, things get even worse when they are required to tackle mixed fractions of the genre:

$$24\frac{1}{2} \div 27\frac{3}{4} = \underline{\hspace{1cm}}.$$

I make my living working with numbers, and I honestly believe that the last time I was ever faced with performing an operation such as this was in elementary school. True, fractional concepts have some applicability to the study of algebra, but their transferability there is probably quite tenuous and the necessary operations would be more efficiently taught *when* they are needed, at which point the term "fractions" wouldn't even be used.

In real-life computations, we use decimals and percentages, not fractions. True, we use language that implies a fractional representation ("Kobe Bryant has just hit 15 out of his last 17 free throws") to calculate decimals or percentages ("Kobe Bryant has hit 88% of his last 17 free throws"), but not fractions (or operations thereon) themselves. We also employ computers or calculators to arrive at the percentages/decimals that we do use.

However, to illustrate just how ingrained the curriculum can become, Texas Instruments came out with a calculator a number of years ago that was designed to perform basic operations on *fractions* rather than decimals for the sole purpose of facilitating elementary school instruction. Talk about getting the cart before the horse! It would be amusing if it didn't illustrate how little thought goes into our children's curriculum, how firmly entrenched some topics are within it, and how little relevance much of it is to children's future needs.

Fractions could just as easily be relegated to vocabulary expansion in the English language curriculum (or to history). There are plenty of other elementary school mathematics topics that should at least be viewed critically, such as whether it is necessity to drill students interminably on computational algorithms like those used for long division. Instruction such as this is both boring and time consuming, yet the only time adults would *ever* sit down and do a long division problem is if they find themselves without access to a calculator, computer, or cell phone (the latter being almost impossible to visualize for anyone below the age of 92). I'm personally not quite this old, but I'm old enough to vaguely remember being taught an algorithm for finding the square root of a number perhaps a half century ago. Naturally, I've long since forgotten that one, even though I use square roots constantly.

Example #2: Cursive Writing

I've never seen the need for teaching children two methods of writing. Cursive writing apparently reached its full development during the 18th and 19th century, before the development of the typewriter, based upon the dual advantages of speed and space requirements, but since the omnipresence of computers it has been gradually falling out of favor.

Many schools continue to teach it, however, even though fewer and fewer people use it even when they need to write something by hand. In fact, in those increasingly rare instances in which we are required to fill out forms via paper-and-pencil rather than online, the instructions usually require us to print, because almost everyone's cursive writing skills over the age of 30 has deteriorated into terminal illegibility. And, although I'm no seer, it may be that in the future we'll see no reason to teach any form of hand-writing. Who knows?

Example #3: The Entire Science Curriculum As We Know It

Although certainly not a candidate for deletion, our elementary school science curriculum is problematic because there is no clear consensus regarding its exact purpose. Should we teach facts, or should we teach the process by which these "facts" are uncovered? Or, should we attempt to teach critical-thinking skills? If one of the latter two options, who is to teach it, or who is to teach the teachers? The average district science education specialist simply doesn't have the training to do this, nor do many schools of education have faculty on board with this sort of expertise. The people with these sorts of talent are so rare (or at least widely dispersed) that the only way I can envision using their expertise at the elementary school level is through digital or virtual instruction of some sort.

So, although these candidates for curricular deletion are only three of a multitude of potential examples, I think it is obvious that what is needed for the entire public school curriculum is an ongoing review of what is absolutely essential to teach and why it is essential to teach it. Again, as I see it, there are three and only three reasons to include something in the curriculum: (1) it is useful for some purpose in later life, such as future job performance; (2) it is a prerequisite for learning something else that is essential; and/or (3) it has some sort of recognized aesthetic value. And, unfortunately, I'm not 100% sold on our ability to evaluate Number 3.

Difficulties Inherent in the Curriculum Review Process

Regardless of how we go about it, three problems must be overcome before a truly effective ongoing curriculum evaluation process can be implemented. These involve (a) the difficulty of choosing reasonable criteria for making deletion/addition decisions, (b) the lack of a national curriculum, and (c) the need to identify true versus bogus prerequisites higher up the educational chain.

Criteria

There is nothing sacrosanct about the three criteria just advanced to decide whether or not something should be taught. Each is fraught with it own difficulties. The first is tenuous, because we don't know what the future holds for our children. The second is probably the most objective of the three, as long as we don't overestimate the transferability of elementary school concepts, including the realities that (a) the way we teach concepts to younger children may not be at the same level of complexity they will need to later apply them and (b) subject matter that isn't constantly used requires periodic review or it will be forgotten. We are much more likely to be disappointed than pleasantly surprised when we expect instruction in one arena to transfer or facilitate learning in another. (The best way to ascertain the likelihood of such transfer occurring is to perform a task analysis to ascertain prerequisite concepts involved in learning a targeted objective or skill.[10])

The final criterion, aesthetic value, unquestionably involves the most subjective judgments of all. Every art and science will have its vociferous advocates in a curriculum review process such as I'm suggesting, and there will be equally adamant objections to including many topics simply because of competition for the limited instructional time available.

Personally, I'm not convinced, for example, that universal music and art instruction belong in the school curriculum, but this the opinion of one person who has no knowledge or expertise in either. Individuals who do possess these qualifications therefore need to have input, and their decisions should be made on the basis of what future artistic outcomes will and will not accrue as a function of mastering specific instructional objectives in these arenas. Said another way, these individuals should ask themselves: "What will mastery of, say, each (or all) of the 124 proposed musical objectives accomplish for a student?" Will it make someone more likely to obtain employment as a musician?[11] Achieve self-actualization by either performing for others or for oneself in adulthood? Be more likely to attend concerts that improve his or her quality of life after leaving school? Having the actual objectives in front of these experts when they make their judgments can be quite instructive, because the objectives (if properly written) are what will be taught, and it is only what is taught that must be judged—nothing else.

A caveat: Someone, such as a music (or impoverished children's) advocate, could reasonably argue that the school is the only place where some children will have the opportunity to experience playing an instrument or being a member of a band. My view of schooling, however, is extremely narrow and focused exclusively upon efficiently producing learning, so I would suggest that opportunities such as these should be provided by other institutions or organizations (which could be allowed to use school facilities after hours). I would similarly suggest that competitive sports be organized and supported by interested community groups completely outside of the school's jurisdiction (and of course with no instructional time sacrificed thereto).

National Versus State Curricula

A second impediment to an ongoing curriculum review process of any sort is the fact that the curriculum is the prerogative of individual states. For the elementary school, at least, this is absurd for a number of reasons.

First, states don't prepare students to function solely within their own borders. It is also important to remember that when we're talking about *elementary school* instruction. Every parent in America (and the world for that matter) should be guaranteed that his or her child is being provided with a core curriculum that has been agreed upon by the best minds that can be brought to bear on the subject. And for grades pre-K through 5, how controversial can this be?

Everyone needs to be able to read, to understand what they read, to understand basic mathematical concepts, and to be able to construct coherent sentences on a computer. Elementary schools don't need to teach children that intelligent design proponents are crackpots or that abstinence is/isn't the method of choice to avoid AIDS. It would be nice of course if more emphasis could be placed upon the critical thinking skills needed to arrive at informed opinions regarding some of the more complex and controversial topics that children will be introduced to later on, but there is really no reason to introduce anything controversial into the elementary school curriculum. Let this remain a prerogative of *families* or the specialized institutions of their choice.

Avoiding Fake Prerequisites

A final curricular pitfall involves the necessity of preparing students for completely irrelevant content further up the educational ladder. This often takes the form of arbitrary, indefensible prerequisites or program entry requirements.

As an example, when I entered college, I selected a "premed" course of study that was designed to lead to medical school and, one assumes, to later facilitate the practice of medicine. One of the requirements of that particular curriculum was two years of coursework in either German or French (German being the preferred option) and a successful score on a standardized foreign language test.

The official rationale for this was that many important medical journals, textbooks, and treatises were published in one of those two languages. The only other modern language offered at my university at the time was Spanish, which was disallowed because there was a perception that sufficiently important medical information wasn't published in that language. (Of course, in hindsight, being able to communicate effectively with one's Hispanic patients might have constituted a much more relevant clinical skill.)

As it turned out, my deficiency in precollege instructional time in foreign language prevented what I'm sure we would all agree would have been a most brilliant medical career. From a curricular perspective, however, the German requirement was completely bogus—the purpose for which (I assume) was solely to serve as a crude screening device to discourage undefined undesirables from applying to medical school in the first place.

In my particular case, the strategy was successful, but it constituted an extremely wasteful use of instructional time, requiring other students to devote approximately 10% of their undergraduate coursework to a topic that they would never use in their chosen profession or anywhere else. Today, German has been replaced by physics and calculus in premedical education, both of which are probably equally irrelevant to the actual practice of medicine. The exact thought processes, if any, underlying such curricular decisions are unclear, but may involve rationales such as:

- "We can't allow just anybody into our profession. Obviously we want to make sure that our future physicians are intelligent people from an acceptable social class, so if we can't employ IQ as a criterion because of political correctness issues, then perhaps a few courses in German or calculus will perform the same function."

- "I had to suffer through irrelevant, boring prerequisites and it didn't hurt me."
- "True, I've never used German or calculus in treating a patient, but perhaps that's just a function of my practice. If they weren't important, they wouldn't be required for medical school admittance."

Now, although such issues may appear a bit far removed from our purpose here, the curriculum at each educational level must provide the prerequisites for successfully negotiating the curriculum at the next level. So, while ultimately one would hope that each profession would eventually conduct a realistic and detailed task analysis to delineate the true prerequisites for successful practice, the curriculum at the lower educational rungs is held hostage until this happens.

A FINAL (HUGE) ADVANTAGE OF EXHAUSTIVELY DEFINING THE CURRICULUM

Although I believe that the simple act of exhaustively delineating what we plan to teach in terms of discrete sets of instructional objectives will put us in a much better position to judge its importance and the feasibility of students mastering it, there is another equally important application of this convention. If our schools' curriculum is specified in terms of discrete objectives, and if our schools' instruction is exclusively dedicated to teaching these objectives, then surely it follows that our tests should be exclusively based upon them as well. (Or, even if we completely eschew instructional objectives, shouldn't our testing system at least be based upon what we teach our children in school and nothing else?)

That our standardized testing system does *not* (a) assess school-based learning, (b) reflect any school's actual curriculum, or (c) have any known implications for instruction, rivals anything that Alice encountered when she passed through the looking glass. Thus, testing—the final pillar upon which the process of schooling stands (the curriculum and instruction being the first two pillars of this three legged stool)—is the subject of our next chapter. And, its reform constitutes a crucial step in our goal of maximizing the amount of relevant instruction our schools are capable of delivering.

CHAPTER 8

Using Tests Designed to Assess School-based Learning

Testing is something we all believe in.[1] We have a great deal of first-hand experience with taking tests, whether in school, in applying for college, or in applying for jobs. In education, testing is how we measure learning, how we *think* we evaluate the instruction delivered by our schools, and often the primary component of any political corrective action instituted to improve our schools. It is something everyone associated with the schooling process thinks they understand, and it is one of the few things in education that is "scientific," based as it is upon a well-validated mathematical model.

Unfortunately, this "scientific basis" upon which our current tests were developed is almost a century old and completely obsolete. It was created to enable psychologists to assess things that they could not define or even prove existed (much less specify how they were produced). A daunting task, if you think about it, but one that has little relevance to assessing school learning, which *can* be defined by what is taught (the curriculum) and which we *can* specify exactly how it is produced (by *instruction* and *nothing else*).

It is surprising how few educators seem to recognize just how simple a test of school learning is to construct. No elegant mathematical models are needed. All that is required is to:

1. Specify exactly what a student will (or should be) taught (which for present purposes we will assume to be in terms of discrete instructional objectives).

2. Write several items based upon each of those objectives, some of which will be shared with teachers (so that they understand what needs to be taught), some of which will *not* be shared to ensure the integrity of the testing process.

3. Select (in some systematically defensible manner) the objectives (and the items representing those objectives) that will appear on any given test. (This is necessary because we can't test students on everything they were taught; it would take too long.)

But, if testing is so conceptually simple, why have we made it so complicated? And why do we believe so fervently in these complications that we have imposed on the process when we understand them so poorly?

The answer, I believe, is to be found in the early public relations successes of the intelligence testing industry, which gave us three bogus measurement principles that are completely inapplicable to assessing school learning:

- *Bogus Testing Principle #1: The items which make up a test are of secondary importance to the attribute being measured.* This is absolutely wrong in any type of measurement because the items *are* the test and nothing less. It is an absolutely demented principle as far as school learning is concerned because the items must match what is taught or the test will measure something else: most likely the type of home environment children came from before arriving at school and to which they return each evening.

- *Bogus Testing Principle # 2: The total score achieved on a test can be mathematically converted to something that has considerably more intrinsic meaning than simply how many items were answered correctly.* This too is nonsense. In a test of school learning, if the items don't test what students were taught, multiplying and dividing the resulting scores as dictated by some esoteric formula can't change a pumpkin into a coach. Even transforming scores to grade equivalencies or some quotient (IQ being a prime example) is just a way of renaming them.

- *Bogus Testing Principle #3: The most important quality of a test is how consistently it can rank individuals (both with respect to itself and to other tests designed to measure the same "thing" or "attribute").* Wrong again. What we need from a test of school learning is an accurate estimate of *how* much students learned, *what* they learned, and what they *need* to learn. Rank ordering a set of scores from high to low, whether this is done via percentile ranks or T-scores or z-scores or grade equivalencies, doesn't provide any information relevant to improving instruction and thereby improving learning.

To illustrate, suppose you were informed by your child's teacher that your child had received a percentile rank of 52 on her latest standardized mathematics test. If you called the teacher and requested more information, you might be told that there was nothing for you to worry about since your child actually scored better than 52% of all of the third-grade students in the country and was reading at grade level, as indicated by her grade equivalency of 3.6. (Both grade equivalencies and percentile ranks are normally supplied by testing companies and are basically interchangeable.) And, if the person at the other end of the line perceived a hint of doubt on your part, she might also inform you that this was a very excellent test because it was extremely reliable and it correlated quite highly with other tests, such as quantitative aptitude and (with a slight pause) even intelligence tests.

From an educational point of view, however, information of this sort, if not worthless, is close. This would be comparable to receiving a bank statement that tells you only that you have more money in your account than 52% of all U.S. citizens who have a checking account. Although perhaps an interesting piece of trivia, you might want to know a few more details. So, let's pretend that you decided to call your local bank, which resulted in the following conversation with a help-center employee:

- *You*: I'm glad to know that I have more money than the average person in the country, but what I'd like to know is what my balance is. You see, I have a more pressing concern. What I need to know is how much money I have in my account because I want to buy a mattress.
- *Help Center*: I'm sorry, but we don't keep records in that manner. We can provide you with an age-equivalent financial score, and we can predict what that score will be upon your retirement. We can even predict what your percentile rank is in terms of property and stocks, based upon your account. If I may be allowed to put you on hold for 45 seconds, I will provide you with all this information.
- *You*: But I need to know how much money I have in my account. I don't need to know all of this other information. I need to know

if I have enough money to buy a (*expletive deleted*) mattress! And if I don't, I want to be able to figure out how much money I will have to save in order to buy one.

Now, as absurd as this conversation may sound, this is the only type of information that a standardized test is capable of providing. And what does it profit you (or a teacher for that matter) to know how well your child stacked up against other third-graders from Washington State to Florida (whether on the overall test score or on a few subtests)? For one thing, even this odd level of information can be quite misleading if our public schools as a whole are drastically underperforming—which they are. Wouldn't it make more sense to you and your daughter's teacher to know what percentage of the curriculum she had mastered? Even better, to inform the two of you exactly what your daughter hadn't yet learned and how much additional instructional time would be required for her to correct this deficit?

Time, after all, is something that can be quantified and, like money and weight, has so much inherent meaning that no one other than a psychometrician would think of converting it to something less useful. And learning, also after all, is a situation-specific, time-specific, and content-specific dynamic process of change. It is not a hypothetically stable attribute such as aptitude or intelligence; it is a specific response to instruction and therefore should not necessarily be highly correlated with other cognitive tests that are hypothesized not to be responsive to instruction.

And, what applies to the assessment of individual children also applies to the schools in which they are enrolled. Rank ordering schools from highest to lowest on some test (even if by some accident its items did reflect these schools' curricula) doesn't supply useful information. If 90% of the schools are performing at levels far below what they should (or could) be performing, then a percentile rank of 52% is hardly cause for celebration.

And that is why all three of the above-mentioned principles are completely bogus as far as school learning is concerned. Perhaps certain components of them are defensible from the perspective of measuring unobservable, indefinable psychological attributes such as aptitude, ability, achievement, or intelligence—but they are all completely indefensible from the perspective of assessing *school learning*. In fact, the adoption of these three principles by our testing industry guarantees that any test they develop will measure something entirely different from school learning. These are tests that are capable neither of (a) assessing what children *need* to be taught nor (b) evaluating the effectiveness of what they *have* been taught. And naming them "achievement" tests or anything else obviously can't change this sad state of affairs.

Perhaps the easiest way to understand how we arrived at this unfortunate juncture is to make a brief detour through the history of standardized psychological testing, a history that inexorably resulted in an environment in which tests:

- Can be given any name their corporate marketing department chooses,
- Dictate the curriculum to be taught rather than the other way around,
- Determine who will go to college and where,
- Determine entry into choice professions, and
- Play a major role in children's economic futures.

Although I will not attempt to draw point-by-point correspondences between our acceptance of testing proponents' claims and the transformation of the classroom model into the only schooling option we even consider, I believe that both have profited equally from our thoughtlessness, disingenuousness, avoidance, and intellectual laziness. In other words, I offer this little digression as an alternative (but better-documented) parable to J.M. Stephens' history of agriculture. In doing so, I draw liberally upon a lifetime interest in psychometrics, beginning with my exposure to (a) a number of excellent teachers (Professors A. Jon Magoon and James H. Crouse), (b) the work of many of the scholars whose work has already been cited (e.g., Benjamin Bloom, John Carroll, and James Popham), and (c) a number of fascinating books on the topic.[2]

A BRIEF HISTORY OF TESTING

Intelligence Tests

Let's pick up our story in the early years of the 20th century, with the work of a French psychologist named Alfred Binet who, after becoming disillusioned with craniometry (the measurement of head size) as an indicator of intelligence, set out to design a psychological (as opposed to a physical) measure of this cherished attribute. Today, it is difficult to appreciate the difficulty of the task facing Binet because it seems as though we've always had intelligence tests and someone's "IQ" is a crucial part of who and what they are. Indeed, the concept of a single score to measure the thing we call intelligence has become such an integral constituent of our language (and our world views) that we are far beyond the possibility of questioning whether the process by which we arrive at a conclusion regarding someone's level of intelligence makes any sense or not.[3] Instead, we tend to unconsciously and informally estimate other peoples' IQ the first time we meet them, so how can we possibly question the assumptions underlying the measurement of such an ingrained concept, much less its actual existence?

But things weren't this easy for Binet. No one had developed a satisfactory psychological intelligence test, and measuring people's cranial circumference had turned out to be a major scientific dead end. After all, other than that it obviously existed, what did people really know about intelligence in Binet's time? They knew that it was a good thing to have. They knew that educated people had more of it than uneducated people, but it had to be something more than education, because educated people's children seemed to have more of it than uneducated people's children even before they went to school.

In fact, in what is by now a very familiar refrain,[4] one of Binet's avowed goals in developing his test in the first place was to find a method to identify children at risk for experiencing learning problems, so that they could be afforded special remedial education to prevent their falling further and further behind in school. (Of course, a less sophisticated approach would have been to simply teach children, monitor how much they learned, and supply additional instruction as needed.) Unfortunately, there was no strong theory upon which he could draw to help identify what such a measure should look like or what types of items it should contain.

- *The Birth of Bogus Principle #1*: Ignore the items and you can call the test *anything*.

Not to be deterred, Binet simply tried out a wide range of tasks in an attempt to capture as many different facets of a child's "potential for learning" as possible. Since he was interested in assessing learning "potential" rather than learning itself, he naturally concentrated upon concepts that weren't commonly taught in school (or presumably anywhere else) such as attention, memory, and verbal skills. Cognizant of the hodgepodge of tasks he wound up selecting, Binet was initially careful to avoid explicit claims that his test exhaustively described the attribute people thought of as intelligence. After all, how could he? No one knew exactly what intelligence *was*. No one knew what caused it. And, of course, no one had ever directly observed it, so it obviously had to be measured indirectly. Not to be deterred, our hero formulated a generalization based upon his non-theoretical, eclectic approach to selecting his items/tasks, which has turned out to the basic philosophical underpinning of psychological testing, not to mention the unspoken mantra of the modern testing industry:

> *It matters very little what the tests (tasks or items) are as long as they are numerous.*[5]

And thus was born our first standardized testing principle (i.e., ignoring the individual items that make up a test) that helped us get into the mess we now find ourselves with respect to assessing school learning.

- *The Birth of Bogus Principle #2*: Algebra can render non-interpretable test scores *meaningful*.

In the case of measuring an attribute such as intelligence, the adoption of Principle #1 raised an obvious problem to which the solution itself was obvious only in hindsight. If the items themselves don't have any intrinsic meaning, then something had to be done to give the score resulting from them some affective/intuitive appeal. After all, no intelligence test developer could even claim to know how much intelligence it was possible to have or, equally important, *how little was possible*. (There is, in other words, no such thing as *zero* intelligence, unless we are talking about someone in a coma, and there is also no such thing as *total* intelligence.)

However, people's scores on any test, intelligence or otherwise, can always be compared to one another. So, early on, a German psychologist named William Stern came up with the idea of "standardizing" intelligence test scores based upon taking people's ages into account (since obviously a 17-year-old adolescent's score couldn't be compared to that of a seven-year-old child's, because it wouldn't even make sense to give them the same test). This was easily done, however, once enough scores for people at different ages became available by using a relatively simple-minded formula that was defined as the Intelligence Quotient or IQ (which in turn didn't require a lot of heavy translation from the German *Intelligenz-Quotient*):

$$IQ = 100 \times \text{Mental Age/Chronological Age}$$

And thus was the most famous of all "standardized" scores conceived. It had immediate intuitive appeal, because 100 is a nice round number that we can easily relate to. Also, once everyone became sufficiently familiar with it, they tended to forget (if they ever knew) that it was really a mere transformation of a test score. Instead, they began to interpret these nicely converted numbers as the attribute itself: as the person's *degree* of intelligence. After all, it was named an *intelligence quotient* and 100 was indisputably its *average*. Of course it didn't hurt the popularity of the tests that all professionals (and the vast majority of their children) who were in a position to prescribe (or interpret) the results of intelligence tests had above-average IQs.

Now, from a purely logical perspective, we know we can't really measure the *degree* of something that has no high or low endpoints, so what these IQ transformations wound up being was a simple ranking of people's test scores. But, far from a disadvantage, from this simple strategy was born our second principle of standardized testing (the mathematical conversion of the number of items answered correctly to something of more intrinsic meaningfulness).

Today, just about all test scores of all human attributes are standardized (i.e., mathematically manipulated) in some way. Most choose other intuitively appealing averages such as 500 or 50 to replace the actual test scores (which would almost never come out to a nice round number without some algebraic assistance). Standardized elementary school "achievement" tests chose to represent their average scores based upon grade levels or percentiles, but the same principle applies. And, in time, everyone forgets (or never knew) that these numbers simply represented rank ordered test scores, not any absolute amount of whatever the attribute was that was being assessed. Or even that these intuitively meaningful names (intelligence quotient or grade equivalencies) provide no guarantee that the targeted attribute was even being measured.

- *The Birth of Bogus Principle #3*: The name of the game is *stability*.

Formulas were so successful in changing test scores to something that appeared meaningful that the testing industry was absolutely delighted when it found that it had another simple mathematical formula at its disposal that transformed a test's *ranking ability* to an index ranging from 0 to 1.0. This resulting index was called the *reliability* of the test, and it represented the consistency with which a test's scores could rank people from high to low. Test developers also found that the closer this index was to 1.0, the more likely a cognitive test was to rank order people in the same way that other cognitive tests did, and this was called the *validity* of the test.[6] (Note the reassuring and value-laden nature of psychometric terms such as *reliability* and *validity*.) And, although this interrelatedness of seemingly disparate tests could have been seen as problematic, it didn't give IQ proponents pause. They simply assumed that all cognitive tests measured the same underlying inborn mechanism: intelligence. And they were partially correct. It was just that the underlying mechanism wasn't primarily inborn. It was largely reflective of the amount of relevant instruction the test taker had received.

THE BIRTH OF TEST REIFICATION

Returning to our intelligence testing origins, Alfred Binet's relative restraint in reifying (some might call it deifying) his tests wasn't shared by his best-known successor, Lewis Terman, who came up with an adapted version of one of Binet's test, named it the Stanford-Binet, and decreed that it measured *general* intelligence because its items tended to correlate with one another. (The interrelatedness of the items making up a measure is simply one of many other ways to represent the reliability of a test [or the stability with which it ranks individuals] because, algebraically, one formula for calculating this index is to obtain the average correlation among a test's items.) That is, people who performed well on one task tended to perform well on the others. Charles Spearman gave this phenomenon a name, the *g*-factor, and the rest, as they say, is history because *naming* something is an integral part of convincing people that it exists.

The true tipping point for the testing movement, however, coincided with the advent of World War I, when the U.S. military, faced with the prospect of dealing with millions of recruits and not enough officers to command them, inquired of the then-president of the American Psychological Association, Robert Yerkes, if he and some of his colleagues could develop a *group* administered intelligence test based upon Binet's and Terman's work.

What the army needed (or thought it needed) was something that could be administered en masse, capable of grossly discriminating between recruits for two basic purposes: weeding out the obviously mentally defective and identifying others who were a cut above their peers who might serve as officers. Following Binet's lead, Yerkes and his colleagues took an eclectic approach and included items testing such diverse concepts as (a) the use of analogies (which obviously wasn't lost upon future test developers such as the College Board and ETS), (b) mathematical reasoning, and (c) the ability to follow directions. And thus was the Army Alpha test conceived and administered to over a million and a half American soldiers.

And thus did our infatuation with mass testing also receive a major steroidal boost. Few asked whether or not the Army Alpha test was successful or the degree to which it succeeded in performing the tasks for which it was designed. Because no evaluation was ever conducted, no one knew whether it identified the best officer candidates or obviously unfit soldiers. The army itself was fine with the whole process, even though it decided not to blindly follow Yerkes' recommendations that both rank and assigned duties be based upon his test scores. The bottom line was that someone gave the order to develop and administer the test, someone supervised its administration, and we won the war. So, it must have been a good test.

And thus was the art and science of test validation born. For the Stanford-Binet intelligence tests, the Army Alpha test, and all psychological-educational tests that have followed are based upon four or five simple algebraic formulas that demonstrate that *any* test containing enough items to measure something *consistently* (and whose items are neither too easy nor too difficult for the people who answer them) will almost always produce that beauteous bell-shaped curve so beloved of psychologists and educators. (That is something else that Binet was referring to when he said that it doesn't matter what the items/tasks on the test are comprised of "as long as they are numerous.") If a test with a sufficient number of items is administered to the same group of people twice within a relatively brief time frame, the two sets of test scores will produce a very similar rank ordering of the individuals comprising this group. (In other words, people who score higher than their peers on the test the first time they take it will tend—within a specifiable degree of error—to score higher the second time around as well. And, of course, people who score lower than their peers the first time around will find themselves at the bottom of the distribution the second time too.) And again, this is called the *reliability* or *consistency* of a test, and it is the basis of our entire testing industry.[7] (It is also 95% of what its salespersons are referring to when they cite "psychometric theory" in support of their products.)

And, even more conveniently, since the content of the items that make up a test isn't all that important (Bogus Testing Principle #1), *any* test can claim to measure *anything* if its marketers are sufficiently persuasive (some might say disingenuous). Thus, if the developers of a new test could demonstrate that their product and a more established test (sometimes called a "gold standard" if it has sold enough copies) rank ordered individuals similarly, then obviously the new test was fine. If the new test was designed to measure intelligence, and if it and the Stanford-Binet were administered to the same group of people, then the new test automatically became a *valid* intelligence test if the same individuals scored highly on both tests. (*Validity* comprises the other 5% of psychometric theory.)

This in turn made it incumbent upon the developers of any new intelligence test to ensure that it was as similar as possible to the Stanford-Binet, hence giving birth to the testing version of a self-fulfilling prophecy. The end product of all these machinations was a bevy of tests,[8] constructed according to the same basic blueprint that tended to rank order people similarly. And thus was the process of test validation solidified with hardly a thought regarding what the implications would be if the original test happened to be flawed.

Now, all of this isn't to say that tests developed according to this model were not subject to criticism. It wasn't lost on people, for example, that it was difficult to guess exactly what a test was supposed to be measuring based upon a close examination of the items comprising it. This was hardly surprising, given the seemingly unrelated and intuitively unimportant tasks they represented (e.g., recalling lists of random digits), but their constructors found a creative way to circumvent this problem. They simply invented the now-famous psychological adage (attributed to Arthur Jensen) that avoided the need to either defend their tests or the existence of the attribute itself:

Intelligence, by definition, is what intelligence tests measure.[9]

And thus was the second great leap forward in the art and science of test validation accomplished—not to mention the birth of an entire class of self-fulfilling prophesies.

APTITUDE TESTING

One of the earliest applications of intelligence assessment for an exclusively educational test involved the efforts of The College Board: an organization originally founded by 12 university presidents in 1900 for the purpose of creating an "objective," streamlined method of differentiating among college applicants. This organization made little progress for a couple of decades, but, apparently recognizing the opportunity provided by the huge "success" of the Army Alpha tests, it hired one of Yerkes' colleagues, Carl C. Brigham to get the project off the ground.

Brigham was initially commissioned to head a committee whose task was to realize the College Board's original vision (i.e., the development of a test to facilitate the onerous task faced by College Admission Departments of selecting who would and would not be allowed to attend their august institutions). What resulted was the next great success story in American testing. The test, itself, was named The Scholastic Aptitude Test (SAT) and was first administered to high school students in 1926 (and subsequently on a national scale by the Educational Testing Service [ETS] of Princeton). And, not coincidentally (because it too was a type of intelligence test), the SAT also received a major boost when a version of it (called the *Army-Navy Qualifications Test*) was administered to millions of soldiers during World War II.[10]

Initially, the SAT developers faced a similar task to that of their intelligence test predecessors. They needed to measure something ("aptitude") for which no existing "gold standard" existed. They also wanted to distance themselves from the increasingly elitist/racist undertones seemingly endemic to early intelligence test developers/advocates, some of whom were unrepentant racists/eugenicists. Brigham himself had earlier written a book entitled *A Study of American Intelligence*,[11] in which he concluded that the decline of American education was inevitable as long its racial "mixture" continued to accelerate; hence, his first attempts at facilitating the college admissions process involved evaluating the feasibility of using actual intelligence tests as an admission criterion at Princeton University and a couple of other colleges.

But intelligence's increasingly cold, elitist connotations reduced its attractiveness for such an ostensibly egalitarian purpose as deciding who should and should not be allowed to attend college. True, "aptitude" was equally value-laden, but there was something a little softer about it.

A person with aptitude is a person who is likely to do important things, make important discoveries, and contribute to his or her field of endeavor.

And, although the SAT initially measured only two flavors of this attribute (verbal and quantitative), the implication was there that there were many other types of aptitude as well, so no one needed to be without aptitude for *something*—unlike intelligence, which came in a single flavor (at least according to Terman and his supporters). It also made sense that someone who generally had a great deal of aptitude was someone who should be admitted to a prestigious university and thereby provided the opportunity to develop this gift—an institution capable of molding this individual into a productive citizen who would make contributions to his or her field, who would become a leader, and therefore who *deserved* entrance to high-paying jobs and prestigious professions.

But, since the SATs were designed to be administered to high school graduates who were in the process of applying to college, their items had to be constructed accordingly. However, one irritating characteristic of the cherished classic reliability concept is that populating a test with items that the majority of the test takers can correctly answer lowers that test's reliability, makes it more difficult to market, and reduces its ability to predict future events, such as college grades or graduation rates. This, in turn, meant that the SAT couldn't very well be made up of items testing concepts that a typical high school graduate had been taught and expected to have learned. Besides, aptitude was supposed to be something different from learning, hence its developers attempted to include as many items as possible that they thought students *wouldn't* have been taught in school. Items, in other words, much like those that were contained in the old intelligence tests upon which they were modeled. Items which, upon examination, made it exceedingly difficult to nail down exactly what was being measured. *Items that no rational school would ever teach, reflecting content that would useful in no known job*, such as:

A hypotenuse is to an angle as a postulate is to an:
1. argument
2. assumption
3. inference
4. implication

Or:

> Being a man of maxims, he was _____ in what he said.
> - sentient
> - sebaceous
> - transmogrified
> - sententious

And thus did the SATs continue a proud tradition. They were composed of items that gave no hint as to exactly what they were designed to measure, hence the test could be called anything its developers wished (Bogus Testing Principle #1). The scores resulting from these items were then standardized to a scale with a mean of 500, which of course helped disguise the fact that they were really nothing more than test scores based upon an idiosyncratic collection of strange items (Bogus Testing Principle #2). And the items themselves were primarily selected based upon the psychometric properties that ensured the consistency with which they could rank students (Bogus Testing Principle #3).

The SAT therefore grew and prospered. In infancy, it was forced to rely upon exaggerated claims regarding its predictive ability with respect to college grades, even though high school grades did just as well.[12] And, so what if some crank argued that, to the extent that the SAT was successful in including items that *weren't* taught in school, then to that extent the test had to be assessing the home learning environment. Why? *Because anything that has been learned has to have been taught somewhere, and if that somewhere wasn't the school, wouldn't it most likely be the home learning environment?*

But, from another perspective, a nonprofit institution peopled by testing experts named the test the Scholastic *Aptitude* Test, and why would they do that if their test didn't measure aptitude? Of course, this was the same group of experts who claimed that their test/attribute, like the intelligence test developers before them, was impervious to instruction, even as a huge body of evidence grew up disputing the claim (not to mention an even larger industry given over to successfully teaching students how to drastically increase their SAT scores).

But so what? Everyone knows what aptitude is:

Aptitude is what aptitude tests measure.

The art and science of public relations had come a long way from the early days of the 20th century, however, as witnessed by the College Board's recent efforts to ratchet this process of test reification up a notch. Deciding that perhaps aptitude was beginning to take on a negative connotation in our increasingly politically correct world (especially since the parents of certain segments of the student population couldn't afford to pay for multiple SAT preparatory courses and were consequently placed at a major disadvantage in the college admission process), the test's marketers decreed that their product would no longer be called the Scholastic Aptitude Test. Instead, it would simply be called the SAT and nothing else. End of story. End of controversy.

The TEST is what it is.

TESTS DESIGNED TO ASSESS SCHOOL-BASED LEARNING

But what, it is quite reasonable to ask, is the relevance to all of this for the assessment of school learning? The answer is that there shouldn't be *any* because, unlike the measurement of an attribute, we know exactly what causes learning and we can observe this causal process in action. Show children the written word "the," tell them what the three letters in combination represent, repeat this process enough times, and they will eventually be able to identify the word (either orally or via a test item) whenever it is encountered in written form.

Although we might hope that reading is taught a bit less rotely than this, the behavior of telling the children the identity of a written word is a form of instruction. If a child cannot identify that word prior to instruction and can identify it after instruction, then this behavioral change is inferred to represent *learning*. Thus, the causal path here involves an observable behavior on the part of a teacher (instruction) that results in learning (which is *inferred*, based upon an observable behavioral change on the part of a student). We are therefore dealing with a very different situation from the assessment of attributes such as intelligence and aptitude, which their test developers originally claimed couldn't be influenced by instruction.

Of course, we now know full-well that intelligence tests are as malleable as aptitude scores or any other cognitive tests. We know this first because intelligence test scores have been improving steadily now for over a century, which happens to coincide with society's increasing emphasis upon abstract thinking. (Known as the Flynn effect, a century is much too brief a time for the phenomenon to be explained in biological evolutionary terms.[13]) Second, and more importantly, a huge literature has grown up surrounding the experimental manipulation of IQ as reviewed exhaustively in a seminal (and entertaining) book by Richard E. Nisbett,[14] entitled *Intelligence and How to Get It: Why Schools and Cultures Count*. Professor Nisbett, in fact, definitively demonstrates that intelligence (a) improves as a function of instructional time, (b) can be influenced by even relatively brief interventions, and (c) is more influenced by children's home environments than by their genes. I think the best illustration of his common sense approach to the relationship between instruction, learning, and intelligence is the following observation:

> Given that schools directly teach material that appears on comprehensive IQ tests, including information such as the name of the writer who wrote Hamlet and the elements that make up water, as well as vocabulary words and arithmetical operations, it is strange that some IQ theorists doubt that school makes people more intelligent. (p. 43)

And, the only reason that an equally huge industry hasn't grown up around teaching the contents of intelligence tests comparable to the one teaching the SAT contents is that the latter has replaced the former as the guardian of the keys to the kingdom and the bastion of righteousness. That and the fact that higher-educated parents now recognize how high the college entrance test score stakes have become.

But, in the final analysis, what all these tests are really measuring is *learning*, regardless of whether they aspire to assess intelligence, aptitude, or some other theoretically static attribute. Paradoxically, this aspiration for stability and predictive success ensures that any test designed to fulfill these particular objectives will function very poorly as a learning measure. Why? Because learning is not a static attribute. Instead it is extremely dynamic and subject to immediate change anytime instruction occurs).

But unfortunately, the standardized tests our schools use for assessing learning were based on this obsolete psychometric model. And nowhere is their resulting insensitivity to learning changes better illustrated than a recent and very creative analysis performed on seven widely used standardized achievement tests (which are used to assess children's learning, value-added teacher effectiveness, school performance, and just about everything else associated with the public schools). The investigators involved[15] used normative data from the seven testing companies' manuals to estimate how much students improved on each test from the end of one school year until the end of the next. This year by year improvement therefore reflects the average amount that students learn over the course of each school year from the first- to the twelfth- grade *as measured by our standardized testing system.*

I've chosen to graph math scores standardized scores below, but the same basic pattern occurred for reading, social studies, and science scores. The vertical axis of this figure is expressed in terms of effect sizes which provide a convenient way to express the difference between two groups since the magnitude of effect sizes is independent of the type of test used, the number of items each test contains, or the number of students that took the tests.

It doesn't take a very close examination of this little graph to see that something very odd is going on here. Perhaps it isn't so shocking that the effect size representing students' learning in Grade 2 is 10% less than the one representing Grade 1, perhaps children just learn more in first grade or it's due to a statistical fluke of some sort. But isn't it a bit surprising that the effect size for Grade 3 is 14% less than Grade 2's? Why should children learn less at an accelerating rate two years in a row? And that the Grade 4's effect size is 42% less than Grade 3? And we won't even mention Grades 11 and 12, other than to say that if these tests are truly reflective of school learning maybe we should just do away with the upper grades entirely![16]

Now surely these numbers can't really reflect the learning trajectories occurring in our schools. I interpret them as reflecting an increasingly poorer match between standardized tests and what is being taught in school as children progress through the grades.[17] But let's not forget that school learning is what these standardized tests reputably measure and what politicians and educational policy "experts" *believe* they measure.

But just because standardized tests can't measure year-to-year learning changes very well, doesn't mean that they aren't very good at measuring some things. To illustrate, consider the next graph which superimposes the black-white testing gap on the supposed year-to-year learning from Grades 1-12. [For this I've had to use only the only standardized test

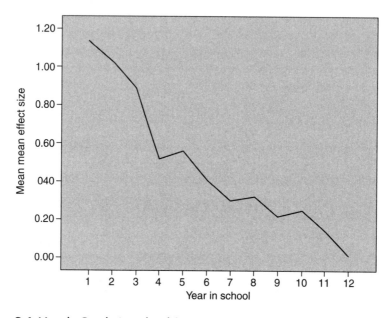

Figure 8.1 Yearly Grade Level Achievement Gains (Mean of 7 Standardized Tests)

(i.e., the *Stanford Achievement Test Series, Ninth Edition*) and grade levels (4, 8, and 11) for which data were available in the second Bloom, Hill, Black, and Lipsey (2008) MDRC publication (see Endnote 15). A very similar basic pattern also occurs when the National Assessment of Education Progress test is superimposed on Figure 8.1 (the average of all 7 standardized tests).

This graph is a little busier than the earlier one, but basically it says that while standardized tests aren't nearly sensitive enough to measure actual learning changes in the later grades (the lower, dashed line), they are very good at measuring differences between home learning environments (the top, solid line). (I choose to consider the top line as representing "home learning environments" because the same exact pattern exists when we superimposed the Hispanic-White testing gap on these grade 4, 8, and 11 learning changes and a reasonably similar one results if we impose students who are ineligible vs. not eligible for reduced price lunches.)

If I believed that grade-by-grade standardized test scores actually reflected school learning, I would be extremely discouraged by Figure 8.2 because taken at face value what these data say are that while the effect

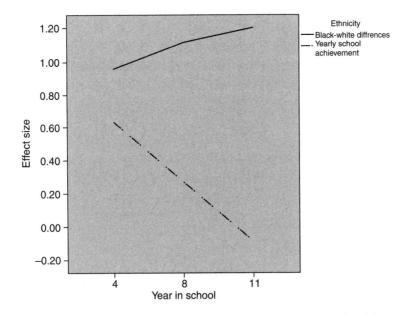

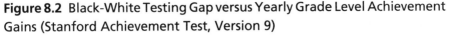

Figure 8.2 Black-White Testing Gap versus Yearly Grade Level Achievement Gains (Stanford Achievement Test, Version 9)

sizes representing school learning decline rapidly over time, the learning gap between Black-White, Hispanic-White, and lower-higher SES students remains constant or actually increases slightly (in the case of the first two comparisons). Not only that, but they remain dramatically higher than the year-to-year effect sizes representing learning gains during successive years.

Since I don't believe that standardized achievement tests really assess school learning, these findings make be more *angry* than discouraged. They say to me that the ethnic gaps in test scores are so great that they will be extremely difficult to close because black, Hispanic, and economically disadvantaged children's school performances are being judged on tests that are fundamentally biased against them. Not biased because of any nefarious conspiracy, but because these tests do not reflect school learning. Instead they reflect the total amount of instruction delivered to children: preschool, extra-school, *and* in-school.

Of course changing our obsolete testing model wouldn't make existing ethnic and social class differences in the *total* amount of instruction disappear – only additional instructional time can overcome deficits in instructional time. Purely curriculum based tests would most likely *reduce* ethnic and social class test differences, however, because some of these differences are due to deficiencies in our tests. And more importantly these "achievement" gaps would be more responsive to the provision of additional instruction.

Is it any wonder then that a testing industry that was created to assess school learning, but constructed its tests according to a completely obsolete testing model, would need to disguise the fact that its test scores not only have no intrinsic meaning but don't actually measure school learning in any meaningful way? What else could it do but fall back on this model's tried and true bogus testing principles and use algebraic manipulations of their scores such as percentiles, standard scores, or *grade equivalencies* to give them some modicum of meaning (Bogus Testing Principle #2)? Even if at the end of the day they all simply wind up rank ordering children's (or schools' or teachers') scores (Bogus Testing Principle #3)? Unfortunate perhaps, but since there is no possible statistical manipulation that can be performed on these scores to tell anyone how *much* students learn in school (or what they *need* to learn), the marketers of these tests avoided the issue of learning altogether and named their attribute of choice: *academic achievement* (Bogus Testing Principle #1: "Ignore the items and you can name the test *anything*").

But, if we are truly interested in school learning, do we really need yet another set of tests designed to assess yet another bogus attribute? Shouldn't we abandon this silly, indirect, old-fashioned approach to assessment altogether? Let us review the reasons why, for our purposes here, it is *necessary* to do so:

1. Unlike psychological assessments that target such nebulous constructs as intelligence and aptitude, school learning can be directly assessed. Why? Because we know what causes school learning. It results from instruction delivered in school. Of course, learning of school-based content can and does result from instruction occurring elsewhere (especially the home environment), but we can't do anything about that other than to ensure that a school learning test does not assess anything that was not taught in school. Furthermore, if we explicitly defined the school curriculum in terms of instructional objectives, each of which is accompanied by sample test items, then the test content would be defined by fiat. We wouldn't have to

resort to such arrogant, ignorant, and transparent statements as *school learning is what school learning tests measure.*

2. Unlike psychological assessments, which can only be marketed if they are demonstrably related to a similar test, a school-based learning test need only be demonstrably based upon the contents of school instruction. Such a test should not be primarily designed to rank order students from high to low, but to assess how much of what was taught in school was learned. Such a test does not need to be related to the results of any other test. In fact, a test of school learning that is highly related to any test designed to measure a stable psychological attribute should be viewed with suspicion.

3. Unlike psychological assessments, a test of school learning does not need to be stable. The purpose of a learning test is not to rank order students; hence, the classical measurement concept of reliability has no relevance. Tests of school learning are designed to assess *change* in knowledge resulting from instruction, and change is almost by definition unstable. True, a properly constructed test of fourth-grade classroom learning will most likely correlate with a comparably constructed fifth-grade test administered the next year to the same students, but certainly not as strongly as current "achievement" tests do. And, as will be recommended shortly, if the test is administered twice per year—once at the beginning and once at the end—the learning gains achieved during the fourth grade will correlate even more weakly with the learning gains achieved in fifth grade.

4. Related to this embracement of instability, there is no need to base item selection upon how well students perform on the items. The ideal item using classic measurement theory is one that approximately half of the testing audience will answer correctly and half will answer incorrectly. This can be mathematically demonstrated as causally related to the ultimate stability of a test and how strongly it correlates with other tests. It has the effect of encouraging test makers to include items that *aren't taught in all schools* (to avoid too many students answering them correctly) but have already been learned *somewhere* by *some* students. However, as I've said before, content that has been learned has to have been taught somewhere, and if this wasn't in school, it must have been in the home environment. Hence, current achievement test constructors have an incentive, indeed a conflict of interest, to include as many items as possible

that are taught via the home environment because this practice will contribute to stability of the test. *This, in turn, automatically provides a nonschooling advantage to children of certain races, cultures, and socioeconomic strata.*

5. Unlike psychological assessments (including current achievement measures), standardization—that is, algebraic manipulation and renaming the resulting scores—is irrelevant for a test of school learning if that test is based upon instructional objectives. Scores generated by an instructional objective–based learning test have intrinsic meaning in and of themselves. If a student answers 70% of the items on such a test correctly, this means that that student has learned 70% of the curriculum (give or take a few specifiable percentage points due to guessing and sampling error). This is completely different from an individual score emanating from a standardized achievement test because such a score has no meaning except in relationship to other peoples' scores. In fact, as we've discussed, that is what standardization means: transforming a test's scores to some other scale of measurement based upon the normal curve, so that we can come up with the percentage of people who did better or worse on the test. Standardization is completely irrelevant for a test of learning because we have no need for semantic window-dressings such as "quotients" or "grade equivalencies." (Of course, since some objectives will take considerably more instruction to learn, we could reasonably weight these objectives by the average amount of time they take to learn.)

6. Unlike psychological and current standardized achievement measures, the individual items of a school learning test have meaning in and of themselves. In fact, they are more important than total scores because each item answered incorrectly represents a discrete instructional objective that was not learned and therefore needs to be *taught* (or taught again). By the same token, each item answered correctly represents one that was learned and does *not* need to be taught. Furthermore, many instructional objectives are logically related to one another in the sense that students who don't know what 4 + 5 equals probably won't know what 7 + 8 equals either, or what either 4 × 5 or 7 × 8 equal. Similarly, students who don't have a basic reading vocabulary will not be able to comprehend written text employing that vocabulary. Hence, if these relationships are

specified a priori, based upon test results, or both, the individual items missed by any given student convey valuable information about that student's instructional needs regarding items that weren't tested. Thus, adaptive computerized testing procedures that take these relationships into account should be able to reduce the testing time required for most students.

7. This preeminent importance of individual items is arguably the second most important distinction between tests actually designed to assess school learning and "achievement" tests built upon the intelligence model. In assessing school learning, the items *are* the test; no item in the test should surprise anyone who has examined the curriculum; and everyone capable of providing instruction to a specific child inside or outside the schooling process should have access to sample items. Which leads to the most important distinction between this type of test and standardized "achievement" tests:

8. The primary *unit of analysis* (or score of interest) for a test of school learning is at the individual student–individual item level. This is because the primary function of a learning test is to inform instruction: to determine what each student needs (and does not need) to be taught.

In addition to the use of tests based solely upon instructional objectives, a number of procedural changes will be required in how we test children, if we are truly committed to assessing school learning. Here are a few of the more important of these:

1. *Testing will optimally occur twice per year, once at the beginning of the school year and once at the end, with the difference between the two constituting the amount of learning that has occurred in that school in that grade during that year.* Our usual practice (there are exceptions) of one testing period per year is fine for rank ordering children and schools, but won't work for learning. If we are interested in assessing Grade Two learning, for example, the difference between the previous end-of-year first-grade test and the end-of-year second-grade test won't suffice for two reasons. First, the previous year's test will be based upon the first-grade curriculum (hence will employ different instructional objectives), and second it will not reflect what goes on in the summer (which for lower

socioeconomic status students not attending summer school primarily involves forgetting what was taught during the previous school year, whereas for their more fortunate counterparts it primarily involves additional instruction provided by an enriched home environment).[18] One very important study, in fact, found that a large part of the socioeconomic disparities in test performance observed in the later grades is more of a function of what is forgotten during the summer months that what is learned during the school year. These researchers, having rare access to a large group of schools that actually did administer standardized tests both at the beginning and end of the school year, found that students from lower socioeconomic families lost ground between May and September, while their higher socioeconomic peers were actually *learning* over the summer. Thus, even though the economically deprived children learned almost as much from September to May as their economically more fortunate peers, they kept getting further and further behind over the years because of this lethal combination—lower socioeconomic academic-deprived home learning environments from May to September coupled with higher socioeconomic learning gains (induced, of course, by their learning-enriched home environments) during the same time period.[19]

Incredibly, however, assessment "experts" trained in obsolete measurement models would argue that the first- and second-grade test scores can be statistically manipulated (i.e., "standardized") to make them equivalent, but this is true only for the purpose for which tests are currently used: to consistently rank order students. Algebraically manipulating scores in this (or any) manner is irrelevant for the assessment of both learning and forgetting.

2. *The test administered at the beginning of the year should also be used to assess individual (and classroom) instructional needs for the upcoming year.* Hopefully, the days of students shading in bubbles on paper answer sheets will soon go the way of the dodo bird. It is scandalous that all students can't take their tests on a computer and have them scored immediately. This would be especially important if the individual items were linked back to the instructional objectives upon which they were based, entered into a database, with the results instantaneously indicating which objectives which students need to be taught.

3. *The test items should not reflect content taught only in some class-rooms and not others (such as in advanced placement courses) or content taught in some schools but not others.* Otherwise, the test will reflect differences in home learning environments just as strongly as do current standardized achievement tests.

4. *The test items should not be written with an eye toward maximizing the test's psychometric properties, such as reliability (which helps to ensure the stability of scores) or validity (which helps to ensure that the test correlates with other tests of desirable, if ill-understood, attributes).* The test items should be clear and unambiguous, but they should not be chosen based upon how well they relate to one another, how well they correlate with other tests, or how difficult they are. They should be chosen based upon how represen-tative they are of the content that is taught. They should be quite straightforward and not "tricky," because otherwise they assess test-taking skills that are often more strongly reflective of the home learning environment than school learning. Test items should not be based upon applications of the material taught unless *those applications* constitute instructional objectives that are themselves taught.

So, allow me to distill all of this into five school testing principles that hopefully can replace the testing industry's three bogus ones:

- *School Testing Principle #1: We don't need tests at any level of school-ing to predict future events. The best predictor of future behavior is past behavior and the best predictor of future performance is past per-formance.* Also, as Gerald Bracey[20] reminds us, probably the most valu-able human attributes (such as creativity, critical thinking, resilience, motivation, persistence, curiosity, endurance, reliability, enthusiasm, empathy, self-awareness, self-discipline, leadership, civic-mindedness, compassion, honesty, resourcefulness, integrity) aren't even tested (and perhaps aren't testable). From this perspective, think what a per-version tests such as the SAT, GRE, MCAT, LSAT, ad nauseum have become. Thinly disguised intelligence tests whose items have no known relevance to anything of importance, but must now be studied assiduously by students who can afford to take the time-consuming, expensive preparatory courses to gain the privilege of being allowed to simply engage in profession training.

- *School Testing Principle #2: Educational tests are worthless if they are not constructed and used in such a way that they can specifically inform instruction.*[21] From this perspective, therefore, the primary interpretive units of an educational test are either an individual student's response to an individual item or the percentage of the curriculum that he or she has mastered—not how the student performed in relationship to his or her peers.
- *School Testing Principle #3: Educational tests cannot inform instruction unless their items accurately reflect the curriculum and nothing but the curriculum.* No one should attempt to interpret a test score without a thorough and intimate knowledge of the items that comprise that test score and how they were selected.
- *School Testing Principle #4: For a test to accurately reflect the curriculum, the curriculum must be explicitly specified via its translation into an exhaustive set of instructional objectives (or a similarly explicit and exhaustive medium).* This, of course, was the subject matter of the previous chapter and encapsulated into our second schooling principle.
- *School Testing Principle #5: Tests are neither God nor His Prophet, nor do they reflect anything of value unless they are constructed based upon Principles #1 through #4.*

TOWARD A THIRD PRINCIPLE OF SCHOOLING

Because of the simplicity of our one-input (instruction), one-output (learning) production model (coupled with the hypothesis that the only way to increase the latter is to increase the former), we have so far felt the need to advance only two simple schooling principles (as opposed to our even more simple *theory of school learning*. These were:

- *Schooling Principle #1: It is exceedingly difficult to improve learning in a typical classroom setting simply because this setting will overwhelm the attempt itself.*

And,

- *Schooling Principle #2: Both instruction and testing should be exclusively based upon a meaningful curriculum and nothing else.*

It is now time for a third principle, necessitated by the preeminent role played by testing in the schooling process. Testing is the only way we know to assess learning (and therefore instruction itself), but testing is a much simpler process than it is made out to be, especially by the marketers of intelligence and aptitude tests who disingenuously pretend that their products are immune to instruction—the sole precursor of *learning*. Hence, our third principle of schooling is advanced to put the roles of testing, instruction, and learning into an appropriately simple perspective:

- *Schooling Principle #3: Anything that can be learned can be taught and anything that can be taught can be tested.*

Hopefully, this principle will further help to demystify both testing and the schooling process itself. For schooling is exceedingly simple, and nothing illustrates this better than the simplest theory of learning ever advanced:

All learning is explained in terms of the amount of relevant instructional time provided.

CHAPTER 9

11 Strategies for Increasing School Learning

It is now time to examine some of the practical implications of our extremely parsimonious theory of school learning. Most of the resulting strategies have already been implemented by some schools in one form or another, and almost all have been alluded to earlier here. I believe it is worth our while, however, to consider them in their entirety, to provide as many options as possible to facilitate the implementation of our fourth and final principle of schooling:

- *Schooling Principle #4*: Since the only way schools can increase learning is to increase the amount of relevant instruction delivered, as much time as possible while students are in school should be devoted to instruction, and every effort should be expended to make this instruction *relevant*.

In all, I will consider 11 such strategies, broadly divided into systemic (or administrative-cultural) changes versus changes in actual classroom instructional procedures. These strategies will be presented from the perspective of the current classroom model, although they would also apply to our proposed learning laboratory. Most would, in fact, be considerably easier to implement in the latter.

INCREASING ACTUAL INSTRUCTIONAL TIME AND CHANGING THE SCHOOLING CULTURE

Three of the four strategies contained in this category involve the physical allocation of additional instructional time. And, although it may seem that children spend more than enough time in school, Elizabeth Graue[1] provides another perspective on how much of this time is devoted to relevant instruction:

> The typical student's allocation of 180 six-hour days in school for 12 years only amounts to 12,960 hours or 16.4% of the potential educative time from birth through age 18 (assuming 12 hours for sleep, meals, and other maintenance activities). Moreover, because of absences, inattention, inappropriate instruction, and managerial and disciplinary overhead during classes, perhaps only a quarter to a half of school time is effectively on-task for typical children, which amounts to 1.6 to 3.1 years of 40-hour weeks, roughly the amount of time required to learn a non-cognate language such as Japanese to near-native capacity. (p. 351)

We've already discussed the research demonstrating just how much individual teachers differ with respect to both the amount of class time they actually devote to instruction and, though some of these discrepancies may be outside of teacher control (such as being assigned an especially unruly group of students), the majority of them probably reflect either teacher preferences or lack of classroom management skills. Classroom teaching is an extremely difficult, demanding job and this is why I advocate the adoption of a learning laboratory model of instruction that provides teachers with the necessary infrastructure to be able to administer more instruction while at the same time making classroom management significantly easier.

Obviously, the amount of variability currently observed in instructional time delivered must be reduced. For the portion that is due to individual teacher preferences, appropriate professional development activities should be routinely administered while the portion that is due to unruly student classroom behavior should simply not be tolerated as a matter of schooling policy.

Thus in addition to the three time specific strategies I present in this first section, I present a fourth, which speaks to increasing student engagement on an institutional basis (i.e., adopting an administrative culture totally intolerant to any type of behavior that interferes with learning). Now, certainly I anticipation a number of criticisms involving the joyless schooling world all of this could create for our children, to which I would respond in three ways. First, a little creativity in the implementation of these strategies could go a long way toward making them more palatable, but my task here is to enumerate the implications of the relevant instructional time hypothesis for a society that desperately needs to increase the learning taking place in its schools, not to coat anything with artificial sweeteners. Second, as *currently* constituted, school is hardly a joyful romp through a magical forest for children who fail to learn or who are terminally bored as material they already know is incessantly repeated. Third, I will present a second category of strategies later in the chapter that do not involve actually increasing the amount of time children spend in school (but would make any additional time that is allocated even more productive).

- *Strategy #1: Complete the full implementation of the pre-kindergarten movement.* In 2008, about 39% of four-year olds attended some kind of public program, such as pre-kindergarten, Head Start, or special education.[2] Our time-on-task hypothesis suggests that all children should be exposed to preschool experiences, and these experiences should be primarily given over to direct instruction, employing academic objectives. As would be expected based upon our hypothesis, children who attend preschool exhibit better achievement results later in school.[3] Further, there is even some evidence that low-income children whose parents are involved in these programs have better learning outcomes later on in school than do those whose parents are not involved.[4]

Of course, there is also no logical reason why an extra grade couldn't be added anywhere in this continuum, either for everyone or for students who need it—but this isn't likely to happen, nor is there any real enthusiasm for such a scheme. Certainly, however, all half-day kindergarten programs should be expanded to a full day.[5]

- *Strategy #2: Increase the length of the school day.* The current length of the school day (approximately six hours) is relatively arbitrary and inconvenient for working parents. The 1983 report, *A Nation at Risk: The Imperative for Educational Reform,*[6] suggested that schools consider a seven-hour day, which could either be devoted to an extra class period or divided up among existing classes. Obviously, this extra time must be exclusively devoted to relevant instruction or it will be wasted. No one really knows how much the market will bear here. Perhaps an eight-hour day is feasible if no homework is assigned, which would allow students, in Etta Kralovec's words, "to go home at night knowing that they have completed a full day of rigorous academic work and that their evening can be spent participating in community events, learning on their own, and enjoying an enriched family life" (p. 11).[7]

- *Corollary Strategy #2a: Devote the entire school day to relevant instruction.* This may seem obvious by now, but as mentioned earlier, a ridiculously large proportion of the school day is given over to activities other than direct instruction. Kralovec details a considerable number of these in her very informative book (*Schools That Do Too Much: Wasting Time and Money in Schools and What We Can All Do about It*), including candy sales, worthless school assemblies, loudspeaker announcements, sports activities,[8] ad nauseam. We should, in other words, attempt to squeeze every minute of instruction into the school day that we can, and the easiest way of doing that is to delete noninstructional activities and disruptive events.

- *Strategy #3: Increase the length of the school year.* This intervention is probably the most often suggested, with calls for extending the school year from its current 180 to 200 or 220 days.[9] It has already been tried in a number of settings (most notably in Japan, which subsequently abandoned it),[10] and its implementation on a national level would also require a bit of creativity and additional resources (e.g., in most parts of this country, classroom air conditioning would be required and teacher salaries would need to be increased to reflect their additional work load), but the strategy constitutes a fertile area for additional instructional time.

Granted, teachers, their unions, and teacher training institutions would argue that the summer months are needed for continuing education and professional development, but no other profession gets the entire summer off, so why should teachers? It is true that lawyers and physicians, say, receive more in the way of a real education in the first place, but since teacher training has no effect upon student learning, why should the continuing education offered by the same culprits be any different?

Four weeks of vacation plus a few assorted holidays during the year is both an excellent job benefit and sufficient for everyone else. It is also sufficient for students, and it would reduce the burden on working parents and increase their productivity. More importantly, however, from our hypothesis' perspective, reducing the length of the summer vacation would be doubly beneficial. It would increase learning via the extra instructional time, and it would decrease forgetting what was learned during the previous school year.

As with the proposed increase in the length of the instructional day, some creativity needs to be applied here, but scheduling problems such as this are not insurmountable. One interesting option mentioned by Sarah Huyvaert in her excellent book entitled *Time Is of the Essence: Learning in Schools* involves a flexible schedule in which instruction is available 240 days, and students may attend all of these or only the state-mandated 180.[11] Of course, regardless of the plan chosen, if students are to be given only four weeks vacation, they obviously can't all be given the same four weeks or the travel-resort economy would suffer and nothing proposed for the schools that disrupts commerce will *ever* be implemented.

Teachers, too, would need their vacations rotated in some way. This could be done by rotating a classroom's vacation dates along with those of their teachers or by moving away from the one teacher per class for an entire academic year model (e.g., by dividing the academic year up into quarters with concomitant teacher changes). Alternatively, the summers could be given over to discrete courses devoted to advanced or remedial topics as indicated. Granted, some versions of this already occur in most school districts, but I would institute it as part of the required schooling process.

Of course, we've had remedial summer school sessions for some time now, and it may be that both students and teachers would prefer to make their nonremedial summer experience different from the standard classroom experience. This would be quite acceptable, to the extent that instruction is delivered in relevant curricular content (in other words, no *Introduction to Basket Weaving* or *Fundamentals of Soccer 101*).

• *Strategy #4: Behavior that prevents or distracts students from learning must not be tolerated*. Regardless of whether the current, obsolete classroom model is retained or a new version adopted, the time-on-task hypothesis implies the necessity of a very different classroom setting, with respect to student behavior, than exists in many American schools. By "behavior that distracts children from learning" I include disorderly conduct in the classroom and uncivil behavior both inside and outside it.

In other words, if some students make it more difficult for their classmates (or even themselves) to attend to the instruction being offered, then an immediate reprimand should be issued. If the behavior occurs a second time, the student should be immediately removed for the remainder of the class. If this doesn't work, the student should be removed for a longer period of time, such as a day, followed by an ever longer and clearly specified period until he or she is transferred to an alternate classroom or school dedicated to such students.

Implicit in this approach is a philosophical shift in which it is not only acceptable, but absolutely necessary, to deal firmly, quickly, and dispassionately with any behavior that conflicts with learning. Obviously, absurd bureaucratic practices such as penalizing schools for suspensions and expulsions must be abandoned. If anything, schools should be rewarded for such actions, as long as they conform to acceptable guidelines. If this means that we have to leave certain children behind because they can't meet behavioral expectations (or we don't know how to enable them to conform), so be it. It's a pity if this dooms such children to a future of menial jobs, incarceration, or populating some street corner waiting for one of the two, but in the meantime they shouldn't be allowed to disrupt other students' learning. Schools exist to teach, not to be law enforcement agencies.

Now, I fully realize that this is a most politically incorrect position, but in some cases political correctness overlaps stupidity, as illustrated in an incident reported in the April 8 2008 *Baltimore Sun*, in which a teacher approached a student to tell her to sit down and be less disruptive. The student told the teacher to back off or she would hit her. The teacher warned the student that if she did so she would defend herself, whereupon the student attacked the teacher, knocked her to the floor and pummeled her for several minutes to the approbation of the rest of the class, as at least one student taped the episode on a cell phone and promptly uploaded it to the internet.

The student was not removed from the class, the teacher was reprimanded by her principal for provoking the attack because she warned the student she would defend herself (which she wound up not doing), and the teacher, on leaving for the day, reputedly walked by her attacker as she bragged to other students about the entire episode. Later the student was suspended briefly (pending "further investigation") but only following public outrage resulting from the ensuing media coverage.

Now, although this may appear to be an extreme example of disruptive classroom behavior, a large number of attacks on teachers occur every year in American schools. It is also worth noting that this incident was precipitated by the teacher attempting to maintain order and asking the student in question to sit down (presumably) so that instruction could continue. In my opinion, any student who commits such an act should be immediately expelled from school, if not permanently, at least for a significant amount of time. Further, anyone who supports such activities (such as via reinforcing applause or video taping it) should be expelled as well.

In general, however, the most common types of learning-disruptive behaviors are not as egregious as actual violence toward teachers, but may be equally deleterious to the learning process because of their prevalence. I realize that parents of children who find it difficult to conform to the types of behavior norms I am proposing would oppose such an unforgiving policy as outlined above, but it is absolutely imperative that classrooms built upon a time-on-task model adopt a culture in which learning is valued and *anything that impedes learning is not tolerated.*

These policies and consequences should also extend to uncivil behaviors such as bullying, pack-like picking on peers, and hurtful denigrating comments occurring anywhere on school property. If some children dread to go to school because they are incessantly teased or physically abused, then they will not be able to concentrate as fully on the instruction presented and will learn less than they otherwise would. This falls under the same principle as classroom misbehavior and is tolerated only at the expense of learning. And it is the elicitation of learning that should constitute the schools' purpose.

Said another way, if a child constantly worries about how he or she is treated by peers or what insult or injury is likely to occur (or has just occurred) during recess, lunch, in the lavatory, or in transit to and from classes, then the instruction received by that child will not be maximally attended to and therefore not maximally *relevant*. So, although this principle may not fit our present conception of what school ambiance should be, it is quite consistent with the types of behaviors required of adults to be allowed to remain on an airliner or to remain employed. Basically, it boils down to the following:

> *If someone isn't willing to learn and isn't willing to allow other students to learn, then they don't belong in an institution whose primary purpose is to foster learning. It's a shame, for the problem may be cultural in nature (or due to cultural deprivation), but it's a problem that schools operating under the precepts of the time-on-task hypothesis don't have the time to deal with.*

Three corollary strategies that might be appended to here are:

- *Corollary Strategy 4a: All classrooms in which violence or disruptive behaviors occur should be electronically monitored to prevent future violence and ensure that appropriate instruction is being delivered.* It is a sad commentary on our society, but there are many, many classrooms in which *no* recognized curriculum is taught, hence *no* learning in any recognized subject matter occurs. These classrooms are easily identified, and documentation should permit immediate remedial action including the removal of disruptive students, the firing of nonperforming teachers, or whatever actions are necessary to bring student learning back on-line.
- *Corollary Strategy 4b: Abusive teacher and administrative behaviors should also be more closely monitored and regulated.* Corporeal punishment is still tolerated in some areas of the south, and some teachers occasionally resort to such inappropriate behaviors as forcibly cutting students' hair that they consider too long or similar humiliating behaviors. It is difficult to calculate how expensive such actions are in terms of total classroom learning, not only for the abused but for the audience as well.
- *Corollary Strategy 4c: Administrative policies should be implemented to reduce absences and tardiness.* Obviously, absences

from school (or missing parts of the school day due to tardiness) have direct time-on-task implications. Not surprisingly, both have been found to be negatively related to student achievement,[12] a fact that needs to be communicated to both parents and students throughout the school year. Reducing absenteeism is a difficult task, but continually stressing the importance of high attendance (and low tardiness) rates throughout the school year and using appropriate (and accelerating) sanctions and incentives, can reduce the problem.

CLASSROOM INSTRUCTION

Now, for some instructional strategies derivable from the time-on-task hypothesis that relate directly to classroom instruction:

- *Strategy #5: The entire curriculum should be transcribed via some exhaustive, detailed, and accessible medium, such as instructional objectives, and computerized testing systems should be developed based solely on this transcription.* I realize that I've already discussed this at length, but I can't conceive of how we can ever substantively improve learning until we get a definitive handle on what is taught and the extent to which it is learned.

  The primary advantage of the use of instructional objectives is their ability to communicate what needs to be learned and what will be tested. Another huge advantage they possess, as well as the tests based upon them, is that the entire package is so naturally conducive to both computerized instruction and testing.

  Few societal arenas are more electronically antiquated than the public schools. Even when computers are freely available, they can't be used efficiently because of the lack of appropriate instructional software. One reason for this deficit is that writing computer programs requires a maddening degree of specificity, and this is exactly what something like instructional objectives, accompanied by sample test items, provides—specificity, incidentally, to a degree that is totally alien to most educators.

  Eventually, the majority of public school instruction will be provided by computers, with or without the use of instructional objectives, with or without acceptance of the time-on-task hypothesis, and with or without the full-blown implementation of a learning-laboratory model of instruction. Nothing, however, would facilitate the implementation of computerized instruction more than the translation of the entire elementary school curriculum to an exhaustive set of instructional objectives to (a) explicitly and exhaustively define and communicate that curriculum, (b) dictate exactly what should be taught, (c) guide the construction of tests that assess school learning (i.e., of what is [or should be] taught and nothing else), and (d) provide the capability of mimicking the tutoring process by:

1. Testing students to identify what they do and do not know,
2. Concentrating instruction upon content that has not been mastered,
3. Retesting students based upon the first two steps, and
4. Reinstruction and retesting as necessary.

But, even if instruction continues to be delivered by teachers, computers are an ideal testing medium since existing spreadsheet software could allow the teacher to generate tests associated with specific content, score the items automatically, and enter this information into a database that could be accessed and sorted in multiple ways (such as targeting groups of students who had not mastered an individual objective or group of related objectives).

- *Strategy #6: Teach only what is useful.* If learning is the purpose of schooling, and instructional time is the sole factor that determines how much learning the schools can produce, then it follows that time should not be squandered on teaching useless material. Said another way, increasing relevant instructional time presupposes that the curriculum is itself relevant!

If 20% of the curriculum is irrelevant to future job performance, civic responsibility, life satisfaction, or any other reasonable criterion, then 20% of our relevant instructional time is being squandered. Or, taking a more optimistic view, if 20% of the curriculum is irrelevant, we've actually been given an ideal way to increase relevant instructional time by 20%.

As I've mentioned, mounting the major initiative implied by Strategy #5 (translating the elementary school curriculum to a universal set of instructional objectives) would constitute a golden opportunity to evaluate whether each objective (or group of objectives) does indeed reflect essential, useful learning content as defined by one of the criteria discussed in Chapter 7.

Naturally, if queried, scientists would undoubtedly lobby for increasing the amount of emphasis upon their discipline, historians would plead for more history instruction, and employers would surely advocate for more time devoted to the skills most needed in their individual workplaces.

But complexity, controversy, and wildly divergent perspectives are facets of modern life, and should be embraced rather than avoided in the educational process. In my opinion, one of the most astonishing shortcomings of our current schooling system is that we have no systematic mechanism in place to periodically review the relevance of the curriculum or to incorporate these diverse viewpoints into informing what we *should* be teaching.

Occasionally, political and economic imperatives do force the schools to change the curriculum, as was the case with Sputnik in the late 1950s and early 1960s. Perhaps the same thing will happen today, as countries such as China and India conspire to replace us in both the economic and educational marketplaces. Unfortunately, educators have little incentive to change their approach to doing business unless they are forced to do so, but the existence of an ongoing curriculum review process should help to keep the curriculum up to date, rather than to allow it to fall as far behind the times as it is currently.

- *Corollary Strategy #6a: Given a choice, opt for direct instruction.* Historically, advocates for various disciplines have used the transferability of their subject matters to other topics as a rationale for inclusion in the curriculum. Latin aficionados, for example, once argued that the study of their discipline "trained the mind" and provided a basis for improving English grammar and reading.

  While no one ever learned how to differentiate a trained from an untrained mind, and we know very little about how transfer of this sort occurs in a classroom setting, we do know that it is a tenuous affair at best—occurring only under disappointing specific and limited conditions.[13] Thus, if I were forced to generalize from classic learning research to the Latin issue, the best I could do is: *If you want to improve students' English grammar and vocabulary, teach English grammar and vocabulary—not Latin grammar and vocabulary.* It may be that certain Latin construc- tions are helpful in vocabulary expansion or for allowing the meaning of a few words to be decoded, but if so, teach *these* constructions—not an entire dead language.[14]

- *Corollary Strategy #6b: Always attempt to foster understanding of the concepts taught.* Although transfer may be a tenuous/ unpredictable affair, ironically it is probably the ultimate goal of learning. Knowledge in and of itself can be useful, but its true payoff occurs when it is applied to generate something new. Transfer, application, and creativity are all facets of this concept and, although we know very little about how to foster them, we do know that if the underlying meaning of a concept isn't under- stood, the concept itself isn't likely to be applied anywhere.

A minimal aspect of understanding involves explaining to the learner why he or she is being taught a topic in the first place. When students are introduced to an algebraic concept, for exam- ple, they should at least be shown a real-world application involv- ing an example of one of the professions that employs it. Although such a minimal effort as this may not actually result in much trans- fer, it may increase learning by encouraging some students to attend to instruction—thereby making it more relevant.[15]

Another aspect of both understanding and transfer resides in teaching common principles that underlie a discipline. This often translates to "why" something works, such as why we "carry" numbers over to the next column in addition algorithms or "borrow" them from the next column in subtraction problems.

- Corollary Strategy #6c: Teach students how to locate reliable information on their own, so that they can learn what they need when they identify gaps in what they've been taught. Obviously, the continuing evolution of the internet has tremendous educa- tional implications. Obviously, too, the schools can never teach students everything they will need to know in life, but they can teach students how to access reliable information on their own and how to judge reliability through the use of critical thinking skills. Such skills (locating information and critically evaluating its reliability) may, in fact, ultimately prove to be more valuable than anything else in the curriculum. (And, as always, they can be specified in terms of discrete instructional objectives. Everything that can be learned or taught can be specified in this way.)

- *Strategy #7*: *Teach at the student's knowledge level.* If instructional content is taught to students who have already learned it, then this instruction is not relevant. If instructional content is taught to students who have not mastered prerequisite content, then *this* instruction is not relevant. If the instructional content is taught to students at an inappropriate rate, then the instruction is not relevant. If some of the students can't read their textbooks, then their use as an adjunct to instruction is not relevant.

Although painfully obvious, all of these practices occur daily in classrooms all over the country because of the truly daunting challenges teachers face in teaching classrooms comprised of students possessing widely diverse knowledge levels. There are only two ways to overcome these challenges. The first is to utilize instructional materials (e.g., computers, exercises, supplementary text books) that permit as much individualization of instruction as possible. The second is to group students into as homogeneous classrooms as possible based upon their prior instructional histories, a strategy often criticized on egalitarian and stigmatizing grounds. (Obviously, if instruction were individualized via computers, the first strategy would be more effective and there would be no need to homogenize classrooms in the first place.)

Heterogeneity in student knowledge has been a major drawback to classroom instruction since its birth. The one-room schools in which my parents first taught represented an extreme historical example of this challenge. Upon querying my mother about the experience, she informed me that there was little choice but to involve older students in helping the younger ones, which undoubtedly reduced the instructional time available to the former. This scenario was so common, in fact, that it spawned an entire genre of schooling research that generated the so-called *Lancaster effect,* in which the learning of students instructing other students was studied. Because this work wasn't sufficiently rigorous to separate out the effects of time from some potential benefit of the teaching act itself, Bill Moody and I conducted an experiment to investigate this effect upon elementary education majors. What we found was that the measurable teacher learning that did occur was due to the amount of time the student teachers prepared for the teaching experience, not to the experience itself.[16]

- *Corollary Strategy 7a: In an educational system primarily based upon instructional objectives and individualized instruction, grade levels and intact classrooms are largely irrelevant.* If the elementary school curriculum is reduced to a set of instructional objectives for each subject, and if students can progress through these objectives at their own pace, a natural question becomes, what does one do with students who master all of the instructional objectives targeted for a particular grade level before their classmates?

    One option for such students is to remain in the same classroom and simply go on to more advanced objectives while their classmates struggle through the objectives mandated for their grade level. Unfortunately, this option could prevent students working on the advanced objectives from receiving the benefits of any relevant didactic classroom instruction targeted at concepts they don't already know—although they could always be invited to attend such experiences targeted at older students working on similar materials.

    One objection to allowing students to progress at their own pace in nongraded, loosely configured classrooms is that it ignores the potential impact of the emotional maturity of students. What would happen, for example, if a second-grader is "thrown in" with students three years older? Would he or she feel completely isolated? Would the older kids "eat him or her alive"?

    In my view of schooling, mastering the curriculum is the primary objective, and if some sort of student cultural mentality impedes this, then it is the culture that must be changed—not instruction. Thus, although it may very well prove to be advantageous to continue to segregate students by age for social reasons, these advantages could decrease over time since an inevitable implication of increasing the amount of instruction delivered during the school day is a concomitant reduction in the amount of social interactions occurring among students.

    Thus, recess, that fertile soil for the formation of cliques and bullying should probably be abolished in its present unstructured form. The same holds for physical education classes, unless they can involve substantial, sustained cardiovascular exercise (or effective antiobesity lifestyle modification). If, as there is some relatively weak evidence to suggest, physical activity can improve student's attention to instruction,[17] then it should be monitored closely.

Lunch time should also be more closely supervised, as should social interaction occurring in lavatories. Serious consideration should be given to outfitting classrooms, halls, school grounds, and staircases with cameras to reduce negative interactions among students.

- *Strategy #8: Teacher behavior should be monitored constantly to ensure the delivery of sufficient instruction, as well as satisfactory coverage of (and minimal departures from) the established curriculum.* Our single-minded focus upon discrete, prespecified instructional objectives implies a very different role for teachers. Historically, many teachers have considered that, as professionals, they have the prerogative to operate autonomously within the confines of their classrooms, including considerable latitude in deciding what parts of the curriculum to stress, what methods to employ, and what optional topics to include.

I would argue that this vision of professionalism is woefully outdated. Professions such as medicine have largely abandoned this intuition-laced mode of operation for a more evidence-based approach accompanied by practice guidelines. Thoracic surgeons, for example, perform the vast majority of their professional tasks according to rigidly prescribed protocols. Of course, they also don't have tenure, and they can be sued if their outcomes are substandard, following divergence from these protocols.

In the past few years, teaching does appear to have been moving toward a more rigidly prescribed practice, although this has occurred in the absence of any reliable or useful evidence or a reasonable infrastructure to facilitate it. It is my hope that one of the contributions of the time-on-task hypothesis will be to correct these deficiencies.

So, although no one would expect all teachers or different instructional software to use exactly the same language or approach in teaching the same instructional content, it is necessary that this content be covered as intensively and as efficiently as possible.

(Remember that Benjamin Bloom and his doctoral students' work predict that all students will exhibit faster learning speeds as they become more familiar with this system.) And teachers should be evaluated on the extent to which they comply with *their* prescribed behaviors—not with respect to student learning (since up to 60% of that is predetermined by children's previous instructional histories).

Of course, some teachers (or learning technicians) will always be better than others (although this is presently quite difficult to consistently document). Some will touch the lives of their students or use their personal experiences to make their presentations more interesting or keep everyone more alert with their playfulness and jokes. A teacher may even introduce topics that are dear to his or her heart or that he or she thinks will be especially interesting to a particular class, but these should not be delivered at the expense of covering the specified curriculum. Every minute of instructional time is precious, and every divergence from the planned curriculum is done so at a cost which, at the very least, should be justified by the fact that (a) the assigned objectives have been achieved or (b) the divergence has the potential of facilitating the attainment of future objectives.

Finally, no matter what we do, some students will also always learn more quickly than others, but these differences may decrease over time (and even if they don't, they can be compensated for by providing slower students with the opportunity to receive more instruction). If the curriculum is extensively specified in terms of hierarchical objectives, however, there should never be a lack of anything to teach or learn, and there should be no need of a "gifted" or "supplemental" or "advanced" set of instructional objectives. Every student should have the opportunity to learn every objective that he or she is willing to devote the time to master. And, of course, resources to facilitate this mastery should be freely available to every student, via either online instruction or the availability of tutoring—financed by the government, parentally administered, or supplied by volunteers.

- *Strategy #9: Use efficient instructional methods.* Although some variability in the ways things are taught may be necessary to maintain interest, elaborate games and group projects should always be avoided because of the amount of time they squander. Using "discovery learning," in which children are "guided" to uncover principles that took some of our best minds centuries to come up with is also contraindicated (and borders upon the ridiculous). It makes a lot more sense to give students the principles they need to begin with, then teach them how those principles are *applied*. A teacher (or someday a learning laboratory technician) should have one eye constantly on the clock and the other on what needs to be taught. It is worth repeating that the basic instructional model should always be (a) test (to find out what is not known), (b) teach, (c) retest (to find out what has and has not been learned), and then (d) find a way to reteach anyone who didn't learn the concepts, without wasting the remainder of the class' time. This model is at the very heart of the proposed learning laboratory, but if it can be achieved by more conventional means, fine.

As one example of instructional *inefficiency*, my son once had a teacher who had an elaborate class project involving building a medieval castle out of popsicle sticks that stretched over a period of several months. Regardless of what the teacher thought she was accomplishing, this is valuable time wasted, regardless of whether it is done in pre-kindergarten or third grade, unless there is an instructional objective in the curriculum mandating the "construction of medieval structures out of popsicle sticks." (And if there is such an objective, one would hope that it would be quickly dropped during our proposed ongoing curriculum review process.)

If the actual purpose for this activity, on the other hand, involves something else, such as "learning to work cooperatively," it (and all similar such activities) should also be dropped unless the curriculum reviewers believe that a significant number of students will someday be involved in the cooperative construction of popsicle-stick medieval castles because *that* is what is being taught here.

And, although teachers should concentrate their instruction on the production of academic learning, rather than attempting to foster social *behaviors*, there are exceptions. There may be social behaviors capable of facilitating success in any institutional setting and if we can identify them they are probably worth teaching. Perhaps because I could have certainly profited from such training, I personally like the Knowledge Is Power Program (KIPP) Academy's "SSLANT" procedure, whereby children are taught to turn and address anyone talking to them, nod, and give that person eye contact among other things. My only caveat to these exceptions is that such skills and behaviors should always be specified very, very specifically. Anything worth teaching is worth an instructional objective.

Of course, there are disruptive behaviors (such as talking to peers instead of engaging in noninstructional activities) that interfere with learning and that don't necessarily merit instructional objectives of their own because they can simply be de-incentivized as necessary. If, on the other hand, something like working cooperatively with others on a group project is considered to be of value, then it should be broken down into more specific behavioral components and applied to *curricular* instructional objectives or their proxies. I would argue, however, that the adoption of the principles listed in this chapter will, to a large extent, make such instructional activities unnecessary.

Thus, returning to the interminable construction projects in my son's early classes, if cooperative behavior is the real instructional target here, then requiring students to be civil to one another in school (*Strategy #4: Behavior that prevents or distracts students from learning must not be tolerated*) may be a better objective. Let our children's future workplaces use the incentives they will have at their disposal when our now adult ex-students actually do need to work with other people. Until that time, the school's job is to produce learning.

I would personally advocate adopting this principle at all levels of education. As an example, during my first year in graduate school (before I became interested in research), I was assigned to videotape my advisor, Bill Moody, teaching a six-year-old genius just about the entire elementary school mathematics curriculum on Thursday nights from 7 to 8 P.M. The taping took place within an observational deck, around which were situated classrooms observable to me through one-way mirrors. It so happened that this was also the time in which another faculty member was teaching a graduate guidance counseling class, which was primarily comprised of everyone breaking up into small groups and attempting to build six-foot chickens out of colored construction paper.

From September to Thanksgiving (and maybe longer, I just stopped taping then and began conducting research), the main activity these graduate students seemed to be engaged in was the attempt to build these huge, ridiculous chickens, so that they would stand vertically with no external supports of any sort. Week after week, the class would work on their chickens and, inevitably, just before one neared the requisite height it would topple over, sending the guidance counselor wannabes back to the drawing board.

What this was supposed to teach anyone (or how it would translate to advising students about their futures) I have no idea, but that's what the graduate students in this particular course did for at least an hour a night for the months that I had the dubious pleasure of clandestinely observing them. I personally suspect that what it really accomplished was to allow the instructor to tread water, since the chances are that at that time no one knew any more about how to train guidance counselors to offer students good advice than how to train teachers how to increase student learning.

- *Strategy 10: Solicit available free or cheap labor sources for supplementary/remedial tutoring and small-group instruction (the latter preferably employing no more than a 1:5 teacher-to-student ratio).* Tutoring and small-group instruction are labor intensive, but they are extremely effective in producing learning. Parents, older students (although not at the expense of their own instructional time), retired persons, or welfare recipients can function as either paid or voluntary tutors in a classroom setting. Whenever such people can be found, they should be employed in direct, small-group instructional activities, rather than used to perform administrative tasks or busy work that will not impact student learning and thereby waste time and money. Paying these workers a few dollars more than minimum wages would not be a budget breaker, even if every classroom in an entire school district had access to at least one per class. The tutoring involved doesn't have to be that complicated, and a high school diploma isn't required to give children (a) practice reading sight words or (b) learning simple mathematical operations via a set of flash cards.

- *Strategy #11: The time-on-task hypothesis constitutes a prediction for what will and will not result in increased student learning within the schooling process. It therefore follows that whenever a new instructional policy or approach is contemplated, the following question should be formally posed: How does this innovation increase the amount of relevant instruction delivered? If no convincing answer is immediately obvious, then the innovation should be scrapped prior to implementation.*

Or, alternately, whenever a new research study is proposed, a variant of the same question should be asked: What can the potential results from this research teach us about increasing relevant instructional time? If no convincing answer is forthcoming, then the research study should not be funded. Which conveniently leads us to the topic of our next chapter: What kind of research, if any, *should* we fund?

CHAPTER 10

Toward a More Focused Science of Education

Every spring, the American Educational Research Association has an annual meeting to which thousands of (primarily) school of education faculty members flock (again primarily) at the public's expense to present thousands of studies—most of them addressing nothing even remotely relevant to school learning. And, year in and year out, decade after decade, the U.S. Department of Education spends hundreds of millions of dollars to fund—with some notable exceptions that I've already mentioned and one that I will discuss shortly—isolated, trivial research. The results of all of these studies pile up, most are forgotten, or they are combined into meta-analyses, which themselves pile up until they too are forgotten. It's no-one's fault really, just a lack of understanding that the sole contributor to school learning is relevant instructional time and investigating anything else is a waste of time and money.

Now, admittedly, this may not be completely fair. The U.S. Department of Education's Institute of Education Sciences' "What Works" Clearing House, for example, is a noble effort to select instructional programs that possess good evidence (e.g., randomized trials with decent sample size) of effectiveness. But what usually isn't controlled in these studies (especially the ones with positive results) is the curriculum and the amount of instructional time delivered, and if our time-on-task hypothesis predicts anything, it is that *any* program (a) that includes more instructional time or

(b) whose curriculum provides a better match with the standardized test used to evaluate it will be judged as more effective (at least if it is properly implemented) than will a program involving less instructional time and/or a less well-matched curriculum.[1]

But, perhaps it isn't really fair to criticize an agency for not basing its funding decisions—or even a profession for not basing its research—on a strong theory which hadn't been either explicitly advanced or proven. (Of course, a theory can never be proven, but evidence can be marshaled for and against its usefulness.) In effect, as I've attempted to demonstrate, marshalling this evidence is exactly what the educational research community (funded, as often as not, by the Department of Education) has been in the process of doing for decades via such efforts as the Beginning Teacher Evaluation Study, the Tennessee Class Size Study, and the Instructional Dimensions Study.[2]

Ironically, however, until early October 10, 2009—22 days before I had to deliver this manuscript to the publisher—there appeared to be a serious negative finding buried within this literature, somewhat at odds with our theory of relevant instruction time. Phrased as a question:

> Why haven't charter schools been shown to produce more learning, given that most of them provide more instructional time and have attempted to implement many of the instructional strategies proposed in Chapter 9?

Given my research experiences (and my total contempt of studies that attempt to negate the effects of previous instructional time emanating from the home learning environment by statistically controlling for socioeconomic status), I simply assumed that the answer lay in our inability (or unwillingness) to randomly assign students to either attend charter or noncharter schools.

And then, in the most recent issue of *Education Week*, I read that such a study (funded by the Department of Education no less) had been performed in New York City. It was made possible by the fact that there were too few charter schools slots available to meet the demand for them (hence a lottery; that is, random assignment) had been instituted to decide who could and could not attend New York City charter schools.

In comparing the students who were "lotteried-in" versus those who were "lotteried-out," the former achieved dramatically higher on all achievement measures. (The two groups were equal on every indicator available to the researcher and should have been equal with respect to every unmeasured indicator such as propensity to learn because of the random assignment [lottery) procedure.) In fact, the investigators estimated that the typical charter student who attended one of these schools from kindergarten to eighth grade would close about 86% of the achievement gap in mathematics and 66% in English in comparison with New York's highest socioeconomic schools (which they provocatively named the "Scarsdale-Harlem achievement gap").[3] Of course projections such as this remain to be proven, but if they ever are I would have to rank them right up there with the most impressive findings in all of educational research, since a typical charter school student was more likely to be black (64% vs. 34%) and poor (91% vs. 72%) than the average New York City student.

Furthermore, analyzing their data to see if certain charter schools were more effective in eliciting achievement than others, the researchers found that schools with the following did indeed produce superior results:

- A longer school year
- A longer school day
- More minutes devoted to English instruction
- A direct instructional style
- A Core Knowledge curriculum
- The use of testing to determine which students had learned what
- A mission statement emphasizing academic performance over other types of educational objectives

For present purposes, I interpret these results in two ways. First, of course, strong (but probably unnecessary) additional evidence is provided for our time-on-task hypothesis. Second, and more germane to the subject of this chapter, support is provided for the contention that we shouldn't even bother conducting research that attempts to substitute statistical control of socioeconomic status (or prior test performance) for *random assignment*. The most powerful predictor of future achievement is prior instructional time (as usually provided by one's home learning environment), and it is absurd to think that we can algebraically equate children from home-enriched versus home-deprived learning environments.

So, assuming that we'll migrate away from research practices as obsolete as our classrooms (research that analyzes and reanalyzes existing databases and conducts experiments that do not employ random assignment), allow me to provide a couple of other examples of relevant schooling research.

RESEARCH DESIGNED TO ANSWER REAL-WORLD, STUDENT LEARNING-ORIENTED QUESTIONS

First, it is important to understand that since education is an *exclusively* practice-oriented discipline, the only conceivable reason for funding educational *research* is the expectation that something potentially useful for facilitating student learning will accrue. So, doesn't it seem reasonable that a few of the tens of thousands of educational research studies published in hundreds of journals by thousands of college of education faculty should be able to answer some relatively simple questions that teachers, school administrators, or parents might have about this particular topic?

To illustrate, what if a parent of an inner-city school student had a concern about the fact that her second-grader could read only about 20 words? If, by some strange happenstance, this parent gained access to a few educational "experts," chances are she might ask them what could be done for her child, and they might very well advise her to engage a tutor. And that would be excellent advice, if the woman could afford one or negotiate the paperwork required by her child's school to access one at public expense. But, what if this parent asked a slightly more specific follow-up question? Something like: *How long will it take Samantha to catch up?*

Now our experts would really be stumped, even if they had access to as much diagnostic information as they wished, such as the fact that Samantha had an IQ of 100, no measurable learning disabilities, and her percentile rank among all second-graders on a standardized reading achievement test. And, if this parent queried your author, he too wouldn't be able to give her a satisfactory answer because *we don't have a clue about how much time it takes a typical student to master a typical instructional objective in any curricular subject.* In fact, we know so very, very little about the amount of time required to learn even common, universal concepts at this point that we have no idea how much children *should* or *could* be learning.

And, as we've discussed, this ignorance is compounded by (if not a direct result of) the fact that our standardized achievement tests give us little or no information about an individual student's specific subject matter mastery or deficits. So, if Samantha's mother knew that her child could read only 20 words, one thing is for sure: She didn't find this out from any standardized test results. All she could find out from such tests is the percentage of children who scored worse (or in Samantha's case better) than her.

Wouldn't it make more sense to at least have the capability of informing Samantha's mother and her teacher what percentage of the curriculum she had mastered? Even better, to be able to inform them exactly what Samantha hadn't yet learned and how much additional instructional time would be required for her to correct this deficit? Time, after all, is something that can be quantified and, like money and weight, it has so much inherent meaning that no one would think of algebraically converting it to something *less* useful (á la Bogus Testing Principle #2).

Obviously, to answer a question such as that posed by Samantha's mother, what we really need to know is how much extra instruction must be delivered to children to ensure that they are learning what they should be learning. It is absurd, if not criminal, that we don't have the capability to do this, right now, because it would be exceedingly easy research to do if the curriculum were specified in terms of instructional objectives. All that would be required would be to tutor (either in person or via computerized instruction) a representative sample of perhaps 50 children on the objectives they haven't learned and see how long it would take them to learn them under ideal conditions. We might have some difficulty extrapolating such results to the conditions characterizing the classroom model, but that would be irrelevant anyway since remedial classroom instruction is presently even more impractical than individual tutoring.

If, however, we ever succeed in implementing the instructional objective–computerized instruction–driven laboratory model, the educational research agenda would be set for decades. The individualization of the resulting instruction would make it possible to conduct hundreds of small laboratory-type experiments simultaneously across the country without disrupting the educational process at all. Students (instead of entire classrooms) working on the same objectives could be randomly assigned to groups, and we could very quickly manipulate all the myriad instructional options (e.g., software, types of assessment items, optimal length of instructional units, instructional presentation, optimal instructional sequence), as well as ascertain the relative difficulty of various types of subject matter (the latter defined in terms of the average amount of instructional time required for mastery). It is *time* that should be the ultimate metric in education in general and educational research specifically; the amount of time needed to learn a topic; the amount of instructional time a new strategy is capable of saving.

In fact, even structural experiments, such as determining optimal numbers of breaks, recesses, and the effects of supplementary parentally supervised computerized instruction (i.e., administered outside of school hours) could be ascertained under carefully controlled conditions. And most exciting of all, *the sciences of what "could be" and "what is" would merge into a single genre of research.*

"Big Science" Questions

But, what if an unusually powerful and proactive politician (Barack Obama) or a socially conscious mega billionaire (Bill Gates) decided that it was time to address the most important question in education and approached your esteemed author for advice on what the topic of such a study should investigate? Of course, you already know that the study would be a randomized, controlled trial and that it would fall squarely within the realm of what *could be*. But, assuming that we had only one shot at answering only one big question, what would that question be?

From our perspective here, surely this would be an absolute no-brainer. Given our view of the institution of schooling as nothing more than an industry (composed of many, many factories) designed to produce learning, obviously the study would involve a strategy for improving the total learning output of this enterprise. From this perspective, then, what is the single greatest impediment to increasing the schooling process' overall output?

This too is a no-brainer, given the huge socioeconomic/ethnic learning disparities inherent in the current system. We need to decrease this gaping discrepancy without affecting the learning output of high-performing students (i.e., those from upper-middle-class families who have already received more instruction than everyone else). In addition to addressing one of our most crucial societal issues, if we could increase the learning output of our instructionally disadvantaged students, we would automatically realize a revolutionary increase in total learning output.

The trial that I have in mind, however, would address an even larger issue:

Given that our current educational system does not substantively reduce the learning gap that exists between children when they walk through the school house door for the first time the question would become:

To what extent can learning disparities among different socioeconomic and/or racial groups be ameliorated by societal action?

Or:

What is the ultimate potential (or limits) of instruction itself?

And, of course, given the person who would propose such a study, it should come as no surprise that the trial would also constitute the ultimate test of our time-on-task hypothesis.

Right now, no educator anywhere would have the remotest idea how to answer a question such as what the ultimate limits of instruction or the schooling process are. And, should a group of competent schooling researchers be posed the same question hypothetically, they would reply that no single experiment could address an issue this large. But it is my contention that in the scientific realm of what *could be* there is a study that *could*.

If our enlightened politician or philanthropist were to be satisfied with an answer to this question based upon collective ignorance, I'd guess that an anonymous poll would indicate the vast majority of the educational establishment does not believe that *any* amount of additional instruction could eradicate existing educational disparities. (Only people like Benjamin Bloom and Barker Bausell were ever this idealistic, and one of us is deceased while the other isn't getting any younger.)

After all, almost everyone associated with the schooling process has been acculturated into (or indoctrinated by) the IQ/ability/aptitude paradigm, which posits that some children have "it," some don't, and that's that. (An especially seductive paradigm, incidentally, for people with advanced degrees and thus who obviously have "it," as do their offspring, because of the massive amounts of extra instruction they provide via the home learning environment—which, not coincidentally, was also probably provided to them by *their* parents.)

Of course, this "I have it" paradigm also conveniently ignores the fact that the two substantive barriers to obtaining an advanced degree are heavily stacked in favor of certain societal classes. The first, lack of money to pay tuition is hardly insurmountable for upper-middle-class students, given the economic capabilities of their parents. Neither is the difficulty of scoring highly on standardized tests such as the SAT (for which upper-middle-class students have been prepped from the cradle and then provided with the resources to obtain all of the testing preparatory help they need).

Another interesting artifact (or self-fulfilling prophecy) this "entitled" assumption ignores kicks in once these fortunate students are admitted to a college or an advanced degree program. Also a facet of test reification, it rests upon the assumption that since aptitude test scores, grades, and progression through higher education are all interrelated, this implies that any student with high enough test scores to be admitted to a program in the first place *deserves* to graduate regardless of his or her performance within said program. Indeed, if a student encounters difficulty in such a prestigious institution, then it is often assumed that there is something amiss with any program faculty who might have had the temerity to issue anything below an "A" (much less a failing grade). Many medical schools, in fact, have graduated close to 100% of their enrollees for years (excluding those who withdraw on their own for nonacademic reasons) and refer students with such seemingly egregious offenses as stealing narcotics from locked medicine cabinets for counseling rather than summarily dismissing them.

But, all of this aside, given the effort and expense we've gone through to fund worthless space shuttle after worthless space shuttle trip (or even the remarkable and potentially useful efforts to decode the human genome, not to mention that of the duckbill platypus), isn't it odd that we have no idea regarding what is involved in saving one underprivileged, educationally deprived, school-age child from the underclass to which the circumstances of his or her birth have delegated him or her? Or even whether or not it is *possible* to do so?

To me, the true promise of the time-on-task hypothesis is its implicit prediction that it is possible to remediate any learning gap not caused by an organic brain condition. Especially since the magic bullet already exists to accomplish this feat in the form of the most low-tech intervention possible: *the administration of additional instruction*. And, although this hypothesis has never been tested, it most definitely *could* be.

Here's how I'd do it.

THE SUPER TUTORING STUDY

First, let me repeat that this study falls squarely under the aegis of the science of "what could be," rather than "what is" or "what is practical." The basic questions it would be designed to address are:

1. Can the educational deficit that inner-city children have in comparison to their upper-middle-class counterparts be eliminated by additional instruction?
2. If so, how much additional instruction would be necessary?

Naturally, I'd design the study based upon a laboratory paradigm, rather than relying upon what occurs within the current classroom/schooling model. We already have a century of experience with what the latter produces. I would therefore totally ignore practicality issues and employ the strongest, most effective mode of instruction known. I would, in other words, conduct a most audacious tutoring trial. (Of course if, by then a progressive company such as Headsprout had finished computerizing the entire elementary curriculum, I'd employ their digital "tutoring" as much as possible and supplement it by intense monitoring and human tutoring when needed to simulate the proposed learning laboratory model of instruction.)

The scientific rationale for the study would be the time-on-task hypothesis because it (a) explains existing disparities in school learning and (b) predicts how these disparities can and cannot be eliminated. Namely, in all but the most drastic cases, currently observed learning disparities are a function of differential instructional time and therefore can be eliminated the same way.

What could be simpler, more explicit, or more straightforward? Some students have received more instruction than others prior to entering school, and continue to receive more instruction afterward as a function of their home environments. Inextricably connected to this additional extra-school instruction is a culture that understands the value of learning and consequently ensures that its young will receive all of the advantages inherent to membership in this club. This is accomplished by parents ensuring that their children have mastered all the prerequisite skills necessary to negotiate the current educational system—even if that system is woefully inefficient and rife with self-fulfilling prophesies.

So, from this class' perspective, if the system doesn't deliver enough relevant instruction to accomplish this, so what? Instruction can be supplemented, and if testing consists of a series of self-fulfilling prophesies, then once understood, they can be gamed. If this gives the scions of these privileged classes a special advantage, again: so what? Third-world children are in the same boat, but no one can do anything about that either. It is a simple accident of the geography of birth—whether continental or regional—but American upper-middle parents can at least ensure that their offspring continue to enjoy all of the perks fortune and extra instruction have bestowed upon them. Indeed, it may be a biocultural imperative that they do so.

So, obviously, from a research perspective, this means that school-age children who have not been the beneficiaries of these huge doses of instruction from birth (not to mention who do not come from a home environment in which the parents are skilled in negotiating the educational system) must be given equivalently huge doses of additional instruction to enable them to perform equivalently to their instructionally enriched peers.

How much more? No one knows; but the seminal study by Risley and Hart discussed in Chapter 4 suggests that we're probably talking about thousands rather than hundreds of hours of additional instructional time here. So, obviously, the relative modicum of extra instruction provided by visionary (and well-intended) initiatives such as Head Start never came close to being enough.

Unfortunately, just as no one knows exactly how much instruction is necessary to eliminate these disparities, no one knows exactly *where* the most pressing learning deficits lie. Certainly, reading is one, but it may be that another involves the effects of grammatically correct oral language, something the schools address only indirectly and timidly.

To anecdotally illustrate the sheer amount of missed instructional time we may be dealing with here, I've both lived and worked in the economically depressed areas of two inner cities and have always been shocked at the linguistic differences between the public verbal behavior of lower- and upper-middle socioeconomic mothers' interactions with their children. Now, I realize such observations may not be representative, but in my experience, a typical response from a lower socioeconomic mother to her child who, say, inadvertently stands in the middle of the sidewalk thereby forcing an adult to walk around him or her, is often comprised of a harshly voiced "Move!" or "Get out of the way!"[4] A middle class parent, on the other hand, is more likely to say something to the effect of "Johnny, you are standing in this person's way. Please stand over here so that she doesn't have to walk around you."

Or, for a more egregious offense, the former may say nothing at all but simply slap the child's behind while her middle class counterpart—even in the rare event that she slaps the child (for it isn't punishment we are interested in here, but *instruction*)—will at least accompany this slap with a rationale for why the behavior is unacceptable and what the consequences will be if it is repeated. In fact, verbal responses to any questions (or observations) initiated by the two children are often equally differentiated. In the one case, the child's comment or question may well be ignored or answered with one or two words. In the other, the parent seizes upon the opportunity to expand upon the child's verbal initiation as both a means of teaching him or her about the world and expanding his or her language repertoire—both grammatical and vocabulary. It is as though one socioeconomic class ascribes to the old ideal that children should be seen and not heard, while the other appears to capitalize on every opportunity to *instruct* its children.

The study by Hart and Risley best illustrates this dramatic and ultimately tragic class difference in our society. These researchers showed that, although informal language instruction begins in infancy in most homes, by the age of three discrepancies in the total amount spoken to children can reached a staggering 20 million words. Twenty million words! And, interestingly, Hart and Risley's research suggests that this discrepancy is due to the culture attendant to socioeconomic status—not race.

Some parents talk to their babies constantly; some even read to them. When these children get older, they are rewarded for practically every verbal interaction or intellectual activity they engage in, all of which is *instruction*, nothing less. It is also extremely *relevant* instruction, especially with respect to preparing children for the types of didactic teaching to which they will be exposed in school.

So, although we may not know exactly how much extra academic instruction would be necessary to make up for the differences in these environments, especially with respect to language, vocabulary, and the simple quantity of factual knowledge taught in the home, it will probably be less difficult to make up the deficits in some of the more traditional academic skills, such as decoding words and learning math facts, as opposed to something like reading comprehension, which is at least partially based upon (a) the amount children have been read to (since this will provide practice and be accompanied by instruction in listening comprehension); (b) the amount of actual reading instruction received; (c) the amount of leisure reading he or she engages in; (d) the sheer number of words in the child's vocabulary; (e) the fact that most reading material is written using upper-middle-class grammatical constructions[5]; and (f) the children's general knowledge (including factual knowledge surrounding the types of topics upon which children's literature tends to be based).[6]

There is absolutely no reason to suspect, however, that these socioeconomic-cultural discrepancies in extra-school instructional time cannot be ameliorated by the provision of what caused the discrepancies in the first place: *extra-school instructional time*. Incredibly, however, despite the tens of thousands of educational research studies conducted, few have bothered to seriously address this issue—a situation that is even more inexplicable given how simple a definitive experiment would be to design.

The Design of the Experiment

All that would be involved would be to locate an inner-city school district and several elementary school principals who were willing to allow the study to be conducted under their auspices. At the beginning of the summer, volunteers would be solicited from families whose children were due to enroll in these schools' pre-kindergarten classes the next school year. (If pre-kindergarten classes weren't available, the study could begin the summer prior to children's kindergarten year.)

The goal would be to obtain a few hundred families willing to allow one of their children to participate once they understood what would be entailed; namely, to have their children tutored for at least one full year (summer and school year) and to make them available for testing throughout their entire elementary school experience.

The overriding purpose of this study would be to determine what the maximum effect of *massive* doses of additional relevant instructional time can be. (Don't forget that in the scientific realm of what could be, the primary purpose is to maximize the differences between the intervention and control groups, not to see how practical the intervention would be in the "real world" of everyday classroom instruction or even whether the intervention would be feasible to implement on a large scale.) We wouldn't be interested in trying to generalize the results of the study to parents who weren't motivated enough, or whose lifestyles didn't permit them, to devote the time and effort necessary to ensure that their children would be available to receive this extra instruction. We also wouldn't be dependent upon teachers' "professional judgment" regarding the extent to which they would implement the intervention. If only 10% of inner-city families' life circumstances allowed them to take advantage of such an intervention, it would be these and only these types of families we would be interested in studying. To enroll children who wouldn't receive the requisite amount of extra instruction would effectively prevent us from answering our overriding question involving the "could" word. As part of the screening process, we would administer a variety of measures in an attempt to screen out as many children with serious development problems as possible: not because these children aren't important, but because our purpose would be to identify the 90%–95% of children who can benefit maximally from extra instruction. In an effort to identify only those families who would be conscientious enough to comply with the experimental protocol, we might be wise to require everyone to come to eight or nine tutoring sessions on content that wouldn't be included in the trial itself (in order to avoid contaminating our experimental effect). The sole purpose of these sessions would be to identify parents who are unlikely to comply with the experimental protocol; hence, only those families who conscientiously brought their children in for both initial testing and tutoring would be permitted to participate in the study and thus be randomly assigned to one of the eight experimental study groups described later.

Naturally, we would carefully train and supervise our tutors (whose credentials we already know won't really matter since teacher training and experience don't count for much). The training would involve instruction in how to tutor children, as well as supervised practice in actually doing so. We would also include practice in using the types of materials that Bill Moody and I once used for the same purpose.

The pre-kindergarten children's instruction would emphasize:

- Elementary phonics (initial consonants, blends, long and short vowel sounds, and the most common rules governing their expression),
- Visual recognition of, say, 100 of the most common sight words,
- Reading brief sentences based upon the child's vocabulary, and
- Elementary number concepts.

Eventually, however, the instruction employed would span the entire elementary school curriculum. It should come as no surprise that we would utilize instructional objectives, build our primary test upon those objectives, and individualize instruction based upon learning gaps identified by constant testing, teaching, and retesting.

We would test all students in the study twice per year—once immediately before school began in the fall and once at the end of the year. The primary assessments would be comprised of items specifically keyed to the instructional objectives to which the curriculum would be reduced, but for public relations purposes we would also employ standardized achievement tests once a year, so that our experimental and control groups could be compared to national norms.

How much tutoring the participants received would depend upon their attention spans and their availability, as provided by their families, but we would make available as much instruction as anyone would be willing to accept. Certainly, we would expect to deliver no less than 12 hours per week during the school year (which would include weekend sessions) and a full schedule during the summer.

If possible, we would like to have the youngest children read to for a few minutes following each tutoring session—optimally with their parents or other family members present. We would also attempt to involve any family members in the process who were interested, such as by (a) providing books with which to read to the children, (b) flash cards with which to work with them at night, and (c) attempting to persuade the family to limit the amount of television viewing available to the child (or, at the very least, ensuring that what was watched was educational in nature—perhaps by providing appropriate DVDs). Certainly, we would realize that these strategies probably wouldn't be implemented with any great frequency unless we could make this child's future a *family* project.

The families would be constantly reminded that the purpose of this experiment wasn't to remediate their school's instruction but rather to prepare their children to excel academically, in order to enable them to reach their full potentials in life. Therefore noncompliance with the experimental protocol (such as only bringing their children in for tutoring when they encountered difficulty in school) would not be tolerated and would result in their children being dropped from the program.

We'd also attempt to open communication channels with the tutored children's classroom teachers to identify other areas that we might work on, although I personally wouldn't expect a great deal here either. For some children, there might even be a degree of informal counseling necessitated, such as in a situation in which the child is too shy to speak in class, or, alternatively, the child might identify areas of personal concern, such as the occurrence of bullying, which perhaps could be resolved.

Naturally, everyone would be free to withdraw their children at any time, and parents would be paid for their time in making their children available for testing, but everyone would need to agree to one relatively harsh provision: They would have no say on when tutoring commenced or for how many years their children would be tutored.

To avoid excessive dropouts from the study, we wouldn't employ a single tutored group and a single control group that received no instruction at all. Instead, assuming the study began the summer before pre-kindergarten, we would randomly assign participating families to one of eight groups (seven if it proved impractical to recruit pre-kindergarten families):

Group 1: The children randomly assigned to this group would begin their tutoring experience the summer before pre-kindergarten and would continue to receive the intensive tutoring intervention from then until the end of fifth grade.

Group 2: Also randomly assigned (as are all of the other groups at the same point in time), these children would not receive the intervention until the summer before kindergarten, but would receive it from then through the end of the fifth grade.

Groups 3–8: Each group would begin the intervention one year later. Group 3 would receive the intervention starting in the summer before first grade all the way through Group 8, which would begin the summer before sixth grade and end at the end of that school year. (This final year of tutoring for Group 8 would be irrelevant for the experimental portion of the trial itself, since the study would effectively end once all the children were tested at the completion of fifth grade.) Of course, their progress would continue to be monitored throughout their schooling experience and, if funds could be obtained, it would be nice if additional supplementary instruction were made available to everyone for as long as they needed it—even if this need extended throughout high school and perhaps college as well!

From my perspective, however, the experiment per se would be over at the end of fifth grade. Some scientists would like to know what the long-term effects of such an intervention would be by ensuring that no addition instruction was made available after the fifth grade, but everyone involved with the experiment would have become so attached to these children by this time that no one would want to cut them off from any additional benefits we might have the resources to provide them.

During Group 1's first year of instruction (the summer before pre-kindergarten and during the pre-kindergarten school year), all seven of the other groups would basically serve as controls to assess the effectiveness of the intervention during that time period. During the following year, the study would lose Group 2 as a control because it would morph into an additional experimental group whose extra-instructional time began one year later in their schooling career than did Group 1 (i.e., during the summer prior to kindergarten, as opposed to prior to pre-kindergarten). The process would then repeat itself for the five remaining years of elementary school, with one control being lost each year and one experimental group being added, until finally only Group 8 remained as a control group for all the previous years. This group would then be lost when its assignees began their tutoring experience during the summer preceding grade six and during the sixth-grade school year, but the study would be effectively over at that point.

Although a bit unwieldy, the huge advantage of this design would be that every family who volunteered would ensure that its child received at least one full year of free tutoring. (The average participant would receive a little over three and one-half years of tutoring.) This would encourage families to volunteer in the first place, as well as to remain in the study until it was over.

Unwieldy or not, there is little question concerning what the initial results would be. Obviously, the children in Group 1 would learn a great deal more during their first year as compared to the children in the other seven groups (because, if for no other reason, the children in the other groups would be receiving very little intense academic instruction in pre-school and probably receive no extra-school instruction). The truly fascinating question, however, is what impact such an intensive and continuing educational intervention would have subsequently. No one knows how much the superiority exhibited at the end of the first summer would increase during the pre-kindergarten year, into kindergarten, during the next summer's instruction, and each year the experiment is continued—only that it *would* increase. And, of course, each time a subsequent group received summer instruction for the first time would prove especially beneficial since it would tend to eliminate the forgetting of what was learned during the previous year—which is so detrimental for children from lower socioeconomic status families.[7]

The major advantage of this design, therefore, would be the definitiveness with which it would answer the following questions:

1. *What is the total effect of children receiving as much extra-school instruction as possible through their entire elementary school experience?* The comparison between Group 1 and Group 8 at the end of the fifth grade would assess the total effect of tutoring children from the summer before pre-kindergarten through the end of elementary school. Based upon my experience and the time-on-task hypothesis, I would expect a truly astounding cumulative learning difference to accrue between these two groups. Potentially as large, in fact, as currently accrues between children from learning-enriched versus learning-impoverished home learning environments.

2. *Is there a point at which extra instruction loses its potential effectiveness (or becomes relatively more effective)?* Our theory of relevant instructional time implicitly predicts that there is no such point, but this question would be definitely answered because each year a different group begins receiving the tutoring intervention (one year later than the previous group, hence receiving one year less additional instruction). Thus, the comparison between Group 3 and Groups 4 through 8 at the end of Grade 1 assessments would assess the effects of beginning tutoring during the summer prior to Grade 1 and throughout the Grade 1 school year. The comparison between Groups 1 versus 2 at the end of kindergarten would address the question: what effect did pre-kindergarten tutoring produce over and above kindergarten tutoring? In other words, if there was very little difference between Groups 1 and 2 at the end of kindergarten, why not simply increase instructional time in kindergarten and leave pre-kindergarten alone? (And, of course, the comparison between Groups 2 and 3 would address the same issue for kindergarten.)

3. *What is the relative effectiveness of extra instruction provided during the summer months, as opposed to extra tutoring occurring*

during the school year? Since students would be tested at both the beginning and end of each school year, it would be possible to assess the differential learning resulting from the intervention during each summer and during each school year for each grade level. These data would also give us a much firmer handle on (a) how much children actually forget during the summer months, (b) what types of content are more susceptible to forgetting, and (c) how much forgetting summer instruction prevented (since there would always be at least one group that received no summer tutoring). Although highly unlikely, these comparisons would also indicate if summer tutoring were sufficient to end learning disparities (or if school year tutoring alone would be sufficient).

There would be many, many additional questions this trial would be capable of answering, but the real question would be nothing less than: "What are the limits of instruction itself?" Said another way, this study would provide us with a first estimate of the magnitude of the effect that an optimal schooling environment *could* have for this long-neglected population. And, paradoxically, my fondest hope would be that the trial would be forced to stop after a couple of years because of ethical concerns. Namely, that the intervention's effectiveness was so dramatic and obvious that it was judged to be unreasonable to deprive the remainder of the study participants (i.e., the delayed treatment groups) of the benefits of the extra instruction.[8] (Of course, if this happened, we would probably still be permitted to continue to assess the children's progress *sans* the randomly assigned control group.)

Research of this genre should have been conducted decades ago. It is the equivalent of big science projects in physics, such as building a multi-mile-long high-energy particle accelerator to answer an equally big question, but ours would provide an answer of greater societal importance at perhaps 1/1000th of the cost. And, although there is no controversy concerning whether, say Group 1 (whose participants were tutored throughout their elementary school tenure) would statistically outperform Group 8 (whose participants were forced to wait until the beginning of middle school to receive their tutoring) each year of the experiment, what no one knows is the magnitude of these effects, nor how rapidly Group 1 would close the gap on their upper-middle-class counterparts as assessed by standardized tests. Certainly, the most dramatic differences between the study groups would occur on our instructional objectives–based tests. Differences on the standardized achievement tests would be next in order of magnitude, and one of the most interesting finding resulting from these tests would be the rate at which the experimental students move upward in percentile ranks in comparison with both their control counterparts and the national norms as a whole. Finally, since we would probably have administered intelligence tests prior to randomization as a screening tool, we would also expect the experimental groups to have improved their "IQ's" substantively over the course of the study. (These improvements would not be as dramatic as the first two comparisons since the children would not receive direct instruction on the intelligence test "tasks," but we would expect perfectly laddered increments corresponding to the amount of total instruction received by each of our eight groups.)

Of course, no randomized trial ever conducted is immune from criticism. One that might be leveled at this one is that the intervention isn't just instruction but involves personal contact with caring adults, mentorship, differences in family involvement resulting from participation in the experiment, and a host of other factors. So, even if the results are breathtakingly positive, how would we ever know exactly what produced them?

And my answer to this question of course is: *Who cares?* The purpose of this study is basically to see what it takes to ameliorate the extra-school learning advantages of not being born into an upper-middle-class family. So, like my own tutoring study conducted, lo, so many years ago, if anyone ever gets the opportunity to conduct this study, they should realize that there may never be a second chance and should therefore unapologetically throw everything into their intervention that has the potential of increasing instructional *time* (which is the *only* thing that can increase learning). What we are talking about here is not simply instruction, but the most intensive, *relevant* instruction that we are capable of delivering. Perhaps it's true that we'll never be able to implement this intervention on a national scale, but we'd at least start at the upper end of the continuum and see what *could* be. Not what *will be* in the world that our research participants have inherited, but what *could be* under the best of circumstances in a world that could be constructed for them. My goal here would be to see the extent to which we *could* change this world. A world so aptly described by Malcolm Gladwell, author of *Outliers: The Story of Success* (Little, Brown, and Co., 2008) in an interview with Charles Blow of the *New York Times*: "I am explicitly turning my back on... these kinds of empty models that say... you can be whatever you want to be. Well, actually, you can't be whatever you want to be. The world decides what you can and can't be."[9]

Yet, if asked if I think such an experiment is truly necessary, I would perhaps surprisingly answer: "*No*, it is not." Those of us left standing who understand (and care about) school learning already know what the results would be, and we now have a theory that definitively explains *why* these results would accrue. So, why not simply replace our obsolete classroom with a learning laboratory in which simulated tutoring is administered to everyone via computerized instruction and be done with it? (And/or, of course, is made available online, so that everyone has access to as much extra instructional time as they have the will to take advantage of.) We know what to do, and we have the technology, so *why not just do it*?

THE SCIENCE OF EDUCATION IN THE LEARNING LABORATORY ERA

If the entire curriculum were translated to discrete instructional objectives, if all students were taught via a simulated tutoring paradigm, and if learning were assessed in terms of what was actually taught, the educational research agenda would receive a sudden and dramatic refocusing. Only two genre of research would be relevant:

- Research involving optimal learning (defined in terms of both the sheer number of objectives achieved and the amount of time required for achieving them).
- Research involving student (and familial) *perseverance*, for now relevant time on task would be a legitimate educational outcome in itself (because anything that could be done to induce a student to spend more relevant time on task would result in more learning).

Gone would be all qualitative research (which almost by definition does not involve how *much* learning occurs). Gone would be attitudinal and other affective research involving passing out worthless questionnaires to teachers and students. Gone would be the huge *variety* of study topics presented at the American Educational Research Association annual meeting each year.

In their place would be research designed around questions such as:

- Can more effective digital presentations of instructional content be designed to facilitate learning, transfer (defined in terms of applying what has been learned to the achievement of future instructional objectives), retention, or perseverance?[10]
- To what types of objectives (or instructional content) are these presentation methods most appropriate?
- How can learning speed (or facility in using digital instruction) be increased?
- What are true versus arbitrary prerequisites for learning? (In other words, what should be taught first, and what doesn't need to be taught at all?)
- At what point (e.g., at what level of mastery or after what amount of unsuccessful instructional time) should students be pulled aside and instructed one-on-one or in small groups by an actual teacher?

Obviously, the list could go on and on, but the main point is that all research would be directed toward improving the learning laboratory model (or its supplemental alternatives such as person-to-person tutoring), so that it would be optimally efficient and attractive to students and their families (defined in terms of willingness to engage in extra-schooling instructional time). From a methodological point of view, a huge amount of such research could be conducted simultaneously because it would not be at all disruptive to the ongoing learning process. There would, in effect, be no control groups that received anything other than the best options currently available to all students. Such experimentation could be constant since it would in no way involve denying instruction or impeding anyone's individual progress through the curriculum, nor would any given experiment necessitate huge numbers of students (because the instructional environment would be so carefully controlled). Students could be matched very carefully according to the number of subject matter objectives they had learned and *then* randomly assigned to, say, an innovative method of presentation versus the standard laboratory method. Since both the standard and the innovation being tested would both be computerized, implementation would be exactly controlled, as would just about every other conceivable variable. And, of course, the experimental outcomes would be automatically collected since they would involve nothing more than how many instructional objectives were mastered within a given period of time (or how much time it took to master a given number of objectives).

Research of this genre would, in other words, be laboratory research conducted in a laboratory. It would be the perfect melding of the science of *what is* and the science of what *could be* since everyday instruction would be administered in the same laboratory setting. It would give the educational research community a focus that it has never had before, comparable in fact to the neurosciences, for which the truly important questions already exist and scientists have no incentive to invent inane, trivial hypotheses. All they have to do is muster the energy to reach up and pluck the low-hanging fruit already available.

CHAPTER 11

Implications for Reducing Racial Disparities in School Learning

Although our time-on-task hypothesis is designed to provide a framework for increasing the learning production in *all* schools, in order for the theory to be more useful than its predecessors it should at least provide some guidance in solving what is arguably the most pressing educational issue facing us today: reducing the racial and socioeconomic disparities in test performance. Unfortunately, I am writing this at a time in which a credit crisis has rocked some of our largest financial institutions, the government has correspondingly committed itself to what some estimate will be an enormous taxpayer bailout to avoid an even more draconian economic de-escalation, and we apparently remain committed to a state of perpetual (and economically expensive) war in Afghanistan and Iraq. And, although we now have a socially conscious president with a personal interest in schooling, he will almost surely not have access to advisors who understand what truly affects school learning.

So how, short of some improbable *deux de machina*, could the necessary processes be put in place for reducing or erasing current learning disparities among our young? The answer is not elegant, but obvious. If no one is available to help you do something, then the Thernstroms' "No Excuses" message is absolutely correct. We must either do it ourselves or not see it done. It seems to me, therefore, that until learning laboratories replace or supplement the classroom model, the only answer (or at least a beginning step) is for the affected cultural and racial groups to get into the instructional business themselves in a very serious way. In effect, these groups need to out-middle-class the middle class by constructing their own version of instruction-intensive home environments.

And, although I realize this advice will be deemed as patently unrealistic, none other than the Reverend Martin Luther King offered the following time-on-task solution several decades ago to African American college students:

> When you are behind in a footrace, the only way to get ahead is to run faster than the man in front of you. So, when your white roommate says he's tired and goes to sleep, you stay up and burn the midnight oil.[1]

And, although equally unrealistic for the vast majority of our current inner-city families, none other than our current president offers yet another time-on-task hint to what is ultimately the only solution to the problem:

> [My mother's] initial efforts centered on education. Without the money to send me to the International School . . . she had arranged from the moment of our arrival to supplement my Indonesian education with lessons from a U.S. correspondence course . . . . Five days a week, she came into my room at four in the morning, force-fed me breakfast, and proceeded to teach me my English lessons for three hours before I left for school and she left for work. I offered stiff resistance to this regimen, but in response to every strategy I concocted, whether unconvincing ("My stomach hurts") or indisputably true (my eyes kept closing every five minutes), she would patiently repeat her most powerful defense:
>
> "This is no picnic for me either, buster." (p. 45-46)[2]

Now, while the Reverend King's advice may be fine for an African American college student and President Obama's experience might resonate with an upper-middle-class African American family, both require a bit of translation to make them applicable to the family of an African American kindergarten child about to enter a completely segregated inner-city school. In fact, advice for families finding themselves in this situation is in short supply, as I think was illustrated by an interview I once saw of Abigail Thernstrom (of *No Excuses: Closing the Racial Gap in Learning* fame) on C-Span.

Abigail, as effete a 95-pound white female intellectual as any caricaturist could have ever created, was well spoken, obviously knowledgeable, and the interview was proceeding quite nicely until the host of the program asked her what advice she would give to an adolescent, single, female, black parent to ensure that her child excelled at school. As I think anyone who didn't happen to be an adolescent, African American single mother would be in the situation, Dr. Thernstrom was quite reluctant to respond and, as I remember, pretty much skirted the issue despite the interviewer's persistence.

I certainly don't blame Dr. Thernstrom, because I could certainly visualize any hypothetical African American single mothers responding with, "Who needs some white woman telling us how to raise our black children?"

And the answer I would have provided this teenager if I had been on the sidelines would be: "You do, if you want your child's life to be any different from yours, because this woman is part of an elite American social class who knows a great deal about preparing children to assume their position in this privileged club."

Or, perhaps our young mother's response might have been: "People like this have no idea what it is like to face what I face everyday of my life."

And, here, she would be absolutely correct, but if she chooses to ignore the rules for entry into Abigail's club, then she will ensure that her child will someday also be absolutely correct in making the same statement. The *only* way to overcome the huge educational disparities afflicting lower socioeconomic groups in this country is (a) the implementation of a supplemental educational program as extreme as the intervention proposed in the seven-year tutoring study described in the last chapter or (b) drastically changing what goes on in most lower socioeconomic homes. So, the way I would have preferred for Abigail Thernstrom, or someone with a bit more ethnic credibility than either of us possess, to have responded to the interviewer's question is:

The learning *culture in the vast majority of impoverished African American households, their extended families, and their communities is not adequate. It may be a warm, caring culture in other regards. It may be fine for teaching children how to cope with poverty and racism, but it will almost absolutely guarantee their being prevented from ever having access to the privileged lifestyle currently enjoyed by the upper middle class.*

Of course, as Gerald W. Bracey[3] very correctly pointed out, poverty is not a culture, but a system or condition or force (like gravity) that that affects everything it touches, so certainly neither I nor Abigail Thernstrom are qualified to tell impoverished, abysmally educated adolescent parents—with no economic hope of their own—how or where to summon the will, energy, and self-sacrifice to begin educating their children from the time they are a few months old.

But I *can* tell these child mothers what will happen to their daughters if such sacrifices are not made. They will be left behind educationally to form the next generation's underclass. Perhaps the inevitability of this status will be easier to accept in the substandard schools they will attend since everyone else will be in the same situation, but the rest of the country's young will begin school already knowing a substantial part of the curriculum and having already been imbued with the belief that, while learning may not always be a lot of fun, it is a worthwhile and absolutely essential activity. I can also reassure these child mothers that they, their mothers, or those support networks available to them, *do* possess the requisite skills to help educate their children. If nothing else, they can begin talking to their children in infancy and always, always encourage them to talk back as early and as often as possible.

Finally, I would mention to this hypothetical mother (if she hadn't already silenced me with a blunt object) that her child will not simply be competing with other poorly educated Americans. She will be competing with children in India and China and countries that she has never heard of who are *hungry* to learn and, in Thomas Friedman's words, whose parents have instilled in them a hunger to take her future job and everyone else's.[4] Her child, in other words, will find herself surrounded by a *world* of competitors, including ever-increasing numbers of poorly educated immigrants for those few lower-paying jobs that can't be geographically outsourced.

But, in the midst of all this doom and gloom, I would remind this young woman that although the *learning* culture in her home and community may need to be completely revamped, her social and familial structures do not. She is probably less likely to be isolated from family and friends (and is more likely to have access to a socially conscious and helpful church) than her privileged suburban counterparts. She is a member of a culture that shares a historic legacy of dealing with (and overcoming) repression. She is a part of a culture and a community that values supporting one another and which values retaining extended family ties, all of which gives her a unique support system that can potentially be channeled to help provide her child with those educational resource denied by the state.

So, I wouldn't address this advice to only our hypothetical young mother. I would address it to *her* mother or her aunts or *anyone* willing to work with her child *every day*. People willing to read to her, work on her educational skills: teaching her to read, making sure that she does read once taught, and creating educational opportunities where none appear to exist. And, lest someone believe they are unqualified for this role, or don't possess the necessary skills, I would reassure them that they do. Or, at the very least they will gain the necessary skills by *teaching* them.

Her child must also be led to understand at a visceral, cultural level that her future is dependent upon learning as much as she can as quickly as she can: that the main job of her childhood must be to learn and excel in school. Her homework must be monitored, the amount of television she is allowed to watch must be limited to educational programs or completely replaced with recreational reading, and her peer group must be carefully screened. She must, in other words, be reared with access to the type of home learning environment in which her suburban peers are raised. It is *not* required, however, that she be reared as though she were a member of the upper-middle-class, white culture. Only that she be provided the same *amount* of extra-school instruction as its children.

But, alas, even providing these home learning opportunities isn't enough. The school, substandard as it may be, will continue to supply the bulk of instructional time that our hypothetical child receives. Her family must therefore establish a presence in the school she attends. The child's teachers and school administrators must know that her family (and therefore she) is a force to be reckoned with. What this means is that someone from the family (not necessarily the mother) should join the PTA and attend (or initiate) parent–teacher conferences. If the child's performance slips, both the child and her teacher must be made immediately aware of the fact that this is unacceptable: the student by being frankly told that she is going to have to do better (underlined by appropriate instructional interventions, consequences, and rewards); the teacher by having the mother/family representative ask what can be done to help the child at home and making a follow-up appointment to ascertain if these interventions are working.[5]

And, through all of this, someone must be on the lookout for better educational opportunities if this child does not thrive in the school our society has provided for her. For, although admittedly a long shot, some private schools give a few diversity scholarships, all modern urban school districts have some kind of transfer policy, and charter schools that routinely offer longer instructional days, briefer summer vacations, and periodic weekend instruction are being formed constantly (the Knowledge Is Power Program [KIPP] Academy being a notable example).[6] Of course, even entry into a truly remarkable school (or dramatically improving the quality of an existing one) would not address the underlying disparities in extra-school instruction, but it will help to a degree. Even a sudden complete migration to the proposed learning laboratory model of schooling wouldn't eliminate this problem, although it would help even more. Only a sufficient amount of extra instructional time has the potential of accomplishing this, thus the mother or her support system should be constantly on the lookout for volunteer tutors or any resource capable of providing extra instruction or increasing the relevancy of what is already available.

So, in the final analysis, the solution is difficult, and my advice is no more helpful than that of Reverent King's: *"When you are behind in a footrace, the only way to get ahead is to run faster than the [person] in front of you."* Neither message is destined to be popular nor is it fair for a child to be destined from birth to fall behind through no fault of her own, but that is the nature of this society and the time-on-task hypothesis itself.

And, after saying this, I can picture Hernstein and Murray sneering at me from the great beyond, Jonathan Kozol calling me a racist, Abigail Thernstrom shaking her head disapprovingly, and J.M. Stephens gazing at me with a disappointed look on his face (for not heeding his repeated pronouncements that no one could depend upon either families or the government getting seriously involved with the process of schooling).

I remain unrepentant, however, because every learning principle and schooling strategy I have delineated in this book is ultimately relevant for decreasing the ethnic/socioeconomic educational disparities. And, although it may take a generation to completely eliminate them, ironically perhaps, the most heartening realization accruing from increasing the *relevance* of the instruction offered in our schools is that it isn't necessary to reduce ethnic learning disparities completely.

For those readers old enough to remember the Neil Simon song about "all the crap" he learned in high school, a translation to our vision of the schooling process is as follows: *Because everything taught in school (and in the home environment) isn't relevant to what students really need to know in the economic marketplace or to prepare them for a college education or for life in general, it follows that the importance or impact of this ethnic/socioeconomic gap in learning may not be as great as it seems.* If we can identify which instructional objectives are truly important and weight our instruction (and tests) heavily with those concepts, then it may be that this will help to reduce racial/socioeconomic disparities in learning with less need for massive extra-school infusions of instructional time. As Richard Nisbett argues in his seminal book (and which Malcolm Gladwell echoes from a completely different perspective), there comes a point at which more *intelligence* (and I would add learning of unused content for its own sake) is neither valued nor useful. At that point, what becomes important to, say, employers are things like ethical behavior, reliability, self-discipline, perseverance, responsibility, communication skills, teamwork ability, and adaptability to change. The same is unquestionably true of learning. If someone can read technically dense text with understanding, write clearly, possess good numerical skills, be digitally proficient, and be able to locate information in a purposeful manner, then that is probably "good enough" for 95% of the economic purposes to which we use education. It is also "good enough" to be able to take advantage of advanced training in colleges and professional schools if we can persuade (or legislatively force) them to abandon such completely bogus entry requirements as SAT and GRE scores.

Of course, the full implementation of the learning laboratory model in our schools would facilitate all of this. Ultimately, movement to some variant of this instructional model will occur, and accompanying it will be the capability of dramatically increasing relevant instructional time, not only within the schools—but within those families willing to devote the necessary time to helping their children master a sensible, useful, and relevant curriculum. I just hope this migration won't take yet another generation to occur.

CHAPTER 12

Getting There From Here

One of the most disheartening predictions made by the time-on-task hypothesis is that no societal intervention yet implemented comes close to supplying the sheer amount of additional instruction necessary to match what upper-middle-class children receive in their homes. For, in the final analysis, the hypothesis and its implications always boil down to time. *Time is all there is. Time is all that counts.*

This means, therefore, that the time-on-task hypothesis suggests that there is no easy solution to either of our most pressing schooling issues: decreasing the learning disparities presently existing within the schooling process or substantively increasing its overall learning production. However, the hypothesis also provides a very optimistic message: There *is* a difficult means of achieving both goals. Furthermore, children's achievement does not need to be constrained by the circumstances of children's birth or their genetic makeup or the type of school they have been designated to attend if they can somehow be provided with the necessary amount of instruction.

How much extra instructional time we supply within the schooling framework (directly or indirectly via the strategies presented in Chapter 9) depends upon the educational aspirations we have for our children. These aspirations should drive the schooling curriculum, however, rather than being reflected in changing students' relative position on black-boxed, irrelevant tests. For, the other side of this coin is that we have no idea the extent to which our most privileged students are being deprived of *their* true potential. In other words, how much more could they learn if their instruction were imbued with some sense of urgency?

But we've already touched on all of these issues, so now it's time to explore how we can get where we want to go from here. How does one transition from a totally obsolete classroom model to a laboratory in which digital tutoring constitutes the bulk of the instruction delivered? Or, at least some version of supplementary digital tutoring which could be accessible 24/7 to students and their families who want access to the opportunities that extra instruction provides? For *this* is the one best chance we have of providing the (a) instructionally deprived segments of our society the opportunity of changing their children's futures and (b) their instructionally advantaged counterparts the option of excelling even more spectacularly.

Or, barring such an ambitious goal, how can we at least obtain a curriculum that is as explicit, transparent, and relevant as our best minds can make it and which is easily accessible to every family everywhere? Or a testing system that would assess only this curriculum and which would be accompanied by sample tests that could be accessed by all participants in the educational process: teachers, students, and parents? Or an instructional process designed to produce learning by the most efficient means possible and not be subject to the idiosyncratic whims of teachers, administrators, testing companies, textbook writers, or anyone else?

One thing is for sure. Our children aren't going to come home one afternoon and report that upon arriving at school they found a computer sitting on their desk and the teacher's desk, littered with monitors and electronic devices, residing on a raised platform at the back of the classroom. Parents aren't going to read in the paper that standardized tests have suddenly been replaced by curriculum-based tests that will actually be designed to assess school learning and to inform instruction. Or that the socioeconomic disparities in test scores have magically dissipated.

That some version of a transition to a more technologically advanced classroom model will occur is inevitable because it has already begun. However, whether this movement approaches anything resembling a learning laboratory, whose first priority is to produce as much learning as possible, is very much open to question. Certainly, it will not happen if its implementation is left to professional educators.

In the delightful book I've mentioned previously (*Disrupting Class: How Disruptive Innovation Will Change How the World Learns*), Clayton Christensen and his colleagues describe how the student-to-computer ratio has improved in schools from one computer for every 125 students in 1981 to one for five in 2001 with practically no accompanying effect upon instructional practice.[1] The schools are *amazingly* impervious to change,[2] and they are likely to continue their idiosyncratic decision making as long as society permits it.

So, is there any way to facilitate this transition? I suppose the only possibility is some sort of initiative on the part of the federal government, the private sector, or the business community. The private sector may hold the most promise—defined as individuals or institutions not solely motivated by a profit motive such as (a) parents, (b) philanthropic organizations, (c) business leaders (who have passed the point in their careers at which quarterly stock prices govern their lives), (d) subject matter experts willing to donate their time to writing instructional objectives, (e) computer programmers willing to help write the shareware upon which computerized instructional programs can be based, (f) database engineers willing to help design the voluminous record-keeping requirements that reliance upon instructional objective–based instruction/testing would require, and (g) legions of ordinary people willing to donate some of their time to providing individual tutoring or small-group instruction to any student who needs it.

Without some sort of governmental or philanthropic intervention, however, it is difficult to visualize from where the impetus for such an initiative could come or how it could be coordinated. Money alone does little good, as witnessed by the Bill and Melinda Gates foundation's efforts which, while well intended, are not primarily targeted at increasing relevant instructional time. Even if all of the volunteer efforts needed to mount such an initiative were available (e.g., tutoring, programming time, curriculum translation, and used hardware donations), the logistics of coordinating it all would be quite daunting.

We do have a president now who may have the political and social capital to at least put these forces into motion. Enough perhaps to even encourage entrepreneurial initiatives based upon the huge potential market that these proposed changes will inevitably create.

Obviously, a book such as this cannot initiate the magnitude of change needed, but I sincerely hope that it has at least provided a roadmap for the explicit direction these changes need to take. Fortunately, everything proposed here doesn't need to be implemented simultaneously, nor must the final product be born fully developed, like Athena leaping from her

father's forehead. The current classroom, although obsolete and inefficient, will continue to teach children something.

I think we run a serious risk, however, that if we don't improve our
public schools, private ones will eventually completely displace them as
producers of our future leaders and scientists, somewhat like the attributed role of the playing-fields of Eton. So, wouldn't it be a shame
if, through our inactivity, we created yet another set of self-fulfilling
prophesies similar to the de facto prerequisites we have permitted our
testing industry to impose upon us? One in which only the privately educated can rise to leadership positions?

Such a future certainly isn't inevitable. There is absolutely no reason
why we can't implement the simple principles that constitute the science
of school learning (as well as the Learning Laboratory itself), one component at a time or one site at a time: be that site an entire state, a school
district, or a single school (public or private). Alternately, a single grade
level could be employed within any one of these units or, even less ambi-
tiously, we could translate the model to one academic subject (preferably
reading because of its preeminent importance) within one grade within
one school! Or, perhaps some version of the digital learning laboratory
could be used exclusively to supply extra-instructional time outside of
the classroom as an entrepreneurial project. (After all, for-profit tutoring
has now evolved into a multibillion dollar industry in this country alone.)
Or, if none of these options proves viable, the conduct of an experiment
such as the tutoring trial proposed in Chapter 10 would at least provide a
significant start on the translation of the curriculum into an instructional
objective format, the development of a set of tests based upon these
objectives, and a validation of the contention that learning discrepancies
are the sole result of discrepancies in instructional time. Or, if even this is
too ambitious, perhaps the existence of a new educational position within
our school districts, dedicated to marshalling, supporting, and facilitating
supplemental parental instructional within the home environment, might
provide extra instruction for at least some children.[3]

However, if I were to prioritize the steps involved in moving toward a
learning laboratory, the first would be the creation of a complete set of
instructional objectives (or some comparable format of equal explicitness)
to represent the elementary school curriculum, accompanied by sample
test items for each objective. Even this task wouldn't be as imposing as it
seems. I would estimate that a relatively small group of educators with

some writing experience could sit down with several sets of textbooks, a collated list of state standards, and translate the entire elementary school curriculum into instructional objectives (with sample items) in a single summer. With a few revisions, this, in and of itself, would permit us to usher in an era of curriculum-based tests—both for use to inform instruction and even more radically to actually evaluate it by measuring *learning*. The fact that these tests could be made freely available to the schools should make their use considerably more attractive.

The existence of such a resource should make it possible to make instruction more relevant, even if no movement toward computerized instruction were in the offing. It would also reduce (but certainly not eliminate) socioeconomic testing disparities because all students would theoretically have classroom exposure to all tested content (as opposed to our current practice of testing content sometimes taught exclusively in the home environment). Further, if the objectives were accompanied by explanations and sample test items as rudimentary as those presented earlier, they would at least provide parents with the capability of providing supplementary instruction at home.

Then, if some sort of standard software platform/template could be developed by which these objectives could be taught—even if little more sophisticated than the simple-minded examples presented in this book—a huge resource would be made available to facilitate supplementary school and home-based instruction. Finally, the securing of computer hardware and a simple method of networking them within each classroom would be needed, along with an architecture by which a teacher (or learning technician) could monitor, supervise, coordinate, and record the learning results taking place on 25 or so computers. If a common software writing package/platform (to avoid a digital Tower of Babel) were also freely available to anyone willing to contribute their time, surely we could develop some version of the entire learning laboratory concept in a reasonably short time

Although not simple, this developmental process is not impossible. It is true that, once developed, the implementation of such a system would be quite expensive, but nothing like as costly as the invasion and occupation of yet another country. It need not even replace our current schooling system, but instead could operate as a shadow, backup, or supplementary system to it—completely constructed by volunteer labor and expertise. A system, accessible to any child or any family with access to a computer or a cell phone, which would contain test items to assess mastery of every conceivable school topic, accompanied by digitized instruction for anything not mastered: anytime, anywhere.

I think it behooves us to remember that good things do happen in the world with little or no governmental funding, corporate sponsorship, or institutional support. The Berlin Wall fell. The Internet appeared and morphed into something that no science fiction writer could have imagined 30 years ago. Perhaps 30 years from now classroom instruction will likewise have developed into something that none of us today can envision. Or, more likely, an internet-based, supplementary school system may evolve to allow anyone to achieve 100% mastery of an optimal curriculum.

Regardless of what the future holds for the schooling process, however, one thing is for certain:

> *The only way to increase school learning is to increase the amount of relevant instructional time we provide our children.*
>
> So, let's just do it!

Introduction: Obsolete from Every Perspective

1. The analogy is supplied by Lorin Anderson [(1984). (Ed.) *Time and school learning*. New York: St. Martin's Press. (p. 47)] via the following quote: "The cocktail party serves as a fine example of selective attention. We stand in a crowded room with sounds and conversations all about us. Often the conversation to which we are trying to listen is not the one in which we are supposedly taking part." From: Norman, D.A. (1969). *Memory and attention: An introduction to human information processing*. New York: John Wiley & Sons (p. 13).

2. See Kieran Egan's *Getting it wrong from the beginning: Our progressivist inheritance from Herbert Spencer, John Dewey, and Jean Piaget* (2002, New Haven, CT: Yale University Press) for a scathing assessment of the contributions made by these individuals. As a graduate student, I wrote a paper debunking Piaget's contention that his developmental tasks could not be taught out of sequence or before children had reached a given level of "development," which was considered radical at the time but now is conventional wisdom based upon the empirical evidence.

3. Lemann, N. (2000). *The big test: The secret history of the American meritocracy*. New York: Farrar, Straus, and Giroux (p. 334).

4. Some of these alternative purposes of schooling are to (a) provide child care for working parents, (b) prepare children to function in their future workplaces, (c) provide a safe environment for children until they are old enough to work, (d) provide an educated electorate to function in a democracy, (e) guide appropriate social development to allow students to take their places as "productive members of society," and so forth.

Chapter 1: The Science of Learning

1. Edward Thorndike (born in 1874) was perhaps the most influential of these researchers and had a long and distinguished career in the psychology of learning. Most famous for his laboratory work with animals (often involving cats), his "law of exercise" specified that learning would increase with practice and is basically a function of time on task. Thorndike was one of the first researchers to develop learning curves based upon repetitions of stimuli, and he came to believe that all mammals learned in a similar, incremental fashion.

2. The total-time hypothesis and its relevance to our purposes here will be discussed in more detail in Chapter 4. For the best review of it of which I'm aware, see Cooper, E.H., & Pantle, A.J. (1967). The total-time hypothesis in verbal learning. *Psychological Bulletin, 68*, 221-234.

3. Neither concept translates completely satisfactorily from classic learning research to school learning. Forgetting of learning occurs much more quickly and to a much greater

extent in paired-associate learning (because of its obvious lack of meaning or relevance) than in the schooling setting (Semb, G.B., & Ellis, J.A. (1994). Knowledge taught in school: What is remembered? *Review of Educational Research, 64*, 253-286). And, for a more contemporary discussion of facilitating transfer in the classroom, see Pressley, M., Synder, B.L., & Cariglia-Bull, T. (1987). How can good strategy use be taught to children? Evaluation of six alternative approaches. In S.M. Cormier & J.D. Hagman (Eds.). *Transfer of learning: Contemporary research and application* (pp. 121-150). New York: Academic Press; and Brooks, L. W., & Dansereau, D. F. (1987). Transfer of information: An instructional perspective. In S. M. Cormier & J. D. Hagman (Eds.), *Transfer of learning: Contemporary research and applications* (pp. 121-150). New York: Academic Press.

4. Examples of such variables include (a) meaningfulness of the learning task (as just mentioned, meaningful content is hopefully the only type we teach our children and is easier to learn and stays with us longer than things that obviously have no relevance to us) or (b) distributive practice (research subjects usually learned more when tasks were presented in briefer sessions rather than in one long trial). The latter would have more implications for classroom instruction if it weren't for the fact that time was seldom truly controlled in distributive learning experiments, as explained by an early proponent of the total-time hypothesis: "Typically such studies (i.e., those investigating breaking up the learning task into smaller units) provide some rest interval between trials for the spaced group while the massed Ss carry on with the activity. Commonly enough, it is found that the spaced group performs at a higher level than the massed group after the same number of trials. When the spaced group's rests are included, however, it might be found that the total time was far in excess of the apparent advantage in trials, and the massed Ss have learned proportionally more than the spaced (p. 412)." Bugelski, B.R. (1962). Presentation time, total time, and mediation in paired-associate learning. *Journal of Experimental Psychology, 63*, 409-412. Although this may seem rather esoteric, it will ultimately prove important for our purposes here because it basically means that about the only thing we can take away from classic learning theory and apply to classroom learning is the importance of relevant time on task.

5. Meta-analysis is a systematic approach to reaching a conclusion based upon synthesizing previous research studies surrounding a specific topic. It differs from other educational research in the sense that it doesn't involve analyzing data from individual students but instead employs the results from entire studies (or experiments) as data points. Although Gene Glass did not invent the procedure itself, he conducted two extremely influential meta-analyses, one in education (on the learning effects of class size) and one in psychology (on the effects of psychotherapy). He also almost single-handedly introduced this powerful technique to the social and behavioral sciences via the following brief article: Glass, G.V. (1976). Primary, secondary, and meta-analysis of research. *Educational Researcher, 5*, 3-8.

6. Prior to 1979, if educational researchers were polled regarding whether they thought class size was related to learning, the majority would have probably said "no." (Of course, their grandmothers' would have unanimously disagreed.) In that year, however, Gene Glass and his wife (Mary Smith) changed all of that with the publication of their above-mentioned class size meta-analysis, which also included my work in the area. Gene was kind enough to write me a note saying that my studies were among the best conducted in this area, and he even wrote me a letter of support years later when I applied for promotion to full professor at the University of Maryland. The Glass' meta-analysis: Glass, G.V., & Smith, M.L. (1979). Meta-analysis of research on class size and achievement. *Educational Evaluation and Policy Analysis, 1*, 2-16.

7. Benjamin Bloom's research and theory will be discussed in greater detail shortly.

8. Perhaps the best study dealing with teacher-allocated time is found in one of the most important research studies in education, the Beginning Teacher Evaluation Study and

often referred to simply by its acronym: BTES. This study is most exhaustively described in Lieberman, A. & Denham, C. (Eds.). (1980). *Time to Learn. A Review of the Beginning Teacher Evaluation Study.* National Institute of Education, Dept. of Health, Education and Welfare, Washington, DC.

9. The strength of this relationship has been demonstrated repeatedly since Edward Thorndike and his animal studies. It is, in fact, such a well-known and obvious relationship that it hardly needs documentation, and no one in their right mind would prospectively conduct a study whose primary goal was to compare, say, students who were taught mathematics for two hours a day versus students who were taught the same content one hour per day. (The results would be too obvious to merit publication in a peer-reviewed research journal.) There are nuances to the relationship, however, that are worth noting, such as the fact that the amount of time students are actively engaged in the learning process is more powerfully related to learning than is the amount of time schools allocate to teaching a topic. For a review of about a dozen studies showing the importance of active engagement (as opposed to simply being exposed to instruction), see: Smyth, W.J. (1985). A context for the study of time and instruction. In C.W. Fisher & D.C. Berliner (1985). (Eds.), *Perspectives on instructional time.* New York and London: Longman. For other extensive reviews of the relationship between time-on-task and learning, see Borg, W.B. (1980). In A. Lieberman & C. Denham (Eds.). *Time to Learn. A Review of the Beginning Teacher Evaluation Study.* National Institute of Education, Dept. of Health, Education and Welfare, Washington, DC); and Fredrick, W.C., & Walberg, H.J. (1980). Learning as a function of time. *Journal of Educational Research, 73,* 183-193.

10. As demonstrated by an extensive review of recent research studies assessing the effects of homework on academic achievement conducted between 1987 and 2003: Cooper, H., Robinson, J.C., and Patall, E.A. (2006). Does homework improve academic achievement? A synthesis of research, 1987-2003. *Review of Educational Research, 76,* 1-62.

11. Based upon a review of over 90 studies evaluating the effects of summer school: Cooper, H., Charlton, K., Valentine, J.C. & Muhlenbruck, L. (2000). Making the most of summer school: A meta-analytic and narrative review. *Monographs of the Society for Research in Child Development, 65,* 1-118.

12. See Summers, A.A., & Wolfe, B.L. (1975). Which school resources help learning? Efficiency and equity in Philadelphia public schools. *Business Review.* Public Information, Federal Reserve Bank of Philadelphia (also available as a PDF from ERIC – ED102716); and Fredrick, W.C., & Walberg, H.J. (1980). Learning as a function of time. *Journal of Educational Research, 73,* 183-193.

13. Wiley, D.E., and Harnischfeger, A. (1974). Explosion of a myth: Quantity of schooling and exposure to instruction, major educational vehicles. *Educational Researcher, 3,* 7-12. John Carroll had earlier argued that, in the learning of complex skills, such as foreign languages, the relationship between time and learning can be approximately linear (e.g., twice as much instruction or study time yields twice as much learning). Carroll, J.B. (1963). *Programmed self-instruction in Mandarin Chinese: Observations of student progress with an automated audiovisual instructional device.* Wellesley, MA: Language Testing Fund. (ERIC Document Reproduction Service No. ED 002 374.)

14. Coleman, J.S., et al. (1966). *Equality of educational opportunity.* Washington, DC: U.S. Department of Health, Education and Welfare.

15. See for example: Bloom, B.S. (1976). *Human characteristics and school learning.* New York: McGraw Hill; or Bracht, G.H., & Hopkins, K.D. (1972). Stability of educational achievement. In G.H. Bracht, K.D. Hopkins, & J.C. Stanley (Eds.), *Perspectives in educational and psychological measurement.* Englewood Cliffs, NJ: Prentice-Hall.

16. Most commonly, intelligence, verbal ability, and standardized achievement tests, all of which are strongly related to one another.

17. Sirin, S.R. (2005). Socioeconomic status and academic achievement: A meta-analytic review of research. *Review of Educational Research, 75*, 417-453.

18. Based upon an analysis of the National Assessment of Educational Progress as presented in an extremely clear manner in: Thernstrom, A., & Thernstrom, S. (2003). *No excuses: Closing the racial gap in learning.* New York: Simon & Schuster.

19. These relationships extend all the way to dropping out of high school [Coleman, J.S. (1988). Social capital in the creation of human capital. *American Journal of Sociology, 94*, S95-S121] to elementary school achievement: Luster, T., & McAdoo, H.P. (1995). Factors related to the achievement and adjustment of young African American children. *Child Development, 65*, 1080-1094; and Dubow, E.G., & Luster, T. (1990). Adjustment of children born to teenage mothers: The contribution of risk and protective factors. *Journal of Marriage and the Family, 52*, 393-404.

20. Blow, C.M. (2009). No more excuses? *NewYork Times*, January 24, p. A19.

21. Coleman, J.S. (1988). Social capital in the creation of human capital. *American Journal of Sociology, 94*, S95-S121.

22. Kellaghan, T., Sloane, K., Alvarez, B., & Bloom, B.S. (1993). *The home environment and school learning: Promoting parental involvement in the education of children.* San Francisco: Jossey-Bass Publishers.

23. Senechal, M., & LeFevre, J. (2002). Parental involvement in the development of children's reading skill: A five year longitudinal study. *Child Development, 73*, 445-460.

24. In a review of 23 studies, the effects of watching television was relatively small but negative (although the relationship was somewhat stronger for students who watched an inordinate amount). [Williams, P.A., Haertel, E.H., Haertel, G.D., & Walberg, H.J. (1982). The impact of leisure-time television on school learning: A research synthesis. *American Educational Research Journal, 19*, 19-52.] Of course, the type of television watched matters, as illustrated in a longitudinal study of German children, which found the amount of time watching educational programs was positively related to reading achievement, whereas time spent watching noneducational television was negatively related [Ennemoser, M., & Schneider, W. (2007). Relations of television viewing and reading: Findings from a 4-year longitudinal study. *Journal of Educational Psychology, 99*, 349-368]. The effect of video-games on learning has not been researched extensively. One extremely creative recent experiment, however, randomly supplied boys who did not already own game systems with same to measure the effects upon both engagement in learning activities at home and academic performance and found deleterious results on both: Weis, R., & Cerankosky, B.C. (2010). Effects of video-game ownership on young boys' academic and behavioral functioning: a randomized, controlled study. *Psychological Science, 21*, 463-470.

25. Bus, A.G., van Ijzendoorn, M.H., & Pellegrini, A.D. (1995). Joint book reading makes for success in learning to read: A meta-analysis on intergenerational transmission of literacy. *Review of Educational Research, 65*, 1-21.

26. See, for example, Adams, M.J. (1994). *Beginning to read: Thinking and learning about print.* Cambridge, MA: MIT Press. Also, one pair of researchers found that knowledge of letter names was the single best predictor of early reading success in school, and knowledge of letter sounds was second: Bond, G.L., & Dykstra, R. (1967). The cooperative reading program in first-grade reading instruction. *Reading Research Quarterly, 2*, 5-142.

27. For an extensive review on this topic, see: Ehri, L.C., Nunes, S.R., Stahl, S.A., & Willows, D.M. (2001) Systematic phonics instruction helps students learn to read: Evidence from the national reading panel's meta-analysis. *Review of Educational Research, 71*, 393-447. Yet, despite the evidence, for some reason the efficacy of phonics instruction keeps being questioned and its attackers keep being silenced for a time by new evidence, for example, Stuebing, K.K., Barth, A.E., Cirnio, P.T., Francis, D.J., & Fletcher, J.M. (2008). A response to recent re-analyses of the National Reading Panel Report: Effects of

systematic phonics instruction are practically significant. *Journal of Educational Psychology, 100*, 123-134.

28. Kemple, J., Corrin, W., Nelson, E., Salinger, T., Herrmann, S., & Drummond, K. (2008). *The Enhanced Reading Opportunities Study: Early impact and implementation findings* (NCEE 2008-4015). Washington, DC: National Center for Education Evaluation and Regional Assistance, Institute of Education Sciences, U.S. Department of Education.

29. Random assignment involves allowing a computer to decide which students, classrooms, or schools will receive either an experimental intervention or no intervention at all (or more commonly, conventional instruction). Randomization is absolutely essential in conducting research designed to assess the effectiveness of an intervention because it helps to eliminate bias and to ensure that two groups (e.g., experimental vs. control) are initially equivalent with respect to factors such as individual student differences in propensity to learn (which it will be remembered account for up to 60% of learning differences and which we simply don't know how to measure with any degree of accuracy—and hence can't possibly adequately control any other way but via random assignment).

30. One exception to the law's almost total reliance upon standardized testing was a provision to supply tutoring (often by private, unsupervised vendors) for students who met certain criteria. Unfortunately well less than 20% (the exact figure is unknown) of qualified students ever received this support service.

31. One of the few exceptions (as discussed in more detail in Chapter Nine) is a randomized trial comparing New York City students who were selected (via lottery) to attend charter schools offering increased instructional time vs. those who were not. The vast majority of the other attempts at evaluating these administrative, choice, and school restructuring "reforms" employed no randomly assigned control groups, but simply attempted to compare the resulting standardized test scores to those obtained by schools serving students with "similar ethnic and demographic characteristics." I personally consider research such as no better (perhaps worse) than no research at all.

32. Ravitch, D. (2010). *The death and life of the great American school system: How testing and choice are undermining education*. New York: Basic Books.

33. Published as: Cronbach, L.J. (1957). The two disciplines of scientific psychology. *American Psychologist, 12*, 671-684.

34. A "disordinal interaction" is the type of aptitude-by-treatment interaction scenario I just described in which Method A is better for one type of student and worse for the other, whereas the exact opposite is true for the effects of Method B. Bracht, G.H. (1970). Experimental factors related to aptitude-by-treatment interactions. *Review of Educational Research, 40*, 627-645.

35. Aptitude × treatment interactions should not be confused with what are sometimes called child × instruction interactions, in which instruction is individualized based upon student's entering skill levels (i.e., teaching what the child needs to be taught vs. a general curriculum). Personalization of instruction in this manner has been demonstrated to be effective: Connor, C.M., Piasta, S.B., Blasney, S. et al. (2009). Individualizing student instruction precisely: Effects of child × instruction interactions on first graders' literacy development. *Child Development, 80*, 77-100; but what studies such as this also demonstrate is that relevant instruction produces more learning than less relevant instruction. It should also not be confused with analyses that demonstrate that, say, lower IQ students learn more slowly than higher IQ students, as can be found in a study conducted by my wife and I showing that parents of special-education students will supply supplementary instruction at home and that significant learning accrues as a result: Vinograd-Bausell, C.R., Bausell, R.B., Proctor, W., & Chandler, B. (1986). The impact of unsupervised parent tutors upon word recognition skills of special education students. *Journal of Special Education, 20*, 83-90.

36. Cronbach, L.J. (1975). Beyond the two disciplines of scientific psychology. *American Psychologist, 30*, 116-127.

37. Rogosa, D., Floden, R., & Willett, J.B. (1984). Assessing the stability of teacher behavior. *Journal of Educational Psychology, 76,* 1000-1027. One very old review focused on this issue, but only found five poorly controlled studies that assessed the stability of long-term teacher effects upon student achievement. Its author concluded that "the current long-term studies show that one cannot use the residual achievement gain scores (i.e., subtracting beginning of year from end-of year test scores) in one year to predict the gain scores in a successive year with any confidence (p. 661)." Rosenshine, B. (1970). The stability of teacher effects upon student achievement. *Review of Educational Research, 40,* 647-662.

38. Nye, B., Konstantopoulos, S., & Hedges, L.V. (2004). How large are teacher effects? *Educational Evaluation and Policy Analysis, 26,* 237-257.

39. In general, the research is equivocal regarding the relationship between variables such as teacher certification and student achievement: Boyd, D., Goldhaber, D., Lankford, H., & Wyckoff, J. (2007). The effect of certification and preparation of teacher quality. *The Future of Children, 17,* 45-68.

40. One study, for example, concluded that students do seem to learn more when they are taught by knowledgeable teachers, but it also found that teachers in schools more likely to serve black students also tended to be less knowledgeable: Hill, H.C., Rowan, B., & Ball, D.L. (2005). Effects of teachers' mathematical knowledge for teaching on student achievement. *American Educational Research Journal, 42,* 371-406. These inequities have also been found for other teacher-preparation indicators as well.

41. For a more in-depth discussion of the difficulties in controlling for socioeconomic status, see: Jeynes, W.H. (2002). The challenge of controlling for SES in social science and education research. *Educational Psychology Review, 14,* 205-221.

42. Sanders, W.L., Wright, S.P., & Langevin, W.E. (2009). The performance of highly effective teachers in different school environments. In *Performance incentives: Their growing impact on American K-12 education,* M.G. Springer (Ed.), Washington, DC: Brookings Institution Press. The percentages presented in Table 1.1 are based upon the fourth panel of Table 8-6 (p. 183) in this paper (p. 183).

43. Aaronson, D., Barrow, L., & Sanders, W. (2007). Teacher and student achievement in the Chicago Public High Schools. *Journal of Labor Economics, 25,* 95-135. The data discussed related to this article are based upon Table 7 (p. 119).

44. Rothstein, J. (2008). *Student sorting and bias in value added estimation: Selection on observables and unobservables.* Unpublished manuscript, Princeton University.

45. For example, "The range of approximately 50 percentile points in student mathematics achievement in this study is awesome!!!!" (Their exclamation marks, not mine) in: Saunders, W., & Rivers, J. (1996). *Cumulative and residual effects of teachers on future student academic achievement.* Knoxville, TN: University of Tennessee Value-Added Research and Assessment Center. These authors might learn from Watson and Crick (certainly not individuals with a propensity to hide their light under a basket), who began a paper detailing the most heralded biological discovery of the 20th century as follows: "We wish to suggest a structure for the salt of deoxyribose nucleic acid (D.N.A.). This structure has novel features which are of considerable biological interest." (p. 737) Watson, J.D., & Crick, F. (1953). A structure for deoxyribose nucleic acid. *Nature, 171,* 737-738.

46. See Baker, A.P., & Xu, D. (1995). *The measure of education: A review of the Tennessee Value-Added Assessment System.* Nashville, TN: Office of Evaluation Accountability; McCaffrey, D.F., Koretz, D.M., Lockwood, J.R., & Hamilton, L.S. (2004). *Evaluating value-added models for teacher accountability.* Santa Monica, CA: Rand Corporation; or Amrein-Beardsley, A. (2008). Methodological concerns about the education value-added assessment system. *Educational Researcher, 37,* 65-75.

47. Popham, W.J. (1997). The moth and the flame: Student learning as a criterion of instructional competence. In J. Millman (Ed.), *Grading teachers, trading schools: Is student achievement a valid evaluation measure?* Thousand Oaks, CA: Corwin Press.

48. Rosenshine, B.V. (1980). How time is spent in elementary classrooms. In A. Lieberman & C. Denham (Eds.). *Time to learn. A Review of the Beginning Teacher Evaluation Study.* National Institute of Education, Dept. of Health, Education and Welfare, Washington, DC.

49. Fisher, C.W., Berliner, D.C., Filby, N.N., Marliave, R., Cahen, L.S., & Dishaw, M.M. (1980). Teaching behaviours, academic learning time, and student achievement: An overview. In A. Lieberman & C. Denham (Eds.). *Time to learn. A Review of the Beginning Teacher Evaluation Study.* National Institute of Education, Dept. of Health, Education and Welfare, Washington, DC.

50. Wiley, D.E., & Harnischfeger, A. (1974). Explosion of a myth: Quantity of schooling and exposure to instruction, major educational vehicles. *Educational Researcher, 3,* 7-12. Other projections of the amount of time spent on effective instruction in schools are similarly dismal (and usually below 50%) such as Rossmiller, R.A. (1983). Time-on-task: A look at what erodes time for instruction. *NASSP Bulletin, 67,* 45-49; and Burns, R.B. (1984). How time is used in elementary schools: The activity structure of the classroom. In Lorin W. Anderson (Ed.), *Time and school learning: Theory, research, and practice.* New York: St. Martin's Press.

51. Popham, W. J. (1971). Performance tests of teaching proficiency: Rationale, development, and validation. *American Educational Research Journal, 8,* 105-117.

52. Bausell, R.B. (1975). *Teacher training, relevant teacher practice, and the elicitation of student achievement.* Doctoral Dissertation, University of Delaware College of Education.

53. Bausell, R.B., & Moody, W.B. (1973). Are teacher training institutions really necessary? *Phi Delta Kappan, 54,* 298.

Chapter 2: Dueling Theories

1. Stephens, J.M. (1967). *The process of schooling: A psychological examination.* New York: Holt, Rinehart, and Winston.

2. Coleman, J.S., et al. (1966). *Equality of educational opportunity.* Washington, DC: U.S. Department of Health, Education and Welfare.

3. Kemp, L.C.D. (1955). Environmental and other characteristics determining attainment in primary schools. *British Journal of Educational Psychology, 25,* 67-77.

4. Bloom, B.S. (1976). *Human characteristics and school learning.* New York: McGraw Hill.

5. Carroll, J.B.A. (1963). A model of school learning. *Teachers College Record, 64,* 723-733. In one of the most influential (and cited) articles in the history of education, Carroll posited the existence of five variables important for learning, three of them direct functions of time: (1) aptitude (the amount of time a student needs to learn a given task), (2) opportunity to learn (amount of time provided to students by the school), and (3) perseverance (the amount of time a student is willing to spend on learning the unit). The other two variables were quality of instruction and ability to understand instruction. Twenty-five years after the publication of this extremely influential article, Carroll himself noted that the most fundamental difference between his model and Bloom's theory was that he (Carroll) believed that "we should seek mainly to achieve equality of *opportunity* for all students, not necessarily equality of *attainment*. In this respect, the model of school learning differs from Bloom's mastery learning concept, which seems to be focused on achieving equality of attainment" (p. 30). [Carroll, J.B. (1989). The Carroll model: A 25-year retrospective and prospective view. *Educational Researcher, 18,* 26-31.] For the record, I agree with Bloom that 90%–95% of all children are capable of learning whatever the schools are capable of teaching although in truth I'm not sure about the actual percentages here.

6. Remember Popham's (and Bill Moody and my) teacher proficiency studies? None of this work would have been possible without explicitly (and prescriptively) defining

exactly what teachers were required to cover during the course of the experimental interval.

7. At least one set of investigators, in fact, have found that the amount of time needed to learn a topic is a better predictor of standardized achievement test scores than is intelligence tests. [Gettinger, M., & White, M.A. (1979). What is the stronger correlate of school learning? Time to learn or measured intelligence? *Journal of Educational Psychology, 71,* 405-412.] Another pair of researchers found that self-discipline (which can be conceptualized in terms of the amount of time someone is willing to devote to learning) is also a better predictor of achievement than is intelligence. [Duckworth, A.L., & Seligman, M.E.P. (2005). Self-discipline outdoes IQ in predicting academic performance of adolescents. *Psychological Science, 16,* 939-944.]

8. Bloom, B.S. (1974). Time and learning. *American Psychologist, 29,* 682-688.

9. Anderson, L.W. (1976). An empirical investigation of individual differences in time to learn. *Journal of Educational Psychology, 68,* 226-33.

10. This fascinating and seminal study was initially designed to identify generic teacher competencies and evaluate teacher education programs. Fortunately, since we already know how the latter evaluation would have come out (á la Popham and myself), the investigators changed their objective to identifying and describing teacher skills that were related to student learning. Fisher, C.W., Berliner, D.C., Filby, N.N., Marliave, R., Cahen, L.S., & Dishaw, M.M. (1980). Teaching behaviours, academic learning time, and student achievement: An overview. In Lieberman, A., & Denham, C. (Eds.). (1980). *Beginning teacher evaluation study.* National Institute of Education, Dept. of Health, Education and Welfare, Washington, DC. Two authors of this report also edited a book that presents more detail on this study and its findings and may be of interest to anyone who wants to delve a bit more deeply into issues related to instructional time: Fisher, C.W., & Berliner, D.C. (1985). (Eds.), *Perspectives on instructional time.* New York and London: Longman. John Carroll's previously mentioned 25-year retrospective on his model of school learning is also reprinted here.

11. Cooley, W.W., & Leinhardt, G. (1980). The Instructional Dimensions Study. *Educational Evaluation and Policy Analysis, 2,* 7-25.

12. Brophy, J. (1986). Teacher influences on student achievement. *American Psychologist, 41,* 1069-1077.

13. Also, don't forget, everything doesn't fall upon teachers. There is also considerable evidence that individual *student* behaviors, such as paying attention in class, being task-oriented, and so forth are positively related to learning. Obviously, students such as these receive more relevant instructional time than their classroom counterparts receiving exactly the same instruction but who exhibit the opposite behaviors. Examples of studies documenting these relationships are McKinney, J.D., Mason, J., Perkerson, K., & Clifford, M. (1975). Relationship between classroom behavior and academic achievement. *Journal of Educational Psychology, 67,* 198-203; and Cobb, J.A. Relationship of discrete classroom behavior to fourth-grade academic achievement. *Journal of Educational Psychology, 63,* 74-80.

Chapter 3: Dueling Political Perspectives

1. Hernrnstein, R., & Murray, C. (1994). *The bell curve: Intelligence and class structure in American life.* New York: Free Press.

2. Thernstrom, A., & Thernstrom, S. (2003). *No excuses: Closing the racial gap in learning.* New York: Simon & Schuster.

3. Kozol, J. (2005). *The shame of the nation: The restoration of apartheid schooling in America.* New York: Crown.

4. Wade, N. (1976). IQ and heredity: Suspicion of fraud beclouds classic experiment. *Science, 194*, 916-919.
5. Kozol, J. (1967). *Death at an early age.* New York: Houghton Mifflin.
6. Isaacson, W. (2004). *Benjamin Franklin: An American life.* New York: Simon & Schuster.

Chapter 4: The Theory of Relevant Instructional Time

1. In an article entitled "Strong Inference," J. R. Platt threw down the gauntlet for potential theorists by suggesting that they not bother advancing any theory for which they were not prepared to answer the following question: "But sir, what experiment could *dis*prove your hypothesis?" Platt, J.R. (1964). Strong inference. *Science, 146*, 347-353.
2. In a review of the total-time hypothesis, two of Benton Underwood's students provided the following explanation of the hypothesis and their "relevance-like" disclaimer: "When task requirements do not exceed simple rehearsal (*Author's note*: which is simply a way of saying when the learning stimuli is presented in a sensible time frame) and when effective time bears a positive linear relationship to nominal time, a fixed amount of time is necessary to learn a fixed amount of material, regardless of the number of individual trials into which that time is divided.... Specification of the relationship between nominal and effective study time in a given situation may prove to be a powerful explanatory concept in many areas of verbal learning" (p. 232). Cooper, E.H., & Pantle, A.J. (1967). The total-time hypothesis in verbal learning. *Psychological Bulletin, 68*, 221-234.

   Although written in a style that only a verbal learning researcher could love, this is an extremely prescient statement from a schooling perspective because it acknowledges the important distinction between the amount of time allocated for instruction and the amount of time that relevant instruction is actually delivered.
3. We know this from the *Beginning Teacher Evaluation Study*.
4. We know this from the work of Coleman, Bloom, and scores of other researchers.
5. And also based upon the work of Coleman, Bloom, and hundreds of studies documenting the relatedness of test score performance over time.
6. For an excellent treatment of the sheer irrelevance of much of classroom time to learning (via activities such as candy sales and organized athletic activities), see:

   Kralovec, E. (2003). *Schools that do too much: Wasting time and money in schools and what we can all do about it.* Boston: Beacon Press. Also recall the finding from the *Beginning Teacher Evaluation Study,* in which teachers who emphasized academic goals over affective ones tended to produce more learning.
7. Other authors prefer to define instructional time in different ways, which impacts its relevance. This is illustrated by a review article on issues and theories related to instructional time defining nine different types of school-related time: Berliner, D.C. (1990). What's all the fuss about instructional time? In M. Ben-Leretz & R. Bromme (Eds.). *The Nature of time in schools: Theoretical concepts, practitioner perceptions.* New York: Teachers College Press. Most are subsumed under my single relevant instructional time construct, but I would probably be remiss if I didn't mention these. They are:
   1. *Allocated time*, time during which someone provides the student with instruction,
   2. *Engaged time*, time during which student appears to be paying attention,
   3. *Time-on-task*, engaged time on the particular kinds of tasks that is wanted,
   4. *Academic learning time*, part of the allocated time in a subject-matter area in which a student is engaged *successfully* in the activities (I personally see this as a learning issue rather than a type of instructional time),
   5. *Transition time*, noninstructional time before and after some instructional activity,
   6. *Waiting time*, time that students must wait for instructional help or to receive an assignment,

7. *Aptitude*, amount of time that a student needs, under optimal instructional conditions, to reach some criterion of learning (also not conceptualized as time per se in our theory),

8. *Perseverance*, the amount of time a student is willing to spend on learning a task or unit of instruction (also called *motivation*, but subsumed under relevant instructional time in my theory), and

9. *Pace*, the amount of content covered during some time period (relevance assumes an appropriate pace).

8. Benjamin Bloom reviewed some of this literature in his book (*Human Characteristics and School Learning*). Also, as mentioned earlier, indicators of self-discipline (which is a characteristic of children of higher socioeconomic status) have been found to be better predictors of academic achievement than are intelligence tests (Duckworth, A.L., & Seligman, M.E.P. (2005). Self-discipline outdoes IQ in predicting academic performance of adolescents. *Psychological Science, 16*, 939-944).

9. If I were forced to choose the two most important studies in education, one of them would be this one as described in: Hart, B., & Risley, T.R. (1995). *Meaningful differences in the everyday experience of young American children.* Baltimore, MD: Paul H. Brookes.

10. For example: Heath, S.B. (1983). *Ways with words.* Cambridge, England: Cambridge University Press, who found that middle-class parents (as opposed to working-class parents and especially non–middle-class African American parents) more often question their children, engage them in extensive discussion, and in general teach the vocabulary, grammar, and thought processes necessary to succeed in school. A more recent perspective on these issues is provided by the sociologist, Annette Lareau (Lareau, A. (2003). *Unequal childhoods: Class race, and family life.* Berkeley: University of California Press.

11. Many of these behaviors are conceptualized as home process variables (for a more thorough discussion, see Kellaghan, T., Sloane, K., Alvarez, B., & Bloom, B.S. (1993). *The home environment and school learning: Promoting parental involvement in the education of children.* San Francisco: Jossey-Bass Publishers. There is a great deal of research detailing the salutary effects of having reading materials in the home. See, for example, Senechal, M., & LeFevre, J. (2002). Parental involvement in the development of children's reading skill: A five year longitudinal study. *Child Development, 73*, 445-460. This is so strongly related to socioeconomic status (SES) that one investigator demonstrated that even *schools* serving high-SES children displayed twice as many books and magazines as schools serving lower-SES children: Duke, N.K. (2000). For the rich it's richer: Print experiences and environments offered to children in very low- and very high-socioeconomic status first-grade classrooms. *American Educational Research Journal, 37*, 441-478. One study even found that this phenomenon extends to entire neighborhoods, with lower-SES communities having practically no book stores or even places to sit and read: Neuman, S.B., Celano, D. (2001). Access to print in low-income and middle-income communities: An ecological study of four neighborhoods. *Reading Research Quarterly, 36*, 8-26. And, finally, with respect to teaching children academic skills prior to attending school, an examination of six longitudinal data sets indicated that the strongest predictors of later achievement were *school-entry* math, reading, and attention skills: Duncan, G.J., Claessens, A., Huston A.C., et al. (2007). School readiness and later achievement. *Developmental Psychology, 43*, 1428-1446.

Chapter 5: The Science of What Could Be

1. Moody, W.B., Bausell, R.B., & Crouse, J.H. (1971). The probability of probability transfer. *Psychonomic Science, 22*, 107-108.

2. Moody, W.B., Abell, R., & Bausell, R.B. (1971). The effect of activity-oriented instruction upon original learning, transfer, and retention. *Journal of Research in Mathematics Education, 2*, 207-212.

3. In 1955, Rudolf Flesch wrote a best-seller entitled *Why Johnny Can't Read* (New York: Harper & Row), which was much reviled by education professors but instrumental in ensuring the reintroduction of phonics into the elementary school curriculum.

4. In this final experiment, the only children allowed to participate were those who could not read the four transfer words written in standard English. Jenkins, J.R., Bausell, R.B., & Jenkins, L.M. (1972). Comparisons of letter name and letter sound training as transfer variables. *American Educational Research Journal, 9*, 75-86.

5. Of course, everyone and their grandmother knew that tutoring was effective, and a decade of so later Benjamin Bloom (based upon laboratory work by his doctoral students) listed it as the most powerful educational intervention known: Bloom, B.S. (1984). The 2 sigma problem: The search for methods of group instruction as effective as one-to-one tutoring. *Educational Researcher, 13*, 4-16. More recently a meta-analysis found that parental tutoring was the most effective form of parental involvement yet identified: Senechal, M., and Young, L. (2008). The effect of family literacy interventions on children's acquisition of reading from kindergarten to grade 3: A meta-analytic review. *Review of Educational Research, 78*, 880-907. Many other forms of tutoring have been shown to be effective as well, including remedial tutoring for children at risk for reading failure [Elbaum, B., Vaughn, S., Hughes, M.T., & Moody, S.W. (2000). How effective are one-to-one tutoring programs in reading for elementary students at risk for reading failure? *Journal of Educational Psychology, 92*, 605-619] and peer and cross-age tutoring of African American and other minority students in math [Robinson, D. R., Schofield, J.W., & Steers-Wentzell, K.L. (2005). Peer and cross-age tutoring in math: Outcomes and their design implications. *Educational Psychology Review, 17*, 327-362].

6. Bausell, R.B., Moody, W.B., & Walzl, R.N. (1972). A factorial study of tutoring versus classroom instruction. *American Education Research Journal, 9*, 591-597.

7. The design of the experiment was somewhat complicated given the number of variables being tested simultaneously (tutoring vs. classroom instruction; high vs. medium vs. low ability levels; trained vs. untrained teachers) and the fact that we had to control for both potential student and teacher differences very carefully as follows:

   • Student ability was controlled by obtaining standardized mathematics test scores and then dividing each classroom into high-, medium-, and low-ability groups based upon those scores. One student from each ability level was then randomly chosen and paired with the classmate who had obtained the most similar (often identical) test score. This resulted in a block of six students: two of whom were extremely closely matched within each of the three ability levels. Next, one student from each matched pair was then randomly assigned to be tutored, while the other was designated to be taught in a classroom setting. (Statistically this ensured that any difference between tutored and classroom-taught students wouldn't be a function of one group having more mathematically gifted students in it than the other.) At the same time, this procedure provided a mechanism by which high-, medium-, and low-ability students' responses to tutoring could be assessed (i.e., the aptitude-by-treatment interaction).

   • Potential "teacher" differences were controlled by requiring each undergraduate to teach the experimental curriculum *four* times: once to an entire classroom (in which the three high-, medium-, and low-ability students randomly assigned to receive classroom instruction were embedded) and three times in a tutorial setting (once for each of the three ability levels). Naturally, the tutored students were excused from the classroom instruction. In all, there were 20 classrooms and 60 tutorial sessions.

8. Actually, today's classroom instruction isn't the most inefficient method ever used. Before the Civil War, a common type of classroom instruction found in cities involved massing together as many as 200 pupils of different ages and academic attainment under the direction of a "master" who was responsible (sometimes along with one or two assistant teachers) for hearing children recite their lessons. (Tyack, D., & Cuban, L. (1995) *Tinkering toward Utopia: A century of public school reform.* Cambridge, MA: Harvard University Press.)

9. Moody, W.B., & Bausell, R.B. The effect of relevant teaching practice on the elicitation of student achievement. The 1973 meeting of the American Educational Research Association at New Orleans.

10. Representing the "science of what is," because the two studies of which I am aware that came up with this finding were not experimental in nature: Hanushek, E.A., Kain, J.F., O'Brien, D.M., & Rivkin, S.G. (2005). *The market for teacher quality*. (Working paper No. 114630. Cambridge, MA: National Bureau of Economic Research - http://www.nber.org/papers/w11154); and Jacob, B.A., & Lefgren, L. (2005). Principals as agents: Subjective performance measurement in education (Working paper No. 114630. Cambridge, MA: National Bureau of Economic Research – http://www.nber.org/papers/w114630).

11. Moody, W.B., Bausell, R.B., & Jenkins, J.R. (1973). The effect of class size on the learning of mathematics: A parametric study with fourth grade students. *Journal of Research in Mathematics Education, 4,* 170-176.

12. Nye, B., Hedges, L.V., & Konstantopoulos, S. (2000). The effects of small classes on academic achievement: The results of the Tennessee class size experiment. *American Educational Research Journal, 37,* 123-151. Interestingly, this study also showed that small class sizes were equally effective for all types of students (i.e., no aptitude-by-treatment interactions). For other descriptions of this important study, see: Mosteller, F. (1995). The Tennessee study of class size in the early school grades. *The Future of Children, 5,* 113-127; or Finn J. & Achilles, C. (1999). Tennessee' class size study: Findings, implications, misconceptions. *Educational Evaluation and Policy Analysis, 21,* 97-109.

13. Persisted, in fact, to the extent that one follow-up study showed that lower socioeconomic students who had at least three years in smaller classes in their early grades were actually more likely to graduate from high school: Finn, J.D., & Gerber, S.B., & Boyd-Zaharias, J. (2005). Small classes in the early grades, academic achievement, and graduating from high school. *Journal of Educational Psychology, 97,* 214- 223.

14. For a general critique of the problems associated with subgroup analyses, see Wang, R., Lagakos, S.W., Ware, J.H., et al. (2007). Statistics in medicine – reporting of subgroup analyses in clinical trials. *New England Journal of Medicine, 357,* 2189-2194. For a specific example of the methodological artifacts often attending the study of aptitude-by-treatment interactions per se, see Gufstafsson, J-E. (1978). A note on class effects in aptitude × treatment interactions. *Journal of Educational Psychology, 70,* 142-146.

15. Campuzano, L., Dynarski, M., Agodini, R., & Rall, K. (2009). *Effectiveness of reading and mathematics software products: Findings from two student cohorts* (NCEE 2009-4041). Washington, DC: National Center for Education Evaluation and Regional Assistance, Institute of Education Sciences, U.S. Department of Education. Earlier research had generally found that more competently implemented computer-based teaching was both effective and efficient. In one review of 51 studies evaluating computer-based teaching, the investigators concluded that "the computer reduced substantially the amount of time that students needed for learning." [Kulik, J.A., Bangert, R.L., & Williams, G.W. (1983). Effects of computer-based teaching on secondary school students. *Journal of Educational Psychology, 75,* 19-26, p. 19.]

16. *Education Week*, April 11, 2007, p. 18

Chapter 6: The Theoretical Importance of Tutoring and the Learning Laboratory

1. One of the major conclusions emanating from the Beginning Teacher Evaluation Study discussed in Chapter 2 was: "The percentage of instructional time during which the student received feedback was positively related to student engagement rate and to achievement." Feedback can take many forms, of course. When it involves frequent

quizzes, it has been shown that the simple process of answering questions on materials just studied is superior to reviewing the materials for a comparable amount of time: Nungester, R.J., & Duchastel, P.C. Testing versus review: Effects on retention. *Journal of Educational Psychology, 74*, 18-22. (I'm not sure whether or not this effect was ever replicated.)

2. The use of the term *mastery* doesn't imply that the student will correctly answer 100% of every question contained on every assessment quiz. Both Carroll and Bloom suggested that a more relaxed criterion would be more efficient. One of Bloom's former doctoral students provided evidence that, under certain circumstances, 75% was a reasonable criterion [Block, J.H. (1972). Student learning and the setting of mastery performance standards. *Educational Horizons, 50*, 183-191]. It has also been suggested that simply employing two learning trials for a task would ultimately be more efficient (i.e., with respect to instructional time) than would unlimited passes through a set of learning materials [Miller, J.W., & Ellsworth, R. (1979). Mastery learning: The effects of time constraints and unit mastery requirements. *Educational Research Quarterly, 4*, 40-48]. Most likely, there are no hard and fast rules for the optimal mastery criterion for all subject matters or all students. However, if computerized instruction were a viable option (or supplementary option), we wouldn't be constrained to a fixed number of instructional passes.

3. The testing process itself has been repeatedly shown to facilitate both learning and retention. Glover, J.A. (1989). The "testing" phenomenon: Not gone but nearly forgotten. *Journal of Educational Psychology, 81*, 392-399.

4. In a classroom setting, teachers by necessity must estimate how much time it will take for their classes to learn a given lesson, but obviously this varies from student to student. In a creative study involving fourth- and fifth-graders, the time needed to master a reading task was estimated for each student, then two scenarios were evaluated: one in which students were given less time than it was estimated they needed and one in which the students themselves were allowed to study the materials as long as they wished before being testing on them. Obviously, learning suffered under the first scenario (since it was already known that the students weren't given enough time). However, those students who chose how much to study (the second scenario), but studied less than the researchers had estimated they required, also learned less. Obvious results, perhaps, but indicative of the importance of instructional time as a determinant of learning and of the fact that the learning of some children in the classroom model will inevitably suffer because they can't be provided all the instruction they need. Gettinger, M. (1985). Time allocated and time spent relative to time needed for learning as determinants of achievement. *Journal of Educational Psychology, 77*, 3-11.

5. Finn, J.D., Pannozzo, G.M., & Achilles, C.M. (2003). The "Why's" of class size: Student behavior in small classes. *Review of Educational Research, 73*, 321-368.

6. See: Rogoff, B. (2003). *The cultural nature of human development.* New York: Oxford University Press. For a relatively accessible treatment of Vygotsky's thought, see: Vygotsky, L. (1986). *Thought and language* (Translated and edited by A. Kozulin). Cambridge, MA: MIT Press.

7. This isn't to suggest that the learning laboratory model will help everyone. Some children won't take advantage of it; some can't for one reason or another. For those who won't, the primary onus will be upon their families to partner with the schools to provide the proper incentives and consequences. For the minority who *can't*, the only more effective intervention we currently have at our disposal is intensive human tutoring so, unless we can somehow find the will or resources to supply tutoring in sufficient quantities to help such children, we'll be no worse off by adopting a laboratory model of instruction. Small consolation, certainly, for these children and their families, but at least they will constitute a much smaller minority than their present failure-to-thrive classroom counterparts.

8. Bloom, B.S. (1984). The 2 sigma problem: The search for methods of group instruction as effective as one-to-one tutoring. *Educational Researcher, 13*, 4-16.

9. If tutoring produces two standard deviations more learning than regular classroom instruction; one way to interpret this is that if two comparable groups of students were compared on the two methods, 98% of the tutored students would perform better on a learning test than the average score obtained by their conventionally instructed counterparts [Bausell, R.B., & Li, Y.F. (2002). *Power analysis for experimental research: A practical guide for the biological, medical, and social sciences*. Cambridge UK: Cambridge University Press]. My research did not produce an effect size this dramatic, but, admittedly, I was contrasting tutoring to an optimal version of classroom instruction (i.e., every moment of classroom instruction was utilized, there were no classroom distractions, instructional objectives were employed, and the test measured only what was taught in that classroom).

10. There are also free instructional programs available on the internet such as Starfall.com, which while not as comprehensive as Headsprout's reading program is still quite impressive in its own right.

Chapter 7: Demystifying the Curriculum

1. Mager, R.F. (1962). *Preparing instructional objectives*. Atlanta, GA: Center for Effective Performance.

2. It is always a good idea to explain to students why they are studying something. There is even some evidence that such explanations can result in increased compliance and learning: Jang, H. (2008). Supporting students' motivation, engagement, and learning during an uninteresting activity. *Journal of Educational Psychology, 100*, 798-811.

3. Perhaps the easiest way to use this resource can be found on the website for a company called Smart: http://education.smarttech.com/ste/en-US/Ed+Resource/Lesson+activities/Notebook+activities/Standards+Search+US.htm

    Another company (McRel) provides useful distillations of standards and benchmarks for various subject matter areas, as well as sequential lists (i.e., which standards are taught first and last): http://www.mcrel.org/topics/products/187/

4. Bloom, B.S. (Ed.), Engelhart, M.D., Furst, E.J., Hill, W.H., & Krathwohl, D.R. (1956). *The taxonomy of educational objectives, the classification of educational goals, Handbook I: Cognitive domain*. New York: David McKay.

5. Anderson, L.W., Krathwohl, D.R., Airasian, P.W., Cruikshank, K.A., Mayer, R.E., Pintrich, P.R., Raths, J., & Wittrock, M.C. (2001). *A taxonomy for learning, teaching, and assessing. A revision of Bloom's taxonomy of educational objectives*. New York: Longman.

6. For anyone interested, this is defined as "knowledge of cognition in general as well as awareness and knowledge of one's own cognition." If the authors truly value this knowledge dimension and understand how it applies to school learning, I apologize for my limitations, because overall their revision of the original taxonomy is a truly impressive and useful undertaking.

7. This was illustrated in a creative experiment a number of years ago using middle school students in which the time needed to learn content assessed at these three levels (recognition of facts, understanding, and application) increased linearly in that order: Lyon, M.A., & Gettinger, M. (1985). Differences in student performance on knowledge, comprehension, and application tasks: Implications for school learning. *Journal of Educational Psychology, 77*, 12-19.

8. Bausell, R.B., & Moody, W.B. (1974). Learning through doing in teacher education: A proposal. *The Arithmetic Teacher, 21*, 436-438.

9. Christensen, C.W., Horn, M.B., & Johnson, D.W. (2008). *Disrupting class: How disruptive innovation will change the way the world learns*. New York: McGraw Hill.

10. If what we teach at one level is a constituent part of a more complex topic, then transfer will most likely occur if what was originally taught hasn't been forgotten. And, even if it has, classic learning research tell us that once-learned (but forgotten) content is relearned with less instructional time the second time around.

11. How likely, for example, is it that any gifted musicians actually developed their talent (or discovered their interest) in the types of musical experiences provided in the public schools?

Chapter 8: Using Tests Designed to Assess School-based Learning

1. Politicians are especially desperate believers in testing because, unlike professional educators, they don't have the luxury of adopting Stephens' "prescription for relaxation," and they see testing as the only way to hold educators responsible for improving learning. It's also an excellent strategy for delaying any substantive action, based upon the knowledge that the public's attention span is very, very brief. Unfortunately, the few conscientious politicians who would like to do something have little understanding of what current tests actually can and cannot achieve. Barach Obama, for example, forcefully declared in his 2008 campaign: "I will lead a new area of accountability in education. But I don't just want to hold teachers accountable.... I want you to hold me accountable." Unfortunately "accountability" means nothing if you have no way to assess school learning (which we currently don't) or you have no notion regarding how to improve it (a deficit which, of course, this book is designed to eliminate). So, with no way to assess learning or any knowledge regarding how to improve it, how can either teachers or presidents be held accountable?

2. Among these very disparate books are Kamin, L.J. (1974). *The science and politics of I.Q.* Potomac, MD: Lawrence Erlbaum Associates; and Gould, S.J. (1981). *The mismeasure of man.* New York: W.W. Norton. (Stephen Gould's book is especially entertaining and readable.) The edited book by Jacoby and Glauberman [Jacoby, R., & Glauberman, N. (Eds.). (1995). *The bell curve debate: History, documents, opinions.* New York: Times Books] is a voluminous response to Hernrnstein and Murray's book discussed in Chapter 3, containing 78 articles, most of which are critical of their deification of IQ, but it also contains some interesting perspectives on testing in general. Jim Popham's common-sense description of the failings of achievement tests (remember he was initially a proponent of tests based upon instructional objectives) is also quite informative and very readable: Popham, W.J. (2001). *The truth about testing: An educator's call to action.* Alexandria, VA: Association for Supervision and Curriculum Development.

3. There have been serious attempts to develop intelligence tests based upon the existence of multiple intelligence, most notably the work of Howard Gardner, who argues that there are at least eight largely independent genre: Gardner, H. (1983). *Frames of mind: The theory of multiple intelligences.* New York: Basic Books.

4. As one intelligence testing expert states: "The main use of intelligence tests has always been and continues to be, prediction of school achievement, whether measured in terms of grades or z scores on standardized tests" (p. 135). [Sternberg, R.J. (1992). Ability tests, measurements, and markets. *Journal of Educational Psychology, 84,* 134-140.] Of course, my perspective on this is, why bother to spend resources on predicting who will and will not succeed in school? Instead, let's just design an optimal learning environment, give everyone unlimited (in terms of instructional time) access to it, and then we'll see who succeeds and who does not with 100% accuracy.

5. A 1911 quote attributed to Binet in Stephen Jay Gould's *The mismeasure of man* (p. 145).

6. There are many forms of validity, but this particular genre is called *concurrent* or *criterion-related validity* and is assessed by a simple correlation coefficient. It, like reliability,

takes the form of an index that ranges between 0 and 1.0, since cognitive tests never bear negative relationships to one another.

7. There are many types of reliability (or consistency) indices. One is referred to as *Cronbach's alpha* (yes, the same Cronbach who sent us all chasing after nonexistent aptitude-by-treatment interactions), which allows the test to be administered only once and is computed on the basis of how well the items correlate with one another. Another approach is called *alternate forms reliability* and is calculated by administering the equivalent forms (i.e., possessing different items designed to measure the same attribute) of the same test. Bausell, R.B. (1986). *A practical guide to conducting empirical research.* New York: Harper and Row.

8. No one knows how many, but by 1940, at least 40 different intelligence tests were on the market. Lawson, D.E. (1992). Need for safeguarding the field of intelligence testing. *Journal of Educational Psychology, 84,* 131-133.

9. Jensen, A.R. (1972). *Genetics and education.* London: Methuen.

10. Lemann, N. (2000). *The big test: The secret history of the American meritocracy.* New York: Farrar, Straus, and Giroux.

11. Brigham, C.C. (1923). *A study of American intelligence.* Princeton, NJ: Princeton University Press.

12. Crouse, J., & Trusheim, D. (1988). *The case against the SAT.* Chicago: University of Chicago Press.

13. Flynn, J.R. (2007). *What is intelligence? Beyond the Flynn effect.* New York: Cambridge University Press.

14. The book, *Intelligence and How to Get It*, should be required reading in schools of education and psychometric programs. It is the perfect antidote for anyone exposed to the Hernstein and Murray "school" of intelligence test reification discussed in Chapter 3, and it gives a balanced picture of some of the methodological difficulties in doing research on intelligence in the first place. It also introduces a line of research that I am ashamed to admit I was unfamiliar with, which involves contrasting the effect upon children's IQ (generally, lower socioeconomic status children) of being adopted by a middle- or upper-middle-class family, as compared to siblings left behind in the family of origin (which translates to an 18-point advantage for upper-middle- versus lower-class upbringing). Nisbett, R.E. (2009). *Intelligence and how to get it: Why schools and cultures count.* New York: W.W. Norton.

15. Hill, C.J., Bloom, H.S., Black, A.R., & Lipsey, M.W. (2008). Empirical benchmarks for interpreting effect sizes in research. *Child Development Perspectives, 2,* 172-177. A slightly more expanded version (with the same authors and the same publication date) of these analyses is available from MDRC entitled *Performance Trajectories and Performance Gaps as Achievement Effect-Size Benchmarks for Educational Interventions.*

16. Effect sizes are themselves just another algebraic method of transforming test scores (or more properly, differences between averages of test scores). A more statistically correct way of interpreting the grade-to-grade changes represented in Figure 8.1 would be that the effect size of 1.14 representing Grade 1 learning can be interpreted as a situation in which 87% of the students who took the Grade 1 tests in May scoring higher than the *average* score obtained by the students who took the same tests in May of kindergarten (if all of the statistical conditions were perfect). Similarly, the effect size for Grade 4 indicates that only 70% of the students who took the tests in May of 4th grade scored above the average obtained on the same tests by students just finishing the 3rd grade. And for Grade 12 there was barely any measurable difference at all in the percentages of students who scored above the mean (50%) between Grade 11 and 12. In other words, although much beloved by educational researchers, effect sizes are simply another way of rank ordering scores.

17. The trouble with all research involving test score data bases is that there are so many uncontrolled factors that there are always alternative explanations for any findings.

Some of these include the cumulative nature of knowledge, teachers' increasing reliance upon reviewing previously taught content, redundancies in the curriculum, the cumulative effects of students' home learning environments, and so on. Regardless of the true explanation, however, these data indicate that something is seriously wrong either with our obsolete system of instruction, our obsolete testing system, or *both*.

18. Burkham, D.T., Ready, D.D., Lee, V.E., & LoGerfo, L.F. (2004). Social class differences in summer learning between kindergarten and first grade: Model specification and estimation, *Sociology of Education, 77*, 1-31.

19. Alexander, K.L., Entwisle, D.R., & Olson, L.S. (2007). Lasting consequences of the summer learning gap. *American Sociological Review, 72*, 167-180. This is an important finding, and would have been discovered a great deal sooner if we used tests more sensibly. Obviously, tests to assess school learning should be administered everywhere in both September and May: How else can tests ever be used to inform instruction? Earlier support for this finding came from a comparison of extended-year programs (210 days) to traditional programs (180 days), in which it was found that the superiority for the former occurred as a function of the additional learning accruing after the end of the 180 days and carried over to the next year. Frazier, J.A., & Morrison, F.J. (1998). The influence of extended-year schooling on growth of achievement and perceived competence in early elementary school. *Child Development, 69*, 495-517. At about the same time as this latter study, a different set of researchers had illustrated that approximately half of the ethnic gap in test scores observable by the 12th grade were present at the beginning of the first grade [Phillip, M., Crouse, J., & Ralph, J. (1998). Does the black-white test score gap widen after children enter school?" In *The Black-White Test Score Gap* (C. Jenks & M. Phillips, Eds.) Washington, DC: Brookings Institute.] A later study also showed that the largest difference in summer learning occurs between the lowest and highest socioeconomic classes: Burkham, D.T., Ready, D.D., Lee, V.E., & LoGerfo, L.F. (2004). Social-class differences in summer learning between kindergarten and first grade: Model specification and estimation. *Sociology of Education, 77*, 1-31.

20. Bracey, G.W. (2004). *Setting the record straight: Responses to misconceptions about public education in the U.S.* Portsmouth, NH: Heinemann.

21. This ideal, while never actually realized, has its own term in the testing lexicon: "formative assessment." In an interview in the September 17 *Education Week* (Vol. 28, No. 4), an ETS spokesperson defended his company's practice of labeling anything it pleased as formative assessment (á la the industry's practice of naming a test anything it pleases á la Bogus Testing Principle #1: *The items which make up a test are of secondary importance to the attribute being measured*) as witnessed by the following quote: "It has become the standard,' he said of the testing industry's practice of labeling some assessment products as 'formative.' I'm not sure if it's good or bad—it's just what the market is looking for." In my opinion, what this has become the standard for is ETS' arrogance and disingenuousness: an organization which I've increasingly become convinced is a source of actual evil in education.

Chapter 9: 11 Strategies for Increasing School Learning

1. Graue, M.E., Weinstein, T., & Walberg, H. J. (1983). School-based home instruction and learning: A quantitative synthesis. *Journal of Educational Research, 76*, 351-360.

2. Barnett, W.S., Epstein, D.J., Friedman, A.H., et al. (2008). The state of preschool 2008. The National Institute for Early Education Research. Rutgers Graduate School of Education.

3. Gromley, W.T., Gayer, T., Phillips, D., & Dawson, B. (2005). The effects of universal pre-K on cognitive development. *Developmental Psychology, 41*, 872-884.

4. Based upon 989 low-income children from the Chicago Longitudinal study. Graue, E. Clements, M.A., Reynolds, A.J., & Niles, M.D. (2004). More than teacher directed or child

initiated: Preschool curriculum type, parental involvement, and children's outcomes in the child-parent centers. *Education Policy Analysis Archives, 12,* 1-36.

5. Beckers, P.M. (1989). *Effects of kindergarten scheduling: A summary of research.* Arlington, VA: Educational Research Service.

6. National Commission on Excellence in Education. (1983). *A nation at risk: The imperative for educational reform.* Washington, DC: U.S. Government Printing Office.

7. Kralovec, E. (2003). *Schools that do too much: Wasting time and money in schools and what we can all do about it.* Boston: Beacon Press. However, as would be expected given the time-on-task hypothesis, homework does result in increased learning. See, for example, Epstein, J.L., & McPartland, J.M. (1976). The concept and measurement of the quality of school life. *American Educational Research Journal, 13,* 15-30; or Wolfe, R.M. (1979). Achievement in the United States. In H.J. Walberg (Ed.), *Educational environments and effects: Evaluation, policy, and productivity.* Berkeley, CA: McCutchan.

8. Etta Kralovec also makes a strong case that all competitive sports should be entirely removed from school sponsorship, citing the European model in which sports programs tend to be part of elaborate club systems that operate at the community level. See also: Snyder, E., & Spreitzer, E. (1983). *Social aspects of sports.* New Jersey: Prentice-Hall.

9. For example, *A Nation at Risk,* cited above. Two other excellent reports are National Education Commission on Time and Learning. (1994; reprinted 2005). *Prisoners of time.* Denver, CO: Education Commission of the States; and Silva, E. (2007). *On the clock: Rethinking the way schools use time.* Washington DC: Education Sector Reports. (The latter provides an interesting history of the issue, including the fact that, in 1840, several city school systems were open for over 250 days per year.)

10. The Japanese also seem to be firm believers in the importance of instructional time in other arenas as well. As reported in the section "Lessons from Abroad" in the above mentioned *Prisoners of Time,* 30% of Japanese students in Tokyo and 15% nationwide attend *jukus,* which are private tutorial services that enrich instruction, provide remedial help, and prepare students for university examinations (http://www.ed.gove/pubs/PrisonersOfTime/Lessons.html). Increasingly, American families are also engaging tutors to supplement instruction at every level of schooling from first grade to graduate school, making tutoring a multibillion dollar industry.

11. Dr. Sarah Huyvaert, a former elementary school teacher and presently a professor at Eastern Michigan University, reports that there are over 60 different scheduling approaches to year-round schooling (although most are adaptations of five basic plans). Her book is definitely recommended for anyone interested in exploring both the relationship between time and learning, and methods of increasing instructional time. Huyvaert, S.H. (1998). *Time is of the essence: Learning in schools.* Boston: Allyn and Bacon.

12. Fredrick, W.C., & Walberg, H.J. (1980). Learning as a function of time. *Journal of Educational Research, 73,* 183-193.

13. Teaching mathematical problem-solving skill (which is a form of transfer) may be an exception here since supplying children with a worked example of a problem seems to transfers to solving new problems [Cooper, G., & Sweller, J. (1987). Effects of schema acquisition and rule automation on mathematical problem-solving transfer. *Journal of Educational Psychology, 79,* 347-362]. Teaching students to apply schemas (which includes grouping problems that require similar solutions into categories) also tends to enhance transfer [Fuchs, L.S., Fuchs, D., Prentice, K., Hamlett, C.L., Finelli, R., & Courey, S.J. (2004). Enhancing mathematical problem solving among third-grade students with schema-based instruction. *Journal of Educational Psychology, 96,* 635-647]. There is also some evidence that teaching certain subjects transfers to learning others, such as from reading to spelling (and vice versa): Conrad, N. (2008). From reading to spelling and spelling reading: Transfer goes both ways. *Journal of Educational Psychology, 100,* 869-878.

14. As a piece of educational trivia, one uncontrolled study compared students who had previously studied Latin with those who had previously studied French to see which group did better when first exposed to Spanish. Those who had studied French did better, which, if the study had been better controlled, would have been evidence of a type of transfer.

15. Although employing college students, one study did show that providing a rationale for working on an uninteresting task resulted in more engagement and learning than did providing no such rationale. Jang, H. (2008). Supporting students' motivation, engagement, and learning during an uninteresting activity. *Journal of Educational Psychology, 100*, 798-811.

16. Bausell, R.B., Moody, W.B., & Crouse, R. (1975). The effect of teaching upon teacher learning. *Journal of Research in Mathematics Education, 6*, 69-75. This study was later replicated, producing the same basic conclusions: Bargh, J.A., & Schul, Y. (1980). On the cognitive benefits of teaching. *Journal of Educational Psychology, 72*, 593-604. There also has been more recent work on reciprocal peer tutoring, but the evidence of tutor learning as a result thereof is, in my opinion, somewhat equivocal because this line of research is not nearly as carefully controlled as the two studies just cited. Roscoe, R.D., & Chi, M.T.H. (2007). Understanding tutor learning: Knowledge-building and knowledge-telling in peer tutors' explanation and questions. *Review of Educational Research, 77*, 34-574. The best evidence suggests that these effects are quite modest, and the best guess is that even if children do learn by tutoring others, this is probably not a particularly efficient use of their (i.e., the tutors') time in the sense that they would learn more if they were provided an equal amount of direct instruction. (That is, an amount equal to the delivered tutoring and the preparation for this tutoring.)

17. Barros, R.M., Silver, E.J., & Stein, R.E.K. (2009). School recess and group classroom behavior. *Pediatrics, 123*, 431-436. Incredibly, this study simply compared schools that offered recess with those that did not, without taking into consideration that more suburban schools allow recess than do inner-city ones. This is typical of the abysmal quality of the research that often receives wide press coverage.

Chapter 10: Toward a Real Science of Education

1. An excellent example of both a high-quality study included in this database, as well as one in which classroom time was not controlled, is a trial in which 34 high schools were randomly assigned to either receive 225 additional minutes per week of literacy instruction (on top of the regular ninth-grade language arts curricula) or not to receive it. Embedded within this design was a comparison of two different instructional methods (both of which received the 225 additional minutes/week of instruction). The results were quite predictable: No difference between the two different instructional methods (since they received the same amount of extra instruction), but both groups improved their reading comprehension skills as compared to the control group, which received less instruction. Kemple, J., Corrin, W., Nelson, E., Salinger, T., Herrmann, S., & Drummond, K. (2008). *The Enhanced Reading Opportunities Study: Early impact and implementation findings* (NCEE 2008-4015). Washington, DC: National Center for Education Evaluation and Regional Assistance, Institute of Education Sciences, U.S. Department of Education.

2. Hart and Risley's seminal home-learning environment study was funded by the National Institute of Child Health and Human Development and the University of Kansas.

3. Hoxby, C. M., Murarka, S., & Kang, J. *How New York City's charter schools affect achievement*, August 2009 Report (Second report in series). Cambridge, MA: New York City Charter Schools Evaluation Project, September 2009. www.nber.org/~schools/charter-schoolseval

4. A considerable amount of research shows that not only do black parents talk less to their children, they tend to do so more harshly. Brooks-Gunn, J., & Markman, L.B. (2005). The contribution of parenting to ethnic and racial gaps in school readiness. *The Future of Children, 15*, 139-168. Further, harsh disciplinary actions have been found to be negatively related to academic achievement. Gutman. L. M., & Eccles, J. S. (1999). Financial strain, parenting behaviors, and adolescents' achievement: Testing model equivalence between African American and European American single- and two-parent families. *Child Development, 70*, 1464-1476.

5. In a study of 217 urban kindergarten–second-grade African American children, greater familiarity with "Standard English" was associated with better reading achievement. Charity, A.H., Scarborough, H.S., & Griffin, D.M. (2004). Familiarity with school English in African American children and its relation to early reading achievement. *Child Development, 75*, 1340-1356.

6. There is considerable support for the contention that reading comprehension is a function of background knowledge, being able to make inferences, specific reading comprehension *strategies*, vocabulary, and word reading, but vocabulary and background knowledge have been found to be the strongest contributors: Cromley, J., & Azevedo, R. (2007). Testing and refining the direct and inferential mediation model of reading comprehension. *Journal of Educational Psychology, 99*, 311-325.

7. Alexander, K.L., Entwisle, D.R., & Olson, L.S. (2007). Lasting consequences of the summer learning gap. *American Sociological Review, 72*, 167-180.

8. Although not routinely mandated in educational research, biomedical trials are normally required to employ a Data Safety and Monitoring Committee that periodically reviews the results in order to ensure that the drug/therapy being tested is not (a) harming anyone or (b) so obviously beneficial that additional research is not required.

9. Based upon his intriguing book, I would like to think that Malcolm Gladwell would endorse the time-on-task hypothesis and definitely not consider it an "empty model." The interview itself appeared in: Blow, C.M. (2009, January 24). No more excuses? *New York Times* Op Ed Page (A19).

10. Actually, some interesting work has already been done in this area, and more surprising findings undoubtedly await us. For example, one study showed that simply personalizing computer-assisted instruction (e.g., including the individual learner's names and a few personal facts about him or her) made it more effective for elementary school children: Anand, P.G., & Ross, S.M. (1987). Using computer-assisted instruction to personalize arithmetic materials for elementary school children. *Journal of Educational Psychology, 79*, 72-78. A similar effect has been found for college students: Moreno, R., & Mayer, R.E. (2004). Personalized messages that promote science learning in virtual environments. *Journal of Educational Psychology, 76*, 165-173.

Chapter 11: Implications for Reducing Racial Disparities in School Learning

1. Quoted from the Thernstrom's *No Excuses: Closing the Racial Gap in Learning* [New York: Simon & Schuster (p. 146)].

2. Obama, B. (2004). *Dreams from my father*. New York: Three Rivers Press.

3. Bracey, G.W. (2004). *Setting the record straight: Responses about misconceptions about public education in the U.S.* Portsmouth, NH: Heinemann.

4. Friedman, T. L. (2005). *The world is flat: A brief history of the twenty-first century*. New York: Farrar, Straus, & Giroux.

5. A huge amount of research has been conducted documenting the positive effects upon grades and achievement of parental involvement in the schools (Black and Hispanic

families tend to be less involved). For reviews of this literature see Pomerantz, E.M., Moorman, E.A., & Litwack, S.D. (2007). The how, whom, and why of parents' involvement in children's academic lives: More is not always better. *Review of Educational Research, 77*, 373-410; Graue, E. Clements, M.A., Reynolds, A.J., & Niles, M.D. (2004). More than teacher directed or child initiated: Preschool curriculum type, parental involvement, and children's outcomes in the child-parent centers. *Education Policy Analysis Archives, 12*, 1-36; Englund, M.M., Luckner, A.E., Whaley, G.J.L. & Egeland, B. (2004). Children's achievement in early elementary school: Longitudinal effects of parental involvement, expectations, and quality of assistance. *Journal of Educational Psychology, 96*, 723-730; and Fan, X. & Chen, M. (2001). Parental involvement and students' academic achievement: A meta-analysis. *Educational Psychology Review, 13*, 1-22.

It has also been shown that the positive results accruing from parental involvement occur equally for both white and minority children: Jeynes, W. H. (2005). A meta-analysis of the relation of parental involvement to urban elementary school student academic achievement. *Urban Education, 40*, 237-269.

6. The majority of charter schools adopt either longer days or longer school years, and children in KIPP schools spend an average of 62% more time in school than do their peers in regular schools. Viadero, D. (September 24, 2008). Research yields clues on the effects of extra time for learning. *Education Week, 28* (5), 16-18. And, as we would predict (and have mentioned repeatedly), controlled research has demonstrated that this additional time translates to increased learning.

Chapter 12: Getting There From Here

1. On the other side of the coin, these authors also detail how a transition toward the use of online (often advanced placement) courses is already occurring within our high schools, as well as the use of supplementary instructional methods (e.g., *Virtual ChemLab*) within traditional courses. Christensen, C.M., Horn, M.B., & Johnson, C.W. (2008). *Disrupting class: How disruptive innovation will change the way the world learns.* New York: McGraw Hill.

2. As also detailed in the Christensen, Horn, and Johnson book, schools, teachers, and administrators have displayed an impressive talent over the years of being able to continue with business as usual once the hue and cry advocating this or that innovation has died down. See also: Tyack, D., & Cuban, L. (1995). *Tinkering toward Utopia: A century of public school reform.* Cambridge MA: Harvard University Press.

3. In the past, many researchers have demonstrated that parents will take advantage of opportunities to supplement their children's instruction, but studies such as this tend to be quickly forgotten, and there is no mechanism to implement them when they obviously work. As one example, a recent well-designed randomized trial tested the efficacy of encouraging over 500 fourth-grade children at the end of school to practice oral reading with their parents (and silent reading comprehension skills on their own) during the summer. Half were then mailed eight books over the course of the summer, matched closely with each student's reading level (and half were given the books after the next school year began). Everyone was tested at the beginning of school and, as would be predicted, those students who received this intervention during the summer improved their reading and comprehension skills more than did those who had not received them at the time of the test. Kim, J.S. (2006). Effects of a voluntary summer reading intervention of reading achievement: Results from a randomized filed trial. *Educational Evaluation and Policy Analysis, 28*, 335-355.

Or, more rudimentarily, my wife and I (in another randomized study) supplied parents of special-education children with flash cards and found that they did indeed use them and their children did indeed learn an impressive number of words in a short period of time. (We then did a little uncontrolled follow-up study to see if parents would make their own flash cards and use them with their children in case it was too big a burden for the schools to supply them. The parents did, and their children learned.) Vinograd-Bausell, C.R., Bausell, R.B., Proctor, W., & Chandler, B. (1986). The impact of unsupervised parent tutors upon word recognition skills of special education students. *Journal of Special Education*, *20*, 83-90.